A Life in the Theatre

BOOKS BY TYRONE GUTHRIE

A Life in the Theatre

Theatre Prospect

Three Plays for the Microphone

Top of the Ladder (a play)
(WITH ROBERTSON DAVIES)

Renown at Stratford

Twice Have the Trumpets Sounded

Thrice the Brinded Cat Hath Mewed

TYRONE GUTHRIE

A Life in the Theatre

LIMELIGHT EDITIONS

New York

First Limelight Edition, October 1985

Copyright © 1959 by Tyrone Guthrie
All rights reserved under international and Pan-American Copyright
Conventions.
Published in the United States by Proscenium Publishers Inc.,
New York and simultaneously in Canada by Fitzhenry & Whiteside,
Limited, Toronto.

Excerpts from Chapter 21 appeared first in *Renown at Stratford* by
Tyrone Guthrie and Robertson Davies, published in 1953 by Clarke,
Irwin & Company, Ltd., Toronto, Canada.

Library of Congress Cataloging-in-Publication Data

Guthrie, Tyrone, Sir, 1900-1971.
A life in the theatre.

Reprint. Originally published: New York: McGraw-Hill, 1959.
    1. Guthrie, Tyrone, Sir, 1900-1971.   2. Theatrical
producers and directors—Great Britain—Biography.
I. Title.
PN2598.G85A3   1985   792'.023'0924 [B]   85-18162
ISBN 0-87910-048-6

CONTENTS

A LIFE IN THE THEATRE

by Tyrone Guthrie

PUBLICATION DATE: September, 1985

PRICE: $10.95   trade paperback

ISBN: 0-87910-048-6

Limelight Editions takes pleasure in
sending you this review copy, and would
appreciate receiving two clippings of
your review notice.

118 East 30th Street, New York, N.Y. 10016 (212) 532 5525

A Life in the
Theatre

I

Early Days

I SUPPOSE few people know precisely why they are occupied as they are. Some accept work which is chosen for them by their parents; some go into work for which they have been trained but for which they have neither aptitude nor enthusiasm. I believe that most people accept their work as being reasonably congenial, a tolerable burden, a way of making a living but not a way of life.

Many do, however, find in their work a means of expression, and pour into it a great part both of their physical energy and also of their fantasy. They can make their work an object, not only of rational planning, contriving and action, but also of dreams, wishes and fears, loves and hates, which belong outside the rational world but nonetheless demand expression.

It is sometimes supposed that self-expression is a privilege reserved for a race apart, beings called artists. This is not my experience. I have known carpenters, cooks, gardeners, engine-drivers—workers of many kinds, who have been able to use their work as a soul-satisfying means of expression. Perhaps, it may be argued, that in so doing they raise cooking or engine-

1

driving to the level of art. I think they do. And, conversely, many artists, persons who profess that painting is their work, or music or literature, are frustrated, miserable creatures who can find in their art no joy, no release of pent-up energies. If so, they are in the wrong job; or maybe their state is such that no work can medicine their disease. These are unhappy people.

I am thankful that my work has been for me a source of great joy, but I claim no credit for having the wit to find a congenial task. I do not know just how or why I came to the theatre. Perhaps heredity had a bit to do with it.

My mother's grandfather, Tyrone Power, was an Irish actor. His friends, many of whom were eminent Victorians, seem to have been impressed by the contrast between the modest man, whom they knew, and the dashing, vivacious figure they saw upon the stage. The dash, the charm and the modesty passed on, not to me, but to his other great-grandson and namesake, my cousin, the late Tyrone Power.

The first Tyrone Power was the leading exponent in his day of Irish comedy. For some years he played at the Haymarket Theatre in London, and twice visited America. The first time, from 1833 to 1835, he made an extensive tour, south to New Orleans and thence up the Mississippi River. His book, *Impressions of America*, published in London in 1836, gave a lively account of his visit.

He came again to America in 1839. At the end of this tour, he returned to New York. The night before he sailed for England he spent on Long Island at the home of his old friend, Judge Emmett. Emmett was the nephew of Robert Emmett, the famous Irish patriot who was executed in Dublin in 1803; he was also the great-grandfather of the playwright Robert Emmett Sherwood.

Emmett questioned his guest about the disposal of the proceeds of the tour, which amounted to a very considerable fortune. Power jokingly told him to mind his own business. "I'll tell you this much," he said. "I've invested it all here.

This country will do well. New York is going to grow. I've put the whole sum into real estate on the outskirts of the city."

He had arranged to buy a large property in the area where now stands Madison Square Garden. He said that a lawyer was handling the deal, but did not mention the lawyer's name.

The next day the Judge waved good-bye to his friend as he sailed away on the steamship *President*, bound for Liverpool. On March 12, 1841, there was a terrific gale. At five o'clock in the afternoon, the *President* was sighted from the bridge of the packet *Orpheus*. She was never seen again. At an inquiry in New York before the British consul, Captain Cole of the *Orpheus* stated that when he had last seen the *President* she was rising on the top of a tremendous sea, pitching heavily and laboring tremendously. It was his belief that the ship did not survive the gale, but foundered with all on board.

It was weeks before the news of her loss reached Mrs. Power in London, further weeks before Judge Emmett tried, on her behalf, and failed to locate either lawyer or fortune.

This much of the story was family legend and had been familiar to me since childhood. Only three years ago I heard a further strange aspect of the tale.

Margaret Webster, a director well known in both the American and British theatre, is the great-granddaughter of Benjamin Webster, part owner and manager of the Haymarket Theatre in London in the eighteen-thirties. He and Tyrone Power had many business relations and were good friends. At lunch one day in her house on Martha's Vineyard —not far, incidentally, from the very spot where the *President* was last seen—Miss Webster told me the following story.

Early in the morning of March 13, 1841, old Benjamin Webster was asleep in his home. He had retired from business and was living in a large house on Blackheath, a suburb in the southeast of London. He was roused by his butler, very agitated:

"Someone is knocking at the hall door. Knocking and knocking. He is calling for you."

It was a night of beating rain and rushing wind. The old man jumped out of bed.

"Don't you know who it is?" he asked the man, as he bundled a heavy coat round his nightshirt.

"It's too dark to see," said the man.

"Didn't you recognize the voice?"

"It sounds like Mr. Power's voice. He keeps calling for you. He's drowned, he says, in the rain."

By this time they were down the stair and along the hall. The old man pulled the bolts and turned the key. No one was there. Nothing was to be seen, nothing heard but the beating rain and rushing wind.

Of Tyrone Power's three sons, the eldest, my grandfather, also called Tyrone, was a professional soldier. Lord Melbourne, who knew his father, bought him a commission in the British army. He was sent to Ireland in the eighteenforties on relief work after the potato famine. There he met my grandmother, Martha Moorehead, in County Monaghan, near the Armagh border. Ten years later, when he returned from the Crimean War, they married. Her home, Annaghma-kerrig, became his and is now mine.

Tyrone Power's second son Frederick was an engineer; he built the trans-Caucasian Railroad. Harold, the third son, was the only one who followed his father's vocation. He acted a little and sang with great charm, though no great power. He married an actress, called Ethel Laffenue, and their son, Tyrone, went early to America where he did well as an actor, mostly in Shakespeare and costume plays. His son, Tyrone, though best known for his good looks and romantic performances in films, was a serious and improving actor. His recent death, before he was yet fifty, cut short a career which might well have matched that of his—and my—great-grandfather, to whom in appearance he bore a distinct likeness.

On the paternal side of my family there were no actors. My father, Thomas Clement Guthrie, was a general medical practitioner and surgeon. He was born in 1867 and educated in Edinburgh, where his father was a minister. His mother, Hannah Kirk, was Irish from County Armagh near the Monaghan border. By an odd coincidence my two grandmothers, though they never met, were born and raised in the same remote part of the Ulster border country.

Of my two great-grandfathers, Dr. Thomas Guthrie, a nationally famous minister of the Scottish Kirk, must have been the more theatrical. With his leonine mane, his rich, ringing voice, his great renown as a mimic and raconteur, Dr. Guthrie was evidently not only a mid-Victorian philanthropist and divine, but more than a bit of a thespian. Pounding the pulpit-cushions is, after all, but a hairsbreadth from treading the boards.

If I "take after" either of these ancestors, it is Dr. Guthrie, to whom I bear a certain facial resemblance and from whom I derive, I suspect, a certain rotund eloquence, a certain Scottish candor and determination to face facts, even, and possibly especially, unpleasant facts, together with a voice which, if not rich and ringing, is remarkably "carrying."

Probably environment weighed heavier than heredity. My mother took me at the age of seven to see *Peter Pan*. For a year I spoke like Pauline Chase, drew Underground Houses with toadstool chimneys, pretended to fly and dreaded, of all things, that I might lose an arm to a crocodile and be obliged to replace my missing hand with a hook.

The following Christmas we went to *The Yeomen of the Guard*. Pauline Chase was forgotten. My admiration transferred itself to a young lady who, as Phoebe, did a spinning-wheel number. As Calais on that of Mary Tudor, her name, which was Miss Beatrice Boarer, is graven on my heart. Henry Lytton was Jack Point. I can still feel the thrill of his last entrance, with chalk-white face; I can still see him stagger and fall dead of a broken heart. I think it was from this moment that, although I did not know it, I felt the theatre must be my life.

Oddly enough, I no longer care very much for *The Yeomen*. Its tuneful, skillful music delighteth me not; its histrionics are an adept bore. *Peter Pan*, on the other hand, still seems a dramatic masterpiece. But why is it always offered as a children's play? I have seen it several times in recent years. At matinees it always plays to hordes of rather listless youngsters. It is the evening performance which comes to life. Then an adult audience hangs on the actors' lips; the poisoning of Tinker Bell produces a hush like death; when Peter comes forward and, with outstretched arms, pleads with the people for the life of Tinker Bell— "If you believe in fairies clap your hands"—then hard-bitten hunting-women from the shires, usurers from the city, field marshals in a bath of tears, rise in their seats and clap and cheer, and clap again, until the twinkling of her light proclaims that Tinker Bell's herself again.

Make no mistake: this is a work of extraordinary theatrical power. If anyone doubts it, let him experience the great moment when the nursery night lights, symbols of Mother's loving protection . . . Mother, you remember, is at this moment out gadding with that miscreant, Mr. Darling . . . when the night lights flicker and fade; and, as they finally die away, the music swells up, the nursery windows swing open and in flies Peter—*flies*, mind you, sails through the night air like a bomber, like a moth.

It would be great to see a production of *Peter Pan* which really drove at the heart of the matter, which presented a version of the Oedipus legend the more horrifying because it is coated with rose-pink, poisoned icing-sugar. An interesting revival of the piece was given in London in the thirties. Charles Laughton played Captain Hook; his wife, a glittering and satiric sprite called Elsa Lanchester, played Peter. Hook, a heavyweight Don Quixote, became the hero of the evening. It was when Peter Pan came on that little children hid their faces in their mothers' skirts and strong men shook with fear.

Between *The Yeomen of the Guard* and my next experience of playgoing a great gulf was fixed. The War of

1914–1918 revolutionized Europe; my school days did something similar to me.

I was sent to an English Public School, called Wellington in honor of the Iron Duke. Wellington specialized in the training of army officers. More than half of us were destined for a career as professional soldiers. Of course during the war, we all were. But, even in normal times, the place had a military atmosphere.

One of the main objects of our training—and a good one—was to make us into responsible leaders. It is true that the sort of leadership envisaged was that of officers, leading things called men, beings of a lower social, intellectual, moral and physical status; of white men leading blacks—justly, humanely, but with no nonsense about who was boss.

On the principle that those who will govern others must first be able to govern themselves, we were entrusted with what was for those days an extraordinary amount of self-government.

We lived in barracklike dormitories, to each boy a tiny cubicle with bed, table, chair and chest of drawers, separated from the cubicle on either side by a partition about seven feet high. Each dormitory was named after one of Wellington's commanding officers, each held about thirty-five boys, and each was governed by a Head Prefect and two other Prefects, senior boys appointed by the Headmaster.

Only at lessons, or as members of opposing teams at football and cricket, did we meet boys from other dormitories. Otherwise the dormitory was our community, to it we owed our loyalty, within it our entire social life was lived, over it as an absolute oligarchy ruled the Prefects. I think it says much for the system that, in my experience, it worked efficiently. For the rulers it was a marvelous moral and practical training in the kind of leadership which was then expected of a British officer; for the subjects it was a harsh, but seldom unreasonable, and never either unintelligible or unjust, discipline.

The physical discomfort of our life was considerable; to Americans it would seem barbarous. There were no baths or

basins in the dormitory; the nearest sanitary arrangements
were down four flights of stairs and across a yard. Each
cubicle, however, was furnished with a small tin bath and a
huge white china po. At six in summer, six-thirty in winter,
our janitor, a retired sergeant in his late eighties, would
thump on each cubicle and say in a pompous tone: "Your
'ot water, sah," as he left a small can of miserably chilly bath
water. Half an hour later we were due at First Lesson, at
which both Masters and boys were too sleepy, and in winter
too cold, to do more than blink and grunt and make pretense
of work.

The food was not good. My school days coincided with
wartime, so I think the school authorities were not to blame.
But, looking back, I see now that for much of the time our
diet was not only drearily monotonous but insufficient.

Towards the end of the war, there was a rebellion. Like almost everything at this school, even rebellion was a disciplined,
highly organized operation. We all ate in one large hall, five
hundred of us, each dormitory at its own long refectory table.
The Masters sat at a high table, set on a dais at right angles
to the rest of us. At the beginning and end of meals the
Master on duty said a brief grace in Latin. On the night of
the rebellion—it was in the winter of 1917—communication
passed from table to table. This in itself was an act of in-
subordination. It was forbidden to speak at meals to those at
other tables. On this occasion Prefects, even Head Prefects,
conspired to break the rule. Notes were secretly handed,
whispers and counterwhispers were exchanged: the margarine
—we hadn't tasted butter for weeks—the margarine was
rancid *again*. Everyone, from the Head Boy, who nearly had
a moustache, down to the merest sucklings of New Boys,
everyone was to leave his pat of margarine untasted, and right
after grace. . . .

The meal ended. Grace was said; and then, instead of
filing out as usual, dormitory by dormitory, in alphabetical
order, we stood, just stood, five hundred of us, each with his
pat of margarine poised on his knife's end.

"What is the matter?" asked the Master in charge.

It was our cue. In silence each of us flipped his margarine as high into the air as he could; many pats struck the ceiling with a soft, soul-satisfying, greasy thud. Then followed something which I shall never forget. The steward, the stern and dignified individual who was responsible for the catering and upon whom we now all fixed our silent, censuring gaze, suddenly hid his face in his hands and fled from the hall in tears. Our rebellion was a fizzle. We had, like all mobs, found a scapegoat for our wrath; our reward for the ritual slaughter was only to be shocked witnesses of the victim's anguish. The margarine continued to be rancid.

It was not, however, the spartan discomfort which I minded, the military discipline or the frequent thrashings at the hands of both Prefects and Masters. If you are used to nothing better, hard conditions do not seem hard; efficiency and justice take the sting out of strictness; a beating is not the most painful or humiliating expiation for crime; better a sore behind than a sin-conscious soul.

But there was one element in our school life which seemed to me, and still seems, soul-destroying. The regimen of our day had been prescribed half a century earlier by the school's first headmaster, an Archbishop, renowned for his gentle and saintly life, on the assumption that the hearts of men, and a fortiori of boys, are deceitful and desperately wicked. Our wickedness was supposed to manifest itself in its most fiendish forms if we were unoccupied, more especially if we were solitary. Therefore our days were arranged to permit of an absolute minimum of solitude and, literally, not one single unoccupied minute.

I now think that the saintly Archbishop was guilty of extreme cynicism, prurience and folly. It was cynical to suppose us desperately wicked; there was a prurient, if tacit, assumption that the wickedness into which an unoccupied and solitary boy would fall was bound to be sexual; it was folly to think that merely by exhausting our bodies he could shield our souls from sin. At the end of our ceaselessly occupied days we certainly fell instantly asleep. But over our dreams not even an Archbishop could hold sway.

To me the lack of solitude was a real torture; not that I realized this at the time. During my school days I was not actively unhappy. I just supposed that Life was like that. It was only later that I realized how unnatural and how violent had been the social pressure to which we had all been subjected. The anthill life of the dormitory demanded absolute social conformity, absolute conventionality, an obedience not merely to the regulations, written and—more important—unwritten, which governed every action but also to the theories which inspired the regulations, which therefore governed almost every thought.

As I grew older, I reacted more and more against this conformity. I developed an exaggerated regard for "originality," an exaggerated dislike of English upper-middle-class routine. Outwardly I conformed, even in the fullness of time became a Prefect. Inwardly I rebelled and seethed with antagonism.

Perhaps I exaggerate the extent to which this was a reaction against school. I was just at the age when all authority becomes irksome, when all adolescents seethe, when they read Shelley—or now, perhaps, Kafka—and dream mad power-dreams and feel that they are surrounded by evil, foolish, elderly conspirators whose one aim is to thwart innovation and retain the scepter in their palsied grasp.

And yet I think, while I felt some of this in relation to my parents, my uncles, aunts and so on, the reaction against them was normal. My reaction against school was far more violent and far less conscious. Indeed, at the time, I was hardly aware of it at all.

Outwardly I conformed, but gradually my energies were withdrawn from the real world and focused themselves upon an imaginary world. This world was only partly of my own imagining; far more it was the creation of the novelists whose books I devoured when I should have been preparing lessons —Dickens, George Eliot and, especially, Thackeray. History,

in which I could "live," into which I could escape from the
real world legitimately because it was work, absorbed me
more and more.

At eighteen I got a History Scholarship to St. John's
college, Oxford.

It must have seemed to my parents the solution of a
problem. A dreamy, overgrown, morbidly timid but "clever"
and rather exhibitionist youth, I clearly was no longer fitting
into their preconception of an Officer and a Gentleman. I
was obviously not the type to become a Merchant Prince.
Oxford opened up a new set of possibilities. If he did well,
the boy might become a don, even in time a professor; there
was the law; there was even the church; worst come to
absolute worst, he could always get by as a schoolmaster.

I think that, absolutely without knowing it, I already felt
that my career would not be in the ordered ranks of a profession. This was probably the main result of those last
seething years at school—a determination to work alone.

I began to feel too, at this time, that I had it in me to
do something original; I had no idea what, but something
which would express what I really felt and thought, not just
conformity with current ideas.

This stage, I think, almost every young person must experience: beginning to be aware, humbly but unmistakably,
of certain gifts, certain capacities, yet utterly unable to find
out how or where to apply them; and acutely, morbidly shy
about discussing the matter or seeking assistance from more
experienced people.

In my case, so extreme was this shyness that, when at a
family Christmas gathering a well-meaning uncle asked me,
right out in front of everybody, right there over the roast
turkey, what I would like to do with my life, I blushed first
as red as fire, then trembled and then started to weep, deeply
embarrassing my parents, and indeed the whole tribe, by
such an exhibition. I think the symptoms were the result of
self-conflict. I wanted enormously, indeed needed, to talk

long and loud about myself, my prospects, hopes and fears.
But I dared not; I felt I must not.

Young people at this stage are at the mercy of environment.
Chance, or predestination, will place them here or there, in
this group of people, that climate; and this will settle what
becomes of them, how they will use their gifts, which furrow
they plough.

In my case there was one factor, to which I have already
alluded: I had A Voice. It was very loud and of penetrating
timbre. Whether it was pleasing or not I had no idea, but
right after I left school, various people said that such a remarkable gift must not be neglected. I must have lessons.

Eventually I was sent to Gustave Garcia, the last of a
famous line of Spanish and Italian singers and teachers.
Although by now he only accepted a very few students, he
agreed to give me lessons. I would like to think that this was
because he thought the voice had such wonderful potentiality.
But in reality I am afraid he thought—and only God knows
why—that I was a gilded amateur, who would pay well and
give no trouble.

For a year I went twice a week to his pretty little house in
Maida Vale. You went in through a low door in the wall,
over which climbed a Clematis montana. You crossed a small
paved garden and were admitted by an enormously stout,
good-natured Italian housekeeper. I think she had been a
contralto in the chorus at Parma.

The large room, in which the maestro taught, was stuffed
to overflowing with furniture and bric-a-brac. Great chairs
covered with black horsehair upon which were laid thick,
cream-colored crochet mats, and a gigantic sofa, loaded with
frilly pillows and fringed rugs, jostled an aged Brinsmead
Grand, also jet black. A black marble mantelpiece was crowded
with black cast-iron statuary—naked men lugging at stal-
lions, stags locked in mortal combat; there was a black marble
clock which, for the whole year, announced the hour as seven
minutes past three. The walls were thick with signed photographs of long-dead operatic stars; big ladies in white nighties

and long plaits, little ladies in saucy bonnets and high-heeled button boots, florid gentlemen in tights and waxed moustaches. In the place of honor was a portrait in oils of Maestro's aunt, Madame Pauline Viardot Garcia—a very great personage of a bygone operatic era. She was a great friend of the Russian novelist Turgenev, and Natalia in A Month in the Country is said to have been a portrait of her. On one side of Pauline was a wax bust of Manuel Garcia, Maestro's father, who invented the Garcia "method," whatever that was; on her other side was a Thing, which hung in a glass case lined with ruby velvet. This was The Laryngoscope. It had something to do with the Garcia method, was regarded with an awe usually reserved for fragments of the True Cross, and was, I am thankful to say, never used upon me.

Maestro stood every inch of four feet eleven, was ninety-three and incredibly formidable and vigorous. He wore a black velvet jacket and a flowing black satin bow, like Rodolfo in La Bohème. The head was enormous and ferociously noble —Mr. Punch, done in ivory, with a fuzz of white, wiry hair and coal-black eyebrows—maybe natural, maybe dyed—which greatly emphasized the brilliance of the great, Spanish eyes— black, in whites which were quite a rich, bright yellow.

Sometimes he would take some trouble over my lessons, but usually none.

"The voice is very large," he would sometimes say. "You can sing at parties. People will ask you out. You will get into nice society."

Once he got angry because I could not manage an exercise in rapid consecutive fourths. Embarrassment over my own incompetence turned to panic as the aged Maestro worked himself into a more and more violent paroxysm.

"How dare you! How dare you waste my time! You are a Jackass! A voice, yes. There is A Voice, but you have no more music in you than that fender."

Whereupon he gave the iron fender a most frightful kick. He then turned a deep plum color and began to cough.

We were alone in the house. Visions of the inquest began

to rise. I had certainly been stupid, oh criminally stupid, but
not to the extent of murder; I would not actually swing. But
six years for manslaughter ... eternal disgrace ... my poor
parents. "Tea!" yelled the corpse, now a much paler shade of
plum. "Go to the kitchen and make tea."

When I returned, he was in the best of humor.

"Sit down. Have a cookie, my boy, I will tell you about my
life."

Then followed an hour, two hours, maybe even three, of
the most high-colored reminiscence I had ever heard. At the
end, we had glasses of cognac. Then he made me take off his
shoes and tuck him up on the sofa, under a rug. I collected my
music off the Brinsmead and turned to say good night. He
was already half asleep. One black and bushy eyebrow rose
a fraction.

"You will not be much of a singer. But you make a good
listener, a good audience. Stick to that."

Was it a compliment? A warning? Or positive advice?

I walked down Warwick Avenue to the bus. It was now
bright moonlight. From the tall, shabby old houses floated
the sounds of music students at practice. A baritone sang
arpeggios. Mine is as good a voice as that, I thought. And
then: "You will not be much of a singer."

A pianist pounded up and down, up and down the scale.
A 'cello wailed. Many are called, I thought, but mighty few
are chosen.

On and on pounded the scales. The 'cello made sounds
like a cow in the last throes. "Ow!" sang the baritone, "Ow
that we tew were Myeing!" *He* wouldn't be much of a singer
either.

It was at that moment that I knew I would not be a singer;
but knew too that I would be some kind of an artist. But
what kind? I was at the bus stop now. A bus arrived, but
I was lost in thought. The bus departed. I was not on board.
What kind of artist? What kind of art?

"You make a good listener, a good audience. Stick to that."

At Oxford, because of my singing, I was thrown into contact with musical people. I was asked to act in a play because the part demanded a song. My performance was praised. This was nice, but at the time I was more interested in lawn tennis. I was asked to act again. Chance, or predestination, was nudging me into position.

This time the cast of the play was more congenial—a group of stage-struck young fellows, some of them brilliant and gifted. None of them eventually went on the stage. One is now a distinguished surgeon, one is a judge, two are professors. We went to plays together and saw the touring companies at Oxford in the West End successes of the date; we saw the Irish Players—Sara Allgood was great in *Kathleen ni Houlihan*; we saw the D'Oyly Carte company in Gilbert and Sullivan; we saw the Carl Rosa Opera Company—the swan in *Lohengrin* entered backwards, beat a hasty retreat and re-entered right way round, but late. We read the notices of London openings and longed to be rich enough to attend. I too was getting stage-struck.

Again I was invited to act. This time in the Oxford University Dramatic Society's annual Shakespearian production. They hired a professional director; they rented the New Theatre for a week; London critics attended and wrote notices with what we never recognized as indulgent condescension.

The play was *Henry IV, Part 1*. My part was Glendower. The director was James B. Fagan, whose work we had all seen and admired, whose work was serious and intelligent, who was an Irishman from Belfast.

My fate was sealed.

2

Oxford

MR. FAGAN was large and genial, with merry blue eyes and an amusing turned-up nose. I do not know what age he was; probably in the late forties. He was very good with the young, neither pompous nor condescending, and treated us undergraduates as reasonable and adult people. There was never any doubt in rehearsal that he was in complete control, but there was no fussy ordering-about or attempt to impress us with masterful airs.

My part of Glendower, the Welsh chieftain, is short but effective. It was a felicitous piece of casting because in this part many of the qualities which prevent my being a real actor became assets, not drawbacks. My overwhelming height, cutting voice and an incurable tendency to emphasize the grotesque and farouche—all these were a help in making something striking and dominant out of a very brief scene.

Fagan directed the scene clearly. He explained to us the relation of the scene to the rest of the play, the sort of effect which he wished the whole scene to make, where, and why, the lights would be placed; showed us where to make the climaxes in the acting, and why, and how—all in a simple and businesslike way.

With me he was too lenient. Instructed to play Glendower as an elderly monarch, I promptly presented a being far older than God, with the phony regality of three emperors laid end to end. But my excesses amused him and he let them pass.

Rehearsing my own scene was fun; but what really interested me was watching the play take shape, watching this man, whom I liked and admired, cope with the inadequacies of a student cast, encouraging and liberating talent when he found it, concealing gross incompetence as much as it could be concealed, gradually shaping the raw material into some approximation to the form he had conceived.

I learned from these rehearsals that the script of a play, even of a great play, a masterpiece, is still only a *part* of the raw material of a performance. The script, the cast, the appurtenances of costume, make-up, scenery, properties and lights, and finally, the audience—these are all ingredients which have somehow to be fused together into a single work of art. Of course, the script is nearly always the most important of these elements; it is the basis. But the script alone has no theatrical existence. It awaits interpretation.

From these rehearsals I began to learn a lesson which many theatre critics might do well to assimilate. It is amazing how many critics, even good ones, in assessing the performance of a masterpiece, *Hamlet* for instance, assume the existence of an ideal performance, which fully realizes the author's intention.

The performance of a play is not merely the re-creation of an already fully realized idea. Even assuming that a dramatic author has in mind a fully realized idea of all that his script may indicate, it would not be possible to achieve a replica of such an idea. For one thing, conditions of performance are never the same. *Hamlet* in a village hall, before a village audience, is of one kind; *Hamlet* in an opera house, before a smart, cosmopolitan audience of quite another. Neither of the two approximates at all closely *Hamlet* in an Elizabethan playhouse before an audience of Shakespeare's contemporaries, which we must suppose to be the kind of performance which Shakespeare had in mind. Or again, *Hamlet* played by Mr. A, who is small and volatile with a light tenor voice, will not be at all like *Hamlet* played by Mr. B, who is a tall and heavy baritone. Yet both may give excellent performances; both interpretations may be equally valid according to the evidence of the text.

Every professional playwright hopes that his work will be good enough to stand revival by many different companies, good enough perhaps to outlast its author and be revived for posterity. He will realize that his intention will not necessarily be perverted if the hero instead of being Mr. A, is Mr. B, if this or that aspect of the whole is treated with different emphasis. The intention, in short, cannot be precise and specific; it must be vague and general to the extent that it permits of a wide variety of interpretation.

Any work of the caliber of a masterpiece carries a load of meaning of which its author is quite unaware. James Bridie, the Scottish dramatist, used often to ask my opinion about his new plays. They usually seemed to me fascinating, witty, original and hard to understand. I would ask "What d'you mean? What is it about?" His invariable reply was "How should I know? I only wrote the thing."

At first I thought this was just an ironic joke. But gradually I came to see that it was profoundly true. Of course he knew in a limited sense what he had tried to say; but he knew also that, if the work were any good, his *conscious* intention was comparatively insignificant. The important part of the work would have, without his conscious intention, often in spite of it, have slipped in "between the lines," over and above his conscious intention. A masterpiece, he used also to say, is like an iceberg; ninety per cent of its meaning lies below the surface of the author's consciousness.

I am told that, according to British Public Library statistics, the demand for books about three particular personalities enormously exceeds that for books about any others. The three are Jesus Christ, Hamlet and Napoleon Bonaparte, in that order.

Can we believe that, when Shakespeare wrote *Hamlet*— and the evidence points to the likelihood of its having been written fast—he deliberately and consciously set out to create a character so fascinating, so mysterious and so alive as to stimulate this extraordinary and abiding interest?

Surely the *conscious* intention was to please the customers with a melodrama about revenge, set in the glamorous environment of a royal court, enlivened with sexual and dynastic intrigue. The central figure became so enormously interesting because Shakespeare poured into it, as any author must into a long and detailed psychological creation, not merely the conscious observation of a good journalist, but his own deepest feelings and intuitions, rather than rational thoughts, about man's predicament in this mysterious and often apparently hostile universe. Unlike most authors, and to a greater degree than any other, Shakespeare had the poetic ability, had the ability to infuse his rational expression with this "over and above" of feeling and intuition.

If this is granted, then it follows that the important part of an author's intention is implicit, not explicit, in his text. Therefore there is no textual evidence as to the most important part of the work. And there can be no objective standard of criticism for the interpretation of this part of the work. Further, there can be no objective standard of interpretation, or any question of fully realizing it; any interpretation must be partial and subjective.

There can, therefore, even in theory, be no ideal representation which fully realizes the author's intention.

Often, I think, dramatic critics, while they sincerely believe that they have in mind such an ideal representation, really have in mind a sort of stereotype, deriving from previously admired representations. Hamlet, for instance, must be melancholy, the Gloomy Dane; Ophelia must be sweet and innocently childlike; King Claudius, with some obligation to smile and smile, must be an obvious villain, the heavy man of a stock company.

Again and again I have read notices warmly commending performances which realize such stereotypes—and notices roundly damning any departure from them.

But, in fact, is the stereotype justified by the text? In my opinion, rarely. To take Hamlet again as the instance: his first scene with Rosencrantz and Guildenstern makes it perfectly clear that he is not habitually a gloomy fellow. If he is played as such, then there is no justification for his mother's concern about him in her first scene with him. It must be surprising, and potentially dangerous, that he refuses to cast his nighted color off, that he is plunged in an *unwonted* melancholy.

His conduct during the subsequent action of the play shows him to be a man of exceptional energy, vivacity and resource. The stereotype has it that he is "unable to make up his mind." In that case, how is it possible to explain the resolute and efficient way in which he carries through the intrigue with the players, the ruthless break with Ophelia, the forcible interview with his mother, the hoisting of Rosencrantz and Guildenstern with their own petard, the grapple with the pirates? Surely a sharp psychological point is blunted if it is not clear that he is a resolute and capable man rendered irresolute and incapable by self-conflict, by qualms of conscience, only in the single matter of avenging his father's death by the murder of his uncle.

Further, to play Hamlet in the stereotyped manner, as a pale, irresolute, moon-struck, constipated weakling is to undermine not only the psychological, but the dynastic elements of the play, which Shakespeare evidently treated seriously and regarded as important. Fortinbras, and even Claudius, would be better Kings of Denmark than such a Hamlet. This belittles the tragedy, which is concerned not with a pathetic royal misfit, but with the jostling out of the succession of a potentially great King, and his destruction through the very greatness of his own nature—a political and public, as well as a merely personal, disaster.

Equally the stereotype of Ophelia as a childlike innocent fails to hold water if you examine the text. I assume it arose because she is a young woman; in stock-company terms, she is the ingénue part. The ingénue is stereotyped as a pure virgin. But there is strong evidence that Ophelia is neither pure nor a virgin.

It is possible to multiply instances of criticism by the standard of similar stereotypes. They exist with respect to all the familiar classics. A great actor interprets a part in a particular way; it may possibly be in a way considerably at odds with the evidence of the text, as were many of Irving's interpretations. The impact of such a performance makes it hard, possibly for generations, to see or hear or imagine the part in any other way.

It is often said that we owe to Mrs. Siddons the "tradition" of Lady Macbeth as a beefy, booming contralto. But this hardly squares with the sort of performance which a boy would have given in the original production; nor, to my mind, with the music and balance of the text. Much the best Lady Macbeth I ever saw was a gifted Welsh actress called Gwen ffrangcon-Davies. She suggested a wildly ambitious spirit in a small and fragile person. I read no professional critic's notice which did not say she was miscast.

Anyone who saw Laurette Taylor as the Mother in *The Glass Menagerie* by Tennessee Williams would find it hard afterwards to read the play, or think about it, without having her image in mind. Clearly the part could be embodied in a number of different ways; endless nuances of performance could differ from Miss Taylor's and be just as valid. Possibly the play would seem to be an even better piece of work if the part, as played by Laurette Taylor, did not so entirely dominate, so exclusively irradiate the whole. Yet so powerful was the impact of this actress that, for at least a generation, performances not merely of the part but of the whole play will be criticized according to their conformity or nonconformity with the image which she created.

Less dominant, but still influential, are the opinions of great critics, the literary rather than theatrical critics. Goethe is largely responsible for the notion of the pale, wavering, Wertherlike Hamlet—probably less by direct influence upon a literary public than through his influence upon the German theatre of his period, thence upon the whole European theatre later in the nineteenth century, thence upon Irving, and upon Gielgud, whose Hamlet has dominated and incalculably influenced all his immediate successors.

As I watched Mr. Fagan at work upon our amateur Oxford production, I traversed little, if any, of this theoretical territory. I was far too green. But I did see that something was being created, that the process of directing a play was something more than merely interpreting an intention which had already been made fully explicit in the text.

It seemed to me then also that, next to the author's, the director's might perhaps be the most creative and interesting, if not the most highly paid or loudly applauded, work in the theatre. This impression was strengthened when, at the technical rehearsals on the stage, I saw how the whole atmosphere of a scene could be influenced by its decor; how the emphasis on this or that could be achieved by light; how critical a matter is the timing of a curtain.

I was still so green that it had not struck me that all this was the result of premeditation and careful rehearsal. You went to the theatre and these things just happened. The curtain fell and it was sometimes rather nice if it fell slowly; lights changed and sometimes a good effect happened—that sinister green on the face of Captain Hook, for instance, as he poisoned Tinker Bell. Now I began to learn how these things were made to happen and, in a very elementary fashion, why.

All this was in the early spring of 1923. That summer I had my final examinations for a degree, and made a most inglorious showing. I was disappointed and considerably dreaded what my father might have to say. His attitude towards me was often, to my way of thinking, stern rather than encouraging. I broke the news. There was a pregnant pause, then in a vague tone: "Oh well, it doesn't matter too much what they think of your abilities. After all, it's a matter of opinion."

The matter was never mentioned again. I doubt if he ever thought of it again; and I realize now that had I achieved a Double First, the Newdigate Prize for Poetry, "Blues" for rowing, boxing, tennis and chess, and—for good measure— the Legion of Honor and the Victoria Cross, his reply would have been exactly the same.

What was I to do next? Before I had really time to examine the cards in my hand, the very highest of which appeared to be the eight of diamonds, an exciting letter arrived from Mr. Fagan. He was opening a repertory theatre at Oxford. In the company he proposed to include three of the cast of *Henry IV* whom he considered to have talent. I was one of the three. Would I be interested?

I replied that instant expressing grateful enthusiasm. I then showed Mr. Fagan's letter to my father and asked his advice. No harm in giving it a try, seemed to be his attitude, and I noticed gratefully that he avoided giving, either by word or tone, the inference that the prospect of a job, even of a job on the stage, was better than no prospect at all.

I heard again from Mr. Fagan. The first season would coincide with the Michaelmas Term at Oxford; eight plays would be done, a new production every Monday, but to give time for more preparation the first two plays were to be ready before we went to Oxford. The first play would be *Heartbreak House* by Bernard Shaw; my part would be Captain Shotover; my salary would be five pounds a week.

This was great. Captain Shotover, a retired seaman of eighty, is the leading part in *Heartbreak House*. Clearly my prowess as Glendower had earned me this plum. To be sure, five pounds a week was no great salary for a leading actor, but

I still just had sense enough to realize that I was but on the threshold of the great histrionic career which now lay before me. In those days five pounds was very reasonable pay for a beginner; one could live—well, keep alive—on three.

I showed the letter to my father. I told him about Captain Shotover and why I thought that I had been offered the part. We agreed that I could live on the salary and even save a little money against the unlikely eventuality of a rainy day. I expressed some gratitude to and admiration of Mr. Fagan, whom my father had never met.

"He sounds a nice man," my father said. Then, after a second: "But put not your trust in Princes."

This sounded almost as ominous as the obiter dictum of the maestro in Maida Vale. I thought it over and got nowhere. Now, nearly forty years later, I have thought it over again. I believe the remark was prompted by jealousy and I realize with sorrow how wounding may have been my naïve enthusiasm for another and substitute father.

During the summer, I played strenuous lawn tennis, learned the words of Captain Shotover and reflected complacently on the good fortune, which had brought my brilliant but hitherto napkin-wrapped talent to the light of day.

Came the first day of rehearsals.

We assembled in a parish hall in London. It was in the basement of one of those tall, damp, dilapidated houses, unlovely and unloved, behind Victoria Station. It was exciting to meet the company. Miss Dorothy Green, a very handsome, auburn lady with a purring voice, had been leading lady at Stratford; her Cleopatra had made quite a stir. Miss Florence Buckton had been at the Old Vic. The gentlemen were no less eminent. Mr. Earle Grey had played leading parts in Shakespeare. Mr. Peter Cresswell had once played in the West End.

The three of us from Oxford felt very young, very small beer. I was the youngest of the three, the youngest person present . . . no, there was a girl younger than I, a tall, dark girl with beautiful gray eyes, who had just left the Royal Academy. Her name was Flora Robson.

Soon Mr. Fagan arrived with Mr. Reginald Denham, who was to direct some of the plays. Goodness! Mr. Denham was quite young, hardly any older than I was, really very, *very* young to be a director. Somehow this seemed a vaguely hopeful sign in an afternoon which was otherwise depressing and ominous.

Now Mr. Shaw appeared and was going to read his play to us. I should like to be able to describe this reading and to give some impression of George Bernard Shaw at this time. It was 1923 and he was finishing *Saint Joan*, which would be produced the following year. Alas, the essentials of the scene have entirely faded from my memory. I cannot remember what Shaw wore nor where he sat. I think we were ranged in a sort of oblong formation round a table with a broken table-tennis net (very "parish hall"). I remember that I was in a wicker chair and, when the reading started, became self-conscious because my chair creaked whenever I took a breath.

Shaw is always said to have read his own plays wonderfully. I cannot remember. I was charmed by the modest gravity of his demeanor when he arrived and received our deferential greetings. Then I recall being a little surprised when, during the reading, he would go into fits of laughter at his own jokes.

The next morning we were to start rehearsal. I was there first, word-perfect, humbly but smugly conscious of being one of the youngest members of the company yet playing the longest part—the wonder-boy. The rehearsal began. The wonder-boy, who had been free all summer and knew the words inside out, strode about, now whispering, now shouting, throwing his arms about in the way which had been so effective in Glendower, making long, thrilling pauses. Miss Green, bless her, was in glasses with her handsome nose pressed to the very small print. Mr. Grey was hardly attempting to act at all, just reading, just mumbling really. I hoped he would eventually do better than that.

When we broke for lunch, Mr. Fagan beckoned me to follow him out of the room. We paced a dingy basement passage—three trash-cans and a door marked "Mr. Fothergill—strictly private."

He took my arm. It had all been a great mistake, he said; he was to blame, not I. He had never realized *quite* how inexperienced I was, not only technically, but in every way.

"After all, you *are* rather young for your age—twenty-one, is it?"

Twenty-three, I had to confess, aware of development abnormally, ridiculously retarded. He was a good psychologist. He did not attempt to gild the pill with flattery. The interest of the whole company, the whole venture, must come before my private interest. I must give up the part. I might leave, if I liked, right then, not come back after lunch; or I might stay on at the same wages, assist the stage manager and make myself as useful as I could.

I could feel that he liked me, that he still felt I had some talent—for something. I could sense and respond to something humorous and merry in the way that he was handling the situation. I suddenly saw that the little episode was not in the least tragic, and not even very absurd. When I said I'd like to stay, he said "Good, I'm glad." And I believe he meant it.

When we resumed after lunch, Mr. Grey read Shotover. I was on the book—theatrical parlance for prompting. No one caught eyes; no one looked at me with contemptuous pity; best of all, no one was obtrusively kind. The next day Mr. Grey invited me out to lunch and we talked of this, that and the other, but never alluded to you-know-what. The episode was closed. I had found my level, and not too painfully. The satisfactory thing was that I had had the chance to leave, to get out, to turn back, and had instinctively, finally rejected it. My foot was on the ladder, albeit upon the very lowest rung. He that is down, I reflected cosily, need fear no fall.

At this moment Mr. Denham addressed me in my new

capacity of Assistant Stage Manager. "We must have somewhere better to rehearse," he said. "Find somewhere for ten
tomorrow, then ring us all up and tell us where."

I felt like the Miller's Son commanded by the Evil Dwarf
to carry ten thousand bushels of corn to the bottom of the
sea. I had no idea what sort of place I was expected to find,
nor how to set about finding it. I did not know London at all
well, nor the first thing about theatrical routine.

I suppose my panic was apparent. Peter Cresswell very
good-naturedly offered to help me. He took me to his club
and we started to telephone from there. After two or three
calls we had got the loan of the bar at the New Theatre. I
was to be there at nine-thirty to arrange the chairs.

I now had leisure to observe my surroundings; till now
I had been too flustered. I had never been in a London club
before. This one was very grand. Was it the Cavalry Club?
Something military. Peter had been a regular soldier. The
walls were covered with field marshals on horseback, field
marshals waving swords and flourishing batons. Field marshals
against backgrounds of flaming cities or devoted Sepoys.

Peter ordered glasses of sherry. There was a tremendous
double staircase. There was a table covered with periodicals,
upon which fierce old gentlemen kept pouncing like birds
of prey... why, goodness, there was the Belfast Telly...
a very, very old man hopped up to two other old men, who
were playing cards. He hopped like a bird.

"Aren't you going to play with me?" They took no notice.

"I wish you'd play with me. Archie and Freddie have gone
home. *Do* play with me."

And now a man in a tail-coat with brass buttons was bringing two glasses of sherry on a silver tray. He handed the
sherry with an absurd air of respect: "Your sherry, sah." Why
did I suddenly think of old John dumping the hot-water cans
outside the doors of our cubicles? It was all extremely uncongenial.

I felt ungrateful to Peter Cresswell, who had been so kind.
I tried to look nonchalant and sophisticated, to make elegant

but manly conversation, not too unworthy of the excellent
sherry, the magnificent staircase, the surrounding marshals.
In the back of my mind something clicked into place. The
subconscious handed me, as it were, a punched card with the
answer. This was Wellington all over again, plushy, not
spartan; dry sherry, not tepid bath water; but the iron conventionality was the same, the absolute priority given to a
kind of dreary negative correctitude, the need for all these
men, most of them quite old, to huddle together, to play at
being boys again, to relive the anthill life of the dormitory.

I fled. I professed, I hope, something of my true gratitude
to my host who had rescued me from panic and despair. But
I fled; and, ever since, I have fled when I have felt come over
me that claustrophobic sensation of being back at school, a
member of the dormitory, forced to conform to rules which I
know to be desperately uncongenial, and believe to be point-
lessly repressive and false. The hearts of men are *not* desperately wicked. It is *not* my duty to lead my men into battle,
nor to impose order on benighted blacks. This is the Temple
of Rimmon. There will I not bow down. I have enough
sense to run out into the rain.

Next morning, I was at the New Theatre betimes to arrange the chairs. What the hell did it mean? The bar was
pink and Louis Quinze and reasonably spacious. There were
quite a lot of chairs and little tables and I decided that the
sensible arrangement was to clear as much space as possible.
I began to pile chairs and tables behind the bar. At this moment a very pleasant-looking man of about forty appeared behind me and took me gently by the elbow. "What cher
doin'?"

"Arranging the chairs."

"Hardly think they'll want yer to 'range 'em like that."

"No?"

"No. What's yer set like?"

I explained. A window there; doors here and here; a sofa
there. He then helped me to arrange the chairs and tables
so that they marked, or indicated, the position of the various

features of the set and the various articles of furniture; he even got down on his hands and knees with a tape measure: "They'll want the dimensions acc'rate, yer know."

Gradually a great light dawned. I saw the point of arranging the chairs. When the company arrived, the stage was set; I was sitting at a table, pencil in hand, before an open prompt book, giving an exaggerated, farouche performance of a theatrical functionary, of whom I had read in the want ads. of theatrical journals: A.S.M. (*fully exp.*)

My bacon had been saved again; and this time I had no idea by whom. It was nearly twenty years later when I met again and recognized this pleasant-looking man as Bronson Albery, the managing director of the wealthy and important company which owns three of the best theatres in London. Twenty years later the thread of my life would again become entangled with his. Again he would come to the rescue, become a valued adviser and staunch friend.

The Playhouse was the name given to our theatre in Oxford. It stood on the fork of two arterial roads and had formerly been a big-game museum. This meant that it was haunted by the ghosts of a moose, an elk and a lion, whose stuffed and moldering corpses had been the melancholy sole exhibits; it also trembled and reverberated like thunder every time a truck or bus went past, that is about every six seconds.

Mr. Fagan announced that our stage was a presentational stage and that we should give Presentational Productions. Nobody quite knew what this meant—not even Mr. Fagan. Everything was white: a white curtain set in a white proscenium; white curtains formed the scenery for all our plays, with either nothing in front of them or the very minimum of chairs and tables to enable the business of the play to proceed.

Much as I admired Mr. Fagan, it was soon apparent that the Presentational Method was not a very good idea. For one thing, the audience became very tired of the white curtains; for another, the white curtains became very tired themselves.

I know this for a fact, because one of my daily duties was to
remove the fingermarks and damnéd spots by rubbing the
beastly things with an ill-smelling concoction called Gudasnu.
Perhaps the most serious objection to the white curtains was
that they threw back the light into the audience's eyes, so
that the actors seemed half-silhouetted; little expression could
be seen on their apparently dark and dirty faces; and the
more light was poured onto them, the darker they seemed
to become. Audiences, straining to see the goings-on in front
of the dazzling background, straining to hear over the thunder
of the traffic, left our performances with splitting headaches
and never came back.

To offset the debit of the Presentational Method, Mr.
Fagan must be credited with a really interesting and ambitious
choice of program; bearing in mind that this was more than
thirty years ago, that the taste of that time is therefore at
the pole from the taste of today, do you agree that the following is a judicious, well-varied and distinguished eight
weeks' season?

1. *Heartbreak House* by George Bernard Shaw
2. *The Importance of Being Earnest* by Oscar Wilde
3. *Mirandolina* by Goldoni, adapted by Lady Gregory
4. *Love for Love* by William Congreve
5. *The Return of the Prodigal* by St. John Hankin
6. *Monna Vanna* by Maurice Maeterlinck
7. *The Man of Destiny* by G. B. Shaw, with *The Land of
   Heart's Desire* by W. B. Yeats
8. *Oedipus Rex* by Sophocles, translated by Gilbert Murray

In addition to many bottle-washing duties, I played various
small parts, to the disconcertment of my colleagues, who
found my towering stature reinforced by a strong instinct for
theatrical effect, as yet entirely undisciplined. I think I had
it in me to be a striking, even powerful, interpreter of a very
limited range of parts; but absolutely not to be a "useful
actor," whose service would be in steady demand. Mr. Fagan
made no pretense that I was anything but a crashing liability

in almost all the parts I played, but still indicated that he thought I had talent; that sometime, somehow, something might be made of me. Meantime I had a living to earn. I foresaw that someone could rather easily be found who would be no less diligent with Gudasnu, and a good deal more presentable as Second Footman, Clerk to the Court, Another Athenian and Captain Spruce, his friend. I started to look around.

James Fagan will not reappear in this book. A very few years after this time, he died of pneumonia in Hollywood, before he had achieved the top rank either as manager, director or playwright. Two of his plays, *And So to Bed*, a charming comedy about Pepys, and *The Earth*, a piece about the newspaper world, were successful in their day but are hardly likely to survive. As a manager and director, his charm, kindness and good sense will be gratefully remembered by all who worked with him, and especially by those who, like myself, owed him the incalculable debt which beginners owe to those who give them encouragement when it is most needed.

3

Belfast

AT THIS TIME a new phenomenon was arising: Radio.
It seemed to offer rather wide possibilities to someone like
myself. As yet there did not appear to be much interest in
its artistic potentiality; the focus was almost exclusively on
the technical and scientific side. The mere fact that you
could poke a wire into a magic box which contained a crystal
and actually hear them talking in London or Paris, actually
hear some faint twanglings, which your nephew told you were
the bands playing that very instant in the Savoy Hotel—'twas
paradise enow. Nobody seemed to mind much *what* they
heard, so long as they heard *something*.

I was not at all interested in the mechanical side. My
mechanical capacities are a little limited. I can pump a bicycle
tire; switch an electric light on—and off; and, if I count twelve
slowly, take a deep breath and clear the mind of cant, I can
recall whether, if you turn it clockwise, you make a screw
go in, or out. But it was clear that other people were intensely interested in the technical development of this new
toy, that they would develop it extremely fast, that in a short
while it would be an important means of communication, and
that the audience would soon accept the miracle of hearing

something and would begin to demand that it be something interesting.

Since the foundations of the house had hardly been dug, I thought there might be some chance of getting in, as they say, on the ground floor. I applied for a job.

After a brief, gruff interview with a retired admiral, I heard a week or two later that I was to be the junior member of the staff of a broadcasting "station," as it was then called, which the B.B.C. was opening in Belfast. This was in June 1924. My appointment did not begin until September. There was time for a last theatrical fling.

My friend Christopher Scaife had written a play. It was in verse, melodious and very melancholy—*The Triumph of Death* was its name. We resolved to get together a group of friends and stage it. I need hardly add that the two leading parts were to be enacted by our two selves.

The Scaifes—quite a tribe—were clever. They were artistic. They had charm and gaiety and dash. They took little thought for the morrow and still less for public opinion. Christopher was the youngest of the tribe, perhaps the most brilliantly gifted. At Oxford he was President of the Union and won the Newdigate Prize for poetry; he was extremely musical and sang delightfully. He was energetic, disciplined and cooperative. Had he wished, he could have had a prominent career in politics, journalism or business—opportunities were offered in all three. He could have quickly made a name and an excellent livelihood as a singer or an actor. It is typical of him that he has chosen a comparatively obscure academic appointment in a Middle-Eastern capital. He has preferred to function as an influence rather than as a creator; in B flat minor rather than C major. I have never met anyone, who could conduct his life in the way which suited him, with such an aristocratic disregard of conventional ideas.

The Triumph of Death was not a full-length bill; so we decided to precede it with *Mirandolina*, Lady Gregory's adaptation of *La Locandiera* by Goldoni, in which Gillian Scaife, Christopher's elder sister and a professional actress of distinction, agreed to play the lead. Molly MacArthur designed and made the clothes; Flora Robson, leaving the Oxford Playhouse, joined us; so did Guy Bolton, an actor friend of the Scaifes, Cecil Bellamy and Robert Speaight, contemporaries of ours, also just leaving Oxford and also stage-struck.

We hired a tiny theatre, converted out of an old barn, at Oxted in Surrey and we gave three performances to an audience consisting almost entirely of aunts, friends and well-wishers of the cast. When the takings were counted, we found that, if each of the company paid ten shillings and Christopher and I each paid a pound, receipts and expenditure would balance.

In September I started my job with the B.B.C. in Belfast. I presume I had been appointed because I am Irish. Not a bad reason. But no one had given me any brief. I had not the faintest inkling of what I was supposed to do. About the policy of the B.B.C., its constitution, finances or function, I had not one clue. I only knew that politics, religion and advertisement were tabu, unmentionable.

When I arrived in Belfast, my colleagues seemed equally vague about the whole business. Our station director was a charming, elderly gentleman of distinguished pedigree. He was mildly interested in dogs and women, keenly interested in pheasant shooting. Belfast, broadcasting, science, art, literature and, especially, office routine he openly and cordially detested.

I was placed in charge of all programs other than music; that is to say all talks, plays, poetry readings, debates—any program which depended, apart from the bare announcement, on the spoken word.

At twenty-three years of age I found myself convening meetings of archbishops, bishops, moderators and ecclesiastical bigwigs of many creeds; the Vice-Chancellor of the University, the Director of Municipal Education and a covey of headmasters; mayors, deputy mayors and town clerks from all over the province; of the officers of local debating, philosophical and dramatic societies in order to break to them the glad news that radio, or broadcasting, as we called it then, had come to the North of Ireland; in order to seek their advice as to how this new medium could most wisely be used; and to induce them to elect some of their number to constitute a Broadcasting Advisory Committee.

I found myself hiring elderly and sometimes distinguished professors to talk about their subjects; hiring local comedians and introducing variety shows; hiring reciters and choosing their programs; ensuring fair do's between the broadcast religious rites of Catholic and Protestant—a ticklish business in Belfast. It was all very interesting and would have been highly unsuitable, if anyone had taken it seriously. But this was early days. No one much was listening, and anyway all they heard was a faint word here and there in between the Morse code of ships' wireless officers exchanging betting tips and the howls and squeals of lost souls, which were called "atmospherics."

The technical aspect of radio still completely dominated not only the public imagination but also that of the B.B.C. An odd instance of the relative importance of the technical staff was the fact that all the office equipment, painting, decoration and upholstery were under the control of the Engineering Department. In consequence, our studio—as we absurdly called the noisome den where performances took place—was one of the ugliest-looking things ever conceived by the mind of man.

It had been, and no expense was spared, lined in curtains of a terrible shade, somewhere between the color of a dandelion and a ginger pudding; upon them there was a "frieze"— a wide stripe arranged in what is called Greek key pattern, in a lurid violet; the floor was covered with a carpet which was meant to match the ginger pudding, but did not quite. The lighting was arranged on the new principle of reflection off the ceiling, then very fashionable and utterly impractical. The ceiling was dazzlingly bright, but down in the depths of the room you could read only with difficulty.

The head engineer had installed a fabulously scientific system of ventilation. A series of gold levers could be pulled and gold arrows pointed to signs on gold dials, which purported to announce the temperature. The room was supposed to be filled with an especially invigorating ozone, which blew in through a golden grille. In fact, the temperature never changed. The room was perpetually cold, but at the same time stuffy.

Some of us were silly enough to think that there was also a very queer smell. The engineers laughed this idea to scorn, and pointed out that it was an aroma of ozone and infinitely healthy. Yet things were better when, from behind the golden grille, the caretaker removed the carcasses of two dead rats.

Gradually it became evident that this new medium was going to exert a tremendous influence upon public opinion and the public imagination. It also appeared that overnight the reputations of actors and politicians, musicians and preachers could be made or ruined; also that there was "big money" to be made. At first many important public figures refused to broadcast on the ground that it was *infra dig*. None of them held out long.

But, as the power of broadcasting became more apparent, and not before it was time, the B.B.C. began to put its house in order. Young men of twenty-three no longer convened its committees and improvised its policy. Regulations, like nettles in a hotbed, took root and flourished exceedingly. Things sobered up, but also dulled down. Gradually a routine of administration evolved. Memos passed from wire basket to wire basket. Questions were asked and answered in triplicate, files bulged, secretaries multiplied. Gradually officials in the B.B.C. became more and more like civil servants, concerned with administrative and not with creative work.

After two years in Belfast, I began to feel the time was coming for a change. Once more I began to look about. They had been for me two happy and formative years. To begin with, these were my first years in an industrial city; they were —and this will seem scarcely credible today—the first years in which I really got to know men and women of a markedly different economic or social environment from my own or met people, markedly older than myself, who were not members of my own family, parents of my friends, or set in authority over me as Masters.

I had been at boarding school from the age of ten till I was eighteen. During that period the year was arbitrarily divided into terms and holidays—terms accounted for thirty-nine of the fifty-two weeks. The two environments—school and home—were, in my case and I think of most other children, in violent and disturbing contrast. At school you never even met any member of the opposite sex, except an occasional elderly housekeeper or Master's wife, and then not on terms of friendship. You never met any grown-up man on anything approaching equal terms. With even the kindest, most approachable Masters the relation was as of nephew to uncle; and our Masters never had time to be more than perfunctorily kind, intermittently approachable.

Even among the other boys we were permitted to develop only the most casual acquaintanceship outside our own dormitories; even within the dormitory it was considered extremely undesirable to associate with anyone more than a few months senior or junior to yourself. Consequently, during the whole ten years my close companions—and I know the same applies to thousands of boys similarly educated—were limited to five or six, none of them chosen because we had any particular affinity, but simply because blind chance, or all-seeing destiny, had planted us like five or six bulbs in a pot.

At home I made friends with youngsters of my parents' friends, but these were only casual contacts. The holidays were too brief for real friendships to develop.

When at eighteen I went to Oxford I had little assurance in meeting new people and strong inhibitions against choosing companions who were not in my immediate orbit. Learning a little technique, gaining some confidence in these matters, was certainly the most valuable lesson I learned at college. But still the environment in which I moved was lamentably circumscribed by my own timidity, which, in turn, was the product of my upbringing.

Let me stress again that such an upbringing was by no means exceptional. Both my parents were liberal-minded, responsible citizens. They considered it their duty to give me the best educational advantages they could afford. One of the principal advantages was to protect us little hothouse sprouts from every avoidable contact with what was wicked, dangerous and vulgar.

Belfast was a salutary shock. To begin with it looked so different from any of the other places where I had lived. Here are no dreaming spires, no gray old colleges. Nature has been kind; the city stands on the estuary of the River Lagan, with soft green hills to the south and southeast; the sea to the east; and to the north, the mountains—Ben Madigan, Divis, the Black Mountain. Man's work is vile. The river is a polluted conglomeration of shipyards, gasworks, coal-basins; into it pours the refuse of the great mills, which send linen and rope to the far corners of the earth. Their chimneys rise like black points of exclamation over the rows and rows of little houses, square as boxes, scarlet as minced beef. Of ancient buildings there is no trace. Before 1750 there was nothing but a row of insignificant huts. The City Hall, which dominates the main square, is younger and scarcely less ugly than the Capitol in Washington, which it dimly resembles. There is a tawdrily pretentious Catholic Cathedral, a dully pretentious Protestant Cathedral, begun in the eighteen-nineties and still unfinished; there are Meeting Houses of Presbyterians and Methodists, of which the architecture is not even lively enough to be pretentious.

With the possible exceptions of Jerusalem and Mecca,

Belfast must be the most religion-conscious city in the world. Of a Sunday evening, in addition to the bulging edifices, there are countless open-air gatherings, caterwauling, depressing and bloodthirsty hymns, usually in a cold, persistent rain. The very public conveniences are inscribed not with the sort of messages which you find in the conveniences of other cities, but with "God Sees You," "Christ died for Sinners," "To Hell with the Pope," "Up Sinn Fein" and, most frequent of all, that eerie query: "Eternity Where?"

For all its great factories, Belfast was still a country town. No one was surprised to see cows walking down the main street and looking in at the windows of the department stores. In those days, more than thirty years ago, you would often see donkey carts and, in the pubs, countrymen accompanied by their sheep dogs. You could look north from the main square up a long, long straight street, with tram lines and electric poles and wires stretching away, away to the great shadowy silhouette of the Black Mountain—very different from Oxford. It was like the pictures of Vancouver or Adelaide, so new, so rawly ugly, but exciting.

I knew nobody at first, except my colleagues at the Radio, who were all older than I and preoccupied with very different interests. When I first arrived, the linen warehouse, which served as our first studio and office, had not been fully "converted." There was nothing to do and nowhere to do it.

In golden weather I roamed the streets, the nearby hills; I took the bus up the Antrim coast or through rural County Down; I roamed the shores of Strangford Lough. It was lonely enough, but I felt affection beginning to grow for this countryside which, though different from any I had known before, had many connections with my forbears.

Gradually we got busier, even extremely busy. Gradually I met people, all sorts of people, whose like I had never met before. I began to choose my companions, a new and thrilling experience; began to get extremely interested in the life of this ugly, fascinating city—its economy, the fierce political and racial differences which rend it apart yet make it strong;

the severe puritanism, Catholic just as much as Protestant, which frowns on so many little pleasures and amenities, usually considered harmless.

Belfast is the capital of a small but highly individual province, with its own marked dialect, its marked difference in character and "ambience" from Celtic, Catholic Ireland, across the border; from England, across the water; and even from Scotland, to which it has much the closest affinity. I had never before lived in a city with this strongly provincial character. London is too huge and cosmopolitan; Oxford too small; anyway, in Oxford, town and gown form two separate communities, and gown feels no provincial or local attachment or even consciousness. I found a great new interest in the effect of locality—through climate, history, economics, religion—upon people's character, behavior, and expressions, especially speech.

This was a period when a great deal was still being written and thought about folk art. Much of this was no more than the nostalgia of well-off and sophisticated people for hard physical work, for a simplicity and contact with nature which they felt they had lost. The nostalgia was frequently genuine; but the cure is to go out and do hard, physical work, to live simply and in close contact with nature. And yet, and yet . . . was it better to be cured? Or was it better to write earthy Georgian poetry in a villa at Sevenoaks or Beaconsfield? To do one's house up with cottagey, naïve wallpapers and arrange dear, simple old flowers in copper jugs? To collect round the Bechstein in Popsie's studio, with its scarlet walls, emerald ceiling and huge black "pouffes," to sing about jolly ploughboys, tarry sailors and milkmaids dabbling in the dew?

It is easy to laugh at the little incongruities and sentimentalities which, obviously in every epoch, beset the intelligentsia in search of something which seems more "real," more simple and satisfying than the expressions and recreations which are currently fashionable. No doubt in the

twenties Oxford undergraduates in white flannels learning
country dances called Rufty Tufty and Lads o' Bunchem were
pretty laughable. But was it more absurd than going to dancing classes to learn the Charleston and the Black Bottom?

Besides, there was more to the folk art revival than just
nostalgia. There was a real attempt to bridge the gulf between the musical and artistic expressions of rich and poor,
high and low. It was part of a general awareness in Britain
that the gap between what Disraeli in the eighteen-forties
had called the Two Nations was far too wide.

Such an awareness had frequently expressed itself in art,
and more practically in legislation, since the forties. The
gross inequalities had begun to be intolerable soon after the
Industrial Revolution had undermined the ancient, feudal
foundations of society. The War of 1914–1918 had enormously
accelerated the pace of social revolution. The equalitarian
notions of the twenties were nothing new. It was just that we
youngsters were more free to express our views than had been
our parents and grandparents, simply because these views
were no longer revolutionary or advanced; they were now
commonplace. When we raised our trumpets and blew, the
Jericho-walls of privilege had already begun to collapse.

In our zeal for folk art we were expressing an aspiration
to make "culture" less snobbish and exclusive, more truly
popular. Surely that is a generous and laudable aspiration. It
is nobody's fault if the apostles of such a cult must always
lay themselves open to ridicule precisely because they are
rarely the embodiment of a popular person, of the common
man.

Is it a mistake to think about other people's culture? Surely
not, in principle. The aspirations of better-educated, more
privileged persons to share their advantages often do express themselves with an air of condescension, with an assumption that an educated person is better equipped by nature, not merely by artifice and accident. That is the result of
the imperfection of human nature. The shortcomings and

human frailties of individual missionaries may discredit the whole idea of mission. But an idea can be discredited by individual instance without being in principle invalidated.

The principle that we should share with others, whom we believe to be less fortunate, possessions which we regard as valuable seems not only morally right but practically inescapable. Joy, like any other emotion, has to be expressed. Maybe the expression, like that of an animal, is no more sophisticated than shouting or capering. Yet surely such shouts and capers are the elements of song and dance, the elements of an artistic expression of emotion.

The joy has to be expressed. The joy of expression is normally greater if it is shared. The impulse to express is hardly separable from the impulse to share.

It is, however, true that individuals exist for whom a pleasure is more intense if it is not shared. Such secret, private pleasure is morbid, like secret drinking.

Some pleasures seem greater if they are shared with a limited and carefully selected group of participants, maybe with a single partner. This is the basis of what we may call the Mandarin view of art. According to this view, works of art acquire merit as they are enjoyable by fewer and better-equipped connoisseurs, or Mandarins. The higher the fewer.

This view seems to me logically defensible, but runs counter to all political and social principles upon which civilized society is built. It is, however, less absurd than its converse; that the greatest works of art are those which are enjoyed not by the smallest but by the greatest number of people.

In fact, do not both the Mandarin view and its converse imply a confusion of quantity with quality? I suggest that pleasure is always greater if shared; that the ideal number of sharers varies greatly with different kinds of pleasure; that the number of sharers in an artistic experience varies greatly with different kinds of works of art; but that the quality of a given work of art is not affected by the number of persons who come under its influence.

In wishing to share a pleasure, it does not necessarily follow that you wish to share it universally. But I think it does follow that you want the experience to be universally available, where anyone who might like to participate is not excluded.

I think that such a viewpoint underlay the folk art revival, which also aimed to keep alive simple and ancient expressions, in danger of disappearing with the change-over from a predominantly agricultural to a predominantly urban and industrial society, and to interest in them people whose environment was cutting them off from many of the healthy and happy features of the old way of life.

Here was the weakness: it was not a spontaneous expression of a popular need, it was sicklied o'er from its inception by the pale cast of intellectual and artistic sophistication. Also, its aspirations, as well as its roots, were firmly bedded in the past. There was something decadent in the insistence upon old tunes, old dances, the glorification of archaism for its own sake, the assumption that hand-beaten, hand-woven articles just must be better than similar articles produced by machinery. There was something plumb idiotic about dancing around Maypoles and recreating Merrie England in the public parks of Liverpool and Birmingham.

Nevertheless, in three important respects the British folk art revivalists were, in my opinion, right. In the face of the powerful and influential Mandarin caste, which exists in every culture, they insisted upon popular, nonexclusive, universally apprehensible values in art. In the face of the powerful centripetal tendencies of modern civilization, they held that London was not the source of all good ideas. At risk of substantiating the charge of being backward-looking fuddy-duddies, they continued the cult of ancient, popular and native arts and crafts, rating them higher than the successive waves of "contemporary" expression, each one of which, if it shows any sign of becoming genuinely popular, is immediately exploited for profit.

The process of exploitation inevitably destroys a work of art. To begin with, in order that there shall be no offense in it, that it contains nothing off-putting to any single hypothetical customer, it must be emasculated, rendered esthetically harmless, therefore esthetically null; secondly, in order to squeeze out of it the last drop of commercial value, it must be produced on such a massive scale, so widely advertised, so over-praised—in a word, so familiarized—that very soon it becomes "common." Even the greatest works of art seem common in the light of a full-scale exploitation. After all, who would want caviar if it were not only cheaper and more available than cod, but if it appeared at every meal; if it were not merely familiar, but inescapable?

Like nearly all the rather artistic and intellectual young people of the time, at Oxford I had been inseminated by the folk art revivalists. The North of Ireland, with its strongly provincial feeling, its wealth of beautiful folk music and legend, was particularly fertile soil in which these seeds might sprout.

The *nouveaux riches*, militantly Philistine people who at that time seemed to dominate Belfast, who poured the accent and the jargon of the Surrey golf clubs over their own accents like treacle over porridge, these people seemed to personify a baneful, enervating vulgarity. With the enthusiastic partisanship of youth, I became militantly provincial, the sworn foe of all that was fashionable and metropolitan.

Another thing happened during my two years in Belfast which considerably influenced my destiny. One of my duties was to choose and direct the plays which, from time to time, were broadcast. I have no idea whether any of these productions were good, but some were quite successful and we were encouraged to include them more and more frequently in the program. Also I found that I had some ability to take rehearsals. I could feel that the actors were happy, that the rehearsals nearly always "went with a swing." My time under Fagan at the Oxford Playhouse had given me confidence and I had, I think, absorbed from him, from Reginald Denham, and the more experienced players in the company not only a little technical know-how but also a professional attitude to

the preparation of a play. Also the fact that I had been "on
the stage," had worked in such good company, gave me a
certain status with the Belfast actors. Most of them were
older than I, and more experienced in every way, but they
were amateurs. Their bread and butter was earned as commercial travelers, in the linen business, the shipyards, the
ropeworks or as teachers. I was, with the exception of occasional guest artists hired from London, the only pro. Even
the guest artists, some of them seasoned and even distinguished veterans, accepted my direction with good grace.

I began to hope that perhaps I was finding my vocation.
I also felt that, though by now I was extremely interested
in the artistic possibilities of radio, its limitations were irksome. I longed to be back in the theatre, but no longer to be
an actor.

Towards the end of my second summer in Belfast I received
an invitation from the Committee of the Ulster Literary
Theatre to direct the first production of their next season.
The Literary Theatre was at that time outstandingly the most
important group of its kind in the North of Ireland. After
the Abbey it was the most important Irish company. The
players were amateurs, but their attitude was serious and
many of them had a great deal of talent. I felt greatly com-
plimented and realized that this invitation confirmed my feeling that the actors had liked working with me and my hope
that I had some potentiality as a director.

At almost the same time, another possibility sailed into
view. The B.B.C. in Northern Ireland was officially supervised from Scotland. From time to time, senior officers would
visit us and see how we were doing. One of these officers
recommended me as a promising director to the Scottish National Players. I was invited for an interview to Glasgow.

4

Glasgow & London

THE LITTLE STEAMER from Belfast crept slowly up the Clyde on a lovely August morning. I was up very early to get a first view of Glasgow. It was impressive. The miles of docks and shipyards, the craft from all over the world; to the north, to our left hand, the strange tower of the University like part of an old-fashioned battleship; the elegant spires of "Greek" Thompson; to our right hand, Govan, a black network of poor streets with brightly colored trams creeping about like insects.

I was struck then with Scotland's air of serious purpose, and still am whenever I return there. It has not the charm of Ireland; but oh, how disciplined and organized it seems! Even the dead in the cemeteries lie in perfectly straight rows. The tombstones stand up in ranks, like guardsmen—*dead* straight. And on the craggy, stern faces what gravity and determination is writ! This is no place to essay the little joke, the gay exaggeration, the butterfly flight of metaphor, indispensable in Irish conversation.

The Scots are sternly literal. They call it truthful. If you

46

lightly, frivolously and, of course, foolishly declare that this must be the wettest summer for years, the most amusing book ever written, the biggest aspidistra in the world, your Scottish interlocutor will, with gentle sternness, rebuke such irresponsible hyperbole... "Oh no; I hardly think that can be so." He will then deploy a platoon of relevant statistics, meteorological, literary or botanic as the case may be, slowly and reasonably *proving* that your remark was inaccurate and therefore silly.

Scots are, and they like to remind you that they are, more sternly educated than people in other parts of the world. They call it better educated. And they like nothing better than "informing" benighted visitors from outside their borders of their encyclopaedic command of a multitude of dull, dry facts.

In Scotland you do not "tell," you "inform." You do not "need," you "require"—"you'll require to make an appointment." You do not "want," you "wish"—to say you "want" a kippered herring implies not desire but deprivation. "D'ye wesh fesh?" is a commonplace of the Scottish restaurant. Most indicative of the subtle difference between Scots and English manners: in Scotland you do not "get a scolding," you "receive a word." What about that for dignified understatement?

Of my interview I remember only that the board of the Scottish National Players appeared extremely Scottish, fanatically national and temperamentally incapable of play. They did not attempt to conceal the fact that they were having difficulty in finding a director. My qualifications were meager enough, but the job was mine. I began in October 1926.

The Scottish National Theatre Society had been founded six years earlier with the hope of doing for Scotland what the Abbey Theatre was doing for Ireland. It aimed "to encourage the initiation and development of a purely Scottish drama by providing a stage and an acting company which will be peculiarly adapted for the production of plays, national in character, written by Scottish men and women of letters."

It was exactly the sort of wheel to which I wanted to put my shoulder. It exactly chimed with my anti-metropolitan, provincial feelings, and there was enough of the Scot in my ancestry to attach me passionately to the nationalist side of what we liked to call The Movement.

I soon found that there was a sterling group of Players, and that most of them knew a great deal more about acting and production than I did. For two years the Players taught me my job; in return, I tried by energy and enthusiasm to create some kind of framework in which we could all function.

We rehearsed four or five productions each season, played them for a week each in Glasgow and toured intermittent "dates," while we rehearsed the next play. The trouble was that there was nowhere suitable in Glasgow for us to act. A warehouse provided an adequate office, rehearsal space and store. But the performances had to be given in a hall attached to the Y.M.C.A. It was very central and accessible; the auditorium was quite nice and about the right size, but the stage was wretchedly small and ill-equipped and the whole institution had about it a depressing odor of sanctity and stewed cabbage. It also stank of amateur theatricals. The alternative was to rent one of the commercial theatres, too expensive for our limited capital, too large for our intimate offerings and, in a different way, just as inappropriate to our style as was the Y.M.C.A.

Every summer, and once in the full force of Scotland's winter, we undertook a tour of one-night stands in country halls. In summer we traveled, a company of eight, our stage fit-up, costumes and properties in a truck and slept in tents. In winter we slept in pubs and lodgings in the villages. I recall in the winter of 1927, when already prices everywhere were rising, paying half a crown (the equivalent of about fifty cents) for an entirely adequate bed and magnificent breakfast of porridge, eggs and bacon.

It was gruelling work. We rose at seven and our day never ended till well after midnight. Each of us had his, or her, own set of tasks, since, as well as the show, we had to fit up the stage, pitch the tents, cater and cook, maintain the wardrobe, install our own lighting plant—an ingenious but dangerous acetylene arrangement, with an unspeakably nasty smell, sell tickets and programs, check the cash. We were frequently wet and frequently cold; we were bitten by midges; we had a fracas with a bull; our truck broke down ... it was physically a hard way to learn, but we all did learn a good deal, about one another, about Scotland, and about our job.

We were faced with two cardinal difficulties: lack of plays and lack of capital. The first we could, and to a considerable extent did, overcome. We eked out the limited Scottish repertory with imports which were possible to transfer into a Scottish setting and to act in Scottish dialect. It was lack of capital which frustrated and eventually killed the enterprise.

The idea was that the efforts of the Players must *earn* the capital to extend our operation and, especially, to build a theatre. At the time this seemed reasonable, but I now think it was putting the cart before the horse.

It should have been apparent to our committee that the standard of performance was high enough to justify faith. There was a group of players who had talent and technique learned in a hard school, and a cohesion and sense of purpose which, though typically Scottish, is also extremely rare. The achievement of our aim now depended upon presenting these players in a manner which would make possible a higher standard of production and a bit more "showmanship" than the Y.M.C.A. permitted; the development of a wider repertory, to which the players were fully equal; and the systematic, businesslike cultivation of a wider clientele than the few hundred "steadies" who supported us because we were a worthy cause.

It should have been faced that, if The Movement were to progress, capital must be raised and invested in a building, a group of talents and an idea.

But what idea? There was the rub. Our board was fatally undecided. There was no single personality who had the rare combination of vision and unscrupulous egotism to take the enterprise by the scruff of its neck and make, or break, it on a clearly defined policy.

Some of our board considered it their duty to press for plays by Scottish authors, and advocated the presentation of even feeble and amateurish scripts if they were written in sufficiently broad vernacular. Others were for good theatre; but hesitated, and very rightly, to define good theatre in terms which could be translated into practical action.

Looking back, I am struck by what exceedingly kind and nice men were on that committee and I blush at the way I treated them: thumping the table, making impassioned speeches, refusing to do this, demanding permission—and money—to do that. The board was a model of douce, gray, dignified discretion. It treated me to mixed doses of cautious admonishment and smiling indulgence. It was an elderly, composite Papa with an uproarious only child.

Their treatment of me was typical of an amiable weakness which finally baffled achievement. They should either have backed me up to the hilt, on the assumption that I had energy, enthusiasm and enough bright ideas to compensate for a great deal of silliness and youthful inexperience; or they should have got rid of me at the earliest possible moment and found a director who would do what they wanted.

But there, again, the old weakness became apparent—a weakness, incidentally, which is surely endemic in lay committees directing the policy of enterprises in which they take a benign interest but about which they have almost no technical knowledge—they knew, neither severally nor collectively, neither in precise nor even in general terms, what they really did want.

Gradually the enterprise fizzled out. From about 1931 it began to dwindle; in 1950 it finally went out of business. The conception of the theatre for which we had all worked, the sort of plays we produced, even the sort we dreamed about producing, the building we dreamed of possessing and never possessed, all these belong to a bygone epoch. Such is the

transitory and fluid nature of existence. No enterprise ever
has fulfilled, or ever can fulfill its purpose completely. The
most you can hope for is to take a respectable shot at an unattainable goal, to succeed partially and intermittently.

It is effort that matters, not achievement. I like to hope
that our effort was respectable. Measured in terms of output
of physical and spiritual energy, unselfish cooperation, risks
taken, fun had, dreams dreamed, the turnover was considerable. I do not imagine that, judged by the highest standards,
any of our efforts was more than a decent shot against heavy
odds. We did not deserve any more "success" than we had;
and our success, in terms of fortune or celebrity, was extremely limited.

Our main achievement was that we provided a valuable
training ground for talent; the best in Scotland, and one of
the best in Britain. A surprising proportion of our people
have done well in many parts of the world. More important,
we were the chief precursor of an indigenous Scottish drama.
The Citizens' Theatre in Glasgow and the Gateway Theatre
in Edinburgh both owe much to past players of the Scottish
National Theatre Society and more to its influence. If there
is a spiritual and cultural renaissance in Scotland at the
present time, and the evidence for believing so is considerable,
then the Scottish National Theatre Society was one of its
many contributory causes. In our small way we helped to
thaw the ice of Calvinism, helped to create the impression
that the arts in general, and the theatre in particular, were
something serious and vital.

The two years I spent in Glasgow were not so violently
developing as my two preceding years in Belfast. I was growing up—and high time, too. In many ways Belfast is like
Glasgow, though on a much smaller scale. It was not for me
a revolutionary change of environment, and I think my development was professional and technical, rather than personal. For one thing, I was working very hard for very long
hours—no hardship when the work is congenial. I had very
little money and did not get about much. My wages from

the Scottish National Theatre Society paid my subsistence;
pocket money was earned by the occasional engagement on
the radio, judging at musical festivals and things like that.

I was beginning to learn some technique. Mr. Fagan's
Presentational Method did not really suit at all for the farm
kitchens, tenement houses or middle-class parlors in which
most of our Scots plays were set. I had everything to learn
in this department, and by process of trial and error I learned
a little. It was very developing, if alarming, to be solely and
obviously responsible. If the production of a play was a mess,
it was my fault.

The B.B.C., even in my day, was such a vast hierarchy that
you could always pass the buck. For a blunder there were endless excuses. High functionaries could always blame lower
functionaries; they, in turn, still lower ones until at last the
blame reached a category so low that no responsibility could
be expected: the cleaning lady's understudy, for instance, or
the office cat. That was behind the scenes. To the public the
excuse was, and is, always the same: "Owing to a technical
fault over which we have no control. . . ."

But the compact organization of the Scottish National
Players permitted of no such evasions. The staff was a one-
man band. If a beat was missed, it was no use glaring at a
nonexistent back desk.

Also, I began to learn something about the money side:
to budget, to calculate business risks, to sacrifice valuable
sprats for a hypothetical mackerel. Hitherto I had only had
to arrange my own money affairs, and the scale of my income
had been such that there was only one way of arranging:
spend as little as possible.

The scale of the Scottish National Theatre enterprise gave
an excuse for the same timid, poor-person's economy. It was
not for me to run the board into debt.

After many years in theatrical affairs, during most of which
I have had some responsibility for other people's money,
I have learned, often painfully, that cheese-paring is just no
good. If you want to make money, you must be ready to spend

it—like water. This does not mean wastefully; it must be spent with care and discrimination, but handsomely. I have come to recognize, though reluctantly, that one of the chief pleasures of the theatre for the audience is to participate in lavish and luxurious goings-on.

This may not be the noblest, highest aspect of theatre-going, but it is very human, especially in the case of people who normally have to be frugal. For the price of their ticket they want not only the pleasure of the play; they want to feel that for a brief and glittering three hours they have bought, and therefore own, something largely, loudly, un-ashamedly luxurious. Isn't this desire rather analogous to the feeling which makes us prefer Becky Sharp to that goody-goody Amelia Sedley? It is fun to live vicariously in *Vanity Fair*. Plain living and high thinking are all very well, but not for a night out, not to celebrate John's homecoming, Millie's birthday, or our silver wedding anniversary.

Is it not the chief reason why managers have always found Ibsen's plays so hard to sell? High thinking takes place in a world of dark-crimson serge tablecloths with chenille bobbles, black horsehair sofas, wall brackets and huge, intellectual women in raincoats and rubbers. Now, if only the dowdy old Master Builder had been a clanking, spanking Colonel in a stunning uniform; if only Hilda Wangel had been a beauti-ful Female Spy, with a series of slinky, shimmering evening dresses, each one cut lower than the last; if only she pro-vocatively waved a great, feather fan, or a bouquet of gar-denias and tuberoses instead of clumping about, poor dear, with that alpenstock.

In those days, however, I would have none of this. There was no money for luxury—why, there wasn't even quite enough for bare necessities. Automatically I pared the cheese and derived a positive pleasure from doing so.

In February 1928 my father died. At the same time my mother, whose sight had been failing for about a year, be-came almost completely blind. I had to leave Scotland. We

took a furnished house in London, to be near the specialist
who was looking after my mother.

From this time I date the end of my childhood. As I was
now nearly twenty-eight, you may consider me rather an
elderly child. But perhaps elderly children are not such a rare
phenomenon as it is usual to pretend.

I now experienced for the first time the feeling of being
out of work, of not knowing when, or even whether, there
would be another theatrical offer. It is not a pleasant feeling.
I am thankful to say it was not only my first, but also my
last, period of unemployment; also that the wolf never got
very near the door, because I had occasional work as an ad-
judicator at amateur drama festivals and of verse-speaking
at musical festivals. Even so, there was a good deal of spare
time and I wrote a play called *Squirrel's Cage*, which the
B.B.C. accepted. I had planned it specifically for radio, because I thought my contacts with B.B.C. officials might make
someone more likely to read it and because I hoped, as a result of my now considerable experience of radio, that I knew
some of the more obvious pitfalls in that medium.

After a few months I was taken back into the employment
of the B.B.C. in London. Now I was a member of the Drama
Department. We worked in Savoy Hill, quite near the Savoy
Hotel. I shared an office with three others. It was very small.
Into its pleasant, large window poured not a single ray of
sun. It overlooked a cemetery.

My job for the first few weeks was to read the scripts of
old musical comedies with a view to adapting them for radio.
It was rather fun, but they were not very adaptable. Shorn of
all sex appeal, all spectacle, they really made odd reading.
The jokes, which had set the Gaiety in a roar in 1906, seemed
flat. The dialogue which led up to Lady Kitty's grand entrance at the head of the double staircase seemed even flatter.
The *coup de théâtre* at the end of the first finale was of an
almost liturgical sameness—the soprano fainting in the arms
of the tenor (naval uniform); the comedian (comic Tyrolean

or *very* Ordinary Seaman) moved to tears—laugh Punchinello; the bass (riding breeches) foiled again.

After a while I was allowed to direct a production: *Paolo and Francesca* by Stephen Phillips, very purpurate and ninetyish. The leading parts were played by Gwen ffrangcon-Davies and Robert Donat, whom I had met in Glasgow when he was there with the Benson Shakespearian Company and who already showed great promise. Also in the cast was Dorothy Green, just as handsome, as purringly contralto and as short-sighted as at Oxford.

Various other productions followed, developingly varied. In those days, if you were on the staff you had to take a whack at anything. I directed a revue, *The Maid of the Mountains, Hamlet* and my own play, *Squirrel's Cage*, written a few months before. It was quite a success; that is to say my colleagues in the Drama Department were gracious and complimentary, and I was encouraged to write some more.

I was also encouraged to feel that as a B.B.C. official, I was, so to say, making the grade. After those months in the desert of the unwanted, was there not something alluring in a prospect of forty years' steady employment at a modest, but modestly increasing, salary? If I never did anything outrageous, if I stuck in—sticking in is the euphuism for not sticking out—and directed *Maids of the Mountains* for forty years, commuting daily—and after twenty years, first class—I would have a little pension; I would have a small villa, with rambler roses; I might even be a member of a good club. A respectful manservant in brass buttons might say: "Your sherry, Sah."

I knew the time had come again to look about.

Was this very snobbish? I don't think so. I did not think myself too good for such a future. I was not looking for something better, but for something else.

The idea of the B.B.C. was a fine one: that radio, this great new vehicle of ideas, should not be subordinated, as in America it already was, to the sale of commodities. I do not see why the only way of applying that idea had to be by the creation of a state monopoly.

Its monopolistic position has been, from the start, the bane of the B.B.C. It has rendered the officials at once complacent, because there was no competition, and timid, because charges that the monopoly was being abused have always been valuable ammunition for its enemies, notably newspapers, jealous of the B.B.C. as a dangerous rival, and politicians who, by asking questions in Parliament, can pose as guardians of public freedom. Further, the B.B.C. officials have never been reliably in touch with public opinion. Broadcasting House has always been an ivory tower.

This remoteness from the customer is a chronic problem in the mass dissemination of ideas. It is not only the B.B.C. which has failed to solve it; commercial radio is beset by it; so are the film and television industries.

Of course there exist elaborate systems for testing public reaction; and no doubt they can, and do, give a reasonably reliable answer—in quantitative terms. But even if the aim of a radio or television program is no higher than to sell, not an idea, but soap, then a merely quantitative estimate of the audience is insufficient. It is necessary to know not only how many people are being reached but also why, and to know in some detail how they react. None of the questionnaires can give reliable information, because only a negligible minority of those questioned knows precisely how it reacted, or why it reacted as it did: only a negligible fraction will be sufficiently articulate and prepared to take sufficient trouble to give a helpful answer.

The only even moderately reliable guide to audience reaction is the spontaneous comeback of those who are present at a performance. But this does not solve the problem for mass distribution. It is, of course, possible to have a studio audience, and this is often done. But the reaction of a studio audience is rarely spontaneous. It is very conscious of a sense of occasion, which is exactly what is absent from the reaction of the mass audience. Also, in order to give to the mass audience the impression that the show is going well, the studio audience is drilled. At appropriate points a card is displayed bearing simple instructions like Silence, Laughter, Applause.

But even if the studio audience's reaction were truly spontaneous and highly favorable, it still does not follow that the program is therefore adapted to its medium. On the contrary, the technique required to stimulate and hold the attention of the audience differs considerably from the technique of writing, production and performance, which suits the camera and the microphone.

Admitting this remoteness, this inability accurately to gauge the ever-changing taste and temper of the audience, most of the great mass-distributing organizations have found it necessary to adopt a style, to give some kind of character to their products which will, they hope, be acceptable. In America, most of the TV and radio programs are offered in a hearty, boisterous, old-fashioned-salesman kind of manner. To the Briton this seems wearisome and vulgar. I shudder to think what Americans must think of the style which the B.B.C. has made its own: the tone of one stranger to another, of slightly lower rank, in a suburban train.

I believe it was a mistake of the B.B.C. to allow its operation to be controlled by a corps of permanent officials. That is what has given to it its civil-service tinge. Better if the vast majority of official appointments had been on a short-term basis—somewhere between six months and two years. The hiring and firing, the maintenance of continuity, could have been left to a small, compact group of solely administrative officers, who alone would have long-term appointments.

Of course, in the early days it was necessary to train people who had no previous experience of a totally new medium. One of the troubles then was that, having used them for some of their best years, it became inhuman and irresponsible to heave them out, because the B.B.C.'s monopoly meant that there was no other home market for their training and experience. Also, short-term hiring would have involved higher rates of pay. Obviously people will accept comparatively low salaries in return for lifelong security.

But it is the policy of hiring on a long-term basis which accounts for so much Bumbledom in British broadcasting. The conditions attract the prudent, rather than daring, men and women; once in, there is every incentive to play safe and none to stick your neck out. Artistic or, for that matter, administrative achievements are only to be had by sticking your neck out as far as ever it will go.

Hardly had I decided that the life of a B.B.C. official was not for me when a great stroke of luck occurred. A lifeline was thrown from an entirely unexpected quarter.

5

Cambridge

A. B. HORNE was very rich and very stage-struck. All his life he had been interested in amateur theatricals. Now and again he had backed a professional production. At this time he cannot have been far short of seventy, but he had decided that it was not too late for a little flutter, had taken a year's lease of the Festival Theatre in Cambridge, and proposed a weekly program of interesting plays during the three eight-week periods of the University term. He needed a director. My old friends, the Scaifes, reminded him of my existence. He had seen our two plays at Oxted a year or two ago. Would I like to direct?

The Festival Theatre was a charming little eighteenth-century building, rather awkwardly placed on a dreary stretch of the main road to Newmarket about a mile from the center of Cambridge. About two years previously it had been rescued from decay by Terence Gray, a wealthy, talented, capricious man, who had done it up in his own idea of an amusing avant-garde style; hired a company and directed it himself in his own idea of an amusing avant-garde style.

His choice of plays was as gaily adventurous as his style of production. He had a considerable flair for showmanship.

But, as always happens, the *dernier cri* of yesterday is the dowdiest possible thing tomorrow. In 1926 Mr. Gray's "moderne" decor of the Festival—triangles of scarlet, black and emerald green; his projections of cerise and mauve light upon a cyclorama; his production of *Romeo and Juliet* in flamenco costume had seemed to the Cambridge intellectuals the last word of dizzy modernity.

By 1927 these delights had lost their gloss; so had the scarlet, black and emerald paint. By 1928 the barometer was falling alarmingly. Even the device of printing the programs in white on transparent black paper, which you had to hold against the light in order to read, created only a mild flicker of interest. The sole bulwark against absolute ruin was the presence in the cast of Miss Leonora Corbett, an extremely handsome girl, to look upon whom her many admirers tolerated the goings-on: avant-garde had become bodyguard.

Terence Gray decided that the theatre needed a change of policy; he let it to Mr. Horne, confident that the managerial taste, though different, would still be respectable, and retired either to tend a vineyard near Bordeaux or to breed racehorses in Eire. Both, perhaps; he was brilliantly versatile.

Mr. Horne—or, to use his stage name, Anmer Hall—made it clear that I was to have an almost completely free hand on the artistic side. Financially, the budget was not such as to permit of extravagance; but, carefully managed, it was enough.

To head the first company, I engaged Robert Donat and, with some difficulty, persuaded Flora Robson to return to the stage. She had quit in despair after a series of wretchedly insignificant parts followed by a long period out of work, and was doing welfare work in a factory.

We opened with Pirandello's *Six Characters in Search of an Author,* in which Flora as the stepdaughter gave an electrifying performance. No one who saw her in that part could doubt that here was the makings of a great actress. I visited Cambridge thirty years later, and a group of senior Fellows over dinner recalled it with the sentiment which we all reserve for the exciting impressions of our youth. Unanimously they declared that in thirty years of subsequent playgoing they had never seen a performance to equal its dazzling originality and force.

We did four seasons at Cambridge—about thirty plays—mostly for a week each. Occasionally, to give more time for rehearsal, we did three plays in a fortnight. The business was not good; we almost always played to capacity on Saturday night, Thursday and Friday were good, but the first three nights in the week were rarely more than half full. Our artistic reputation in Cambridge was quite good, but we never managed to create the body of two thousand regular adherents which would have ensured the theatre's economic life.

Perhaps for a theatre of this kind a University city is not the right place, because of the enormous number of student activities and diversions. But what a wonderful audience these young men and women were; quick on the uptake, warmly and discriminatingly appreciative, scathingly critical of what was shoddy and incompetent.

Anmer Hall was prepared to lose a little money for what he believed to be worth while; and, like the genuine patron he was, did not insist that the program should entirely reflect his own taste. I tried not to make it entirely reflect mine either. Our aim was to be catholic, with a slight classical and conservative bias, because we felt that Cambridge had already had a good dose of avant-garde theatre from Terence Gray.

Here are some of the plays we did: *Naked* (Pirandello), *All for Love* (Dryden), *Six Characters* (Pirandello), *Gentleman Dancing Master* (Wycherley), *The Rivals* (Sheridan), *The Machine Wreckers* (Toller), *Marriage* (Gogol), *Warren Hastings* (Feuchtwanger), *Volpone* (Ben Jonson), *The Cherry Orchard* (Chekhov). Of Ibsen we did *A Doll's House* and *Rosmersholm*; of Shakespeare *Measure for Measure* and *The Merry Wives*. We had a great success with *Lady Audley's Secret*, a mid-Victorian melodrama, produced rather too near burlesque but with a villainess by Miss Robson who managed to be very funny and impressive at the same time; and *Tobias and the Angel* by James Bridie, of which we gave the first performance on any stage. I think our best effort was *Iphigenia in Tauris* in the Gilbert Murray version: Flora Robson again, with Donat very fine as Orestes. The production did woefully poor business but we were encouraged by Gilbert Murray, who saw a matinee and professed himself much moved and impressed.

This was for me a very happy period. It was strenuous—we rehearsed every day from ten till one, and again, except when there was a matinee, from two till about five. Then there was the performance at night. Sunday, instead of being a day of rest, was the busiest day of all. In the morning we struck the scenery of the last production and set up the next. In the afternoon it was lit; in the evening there would be a dress rehearsal, often lasting seven or eight hours.

The company lived as a close and friendly little brotherhood. Five or six of us had rooms in a house attached to the theatre; the rest had lodgings nearby. There was little time or energy for a social life. Our schedule made it very hard to accept invitations to meals. Our salaries were on a scale which precluded all but the simplest entertaining on our part. It was a life of monastic simplicity and concentration.

Professionally, I learned during this time how to put a performance together inside the limits of a very hurried schedule. I am not sure that this has much, if anything, to do with the creative side of direction. But it has a good deal to do with the difference between professional and amateur.

The grind of weekly "rep" must be analogous to being on a daily newspaper. A good journalist must discipline himself to write intelligently and fast; to separate what he believes to be essential in a story from its trimmings; to condense or spread his material as required; above all, to cough it up promptly, and in any and every circumstance—no nonsense about nice, quiet rooms with views, about waiting for inspiration and so on. Newspaper work makes a "pro" of you.

But I can conceive that in knocking the nonsense out of you, it may knock out much of the sensibility too.

So with weekly "rep," or "stock," in the theatre. Everything must be done, perforce, the quickest way; and, as every fool knows, the quickest way is not necessarily the best way.

The advantage of the stock system is that it provides for the young actor or director a quick succession of new productions. That is invaluable. One of the great drawbacks to the current commercial system in the metropolitan theatre is that a production is either a hit or a flop. Either it comes off next Saturday or it runs two years. Either way is disastrous for the young artist.

If the play flops he may easily be out of work for weeks, maybe months; he will not have had time to settle into his part, to find all there is in it, to get the full professional benefit from playing it. If the play has a long run, then, conversely, he has to go on performing his role long after he has explored its limits, until acting becomes merely a matter of forcing himself through a repetitive routine. If you play even a long and complex part hundreds of times, every glance becomes habitual. The routine of the part becomes as automatic as factory work. To keep this routine fresh, and yet keep the performance in its original shape, is a stern test of discipline. But it has nothing to do with creative art; it confines, not enlarges, the technical and imaginative range of the artist.

On the other hand, a weekly succession of new productions is too quick. Even the simplest play, let alone a complex masterpiece, cannot be adequately prepared in a week. There is more to good performance than just knowing the words and the business.

The intuitions of the good actor nearly always occur subsequent to the process of learning the words; they tend to spring not merely out of his own conception of the whole play, but out of glances, small movements, tentative tones which are exchanged between himself and his partners in rehearsal. It is out of these suggestions, out of ideas only half formed in the consciousness of any single individual, that a good director builds up a scene, instinctively feeling, rather than consciously knowing, which of these half-formed suggestions to accept, which to reject. The acceptable ideas must then be coaxed into the full light of consciousness; only if conscious are they repeatable, and only if repeatable can they be incorporated into the finished work of art; be bricks, as it were, in the house which is being built.

Too often performances have to be prepared so fast that there is no possibility for this kind of intuition. Radio and television, where for reasons of economy the preparation must be done as quickly as possible, put a premium upon slickness, upon the ability to achieve a quick and easily acceptable effect; hence, upon technique, know-how. But know-how is not very valuable without know-what and, more important, know-why; and more important still, *feel*-why. Slick and technically efficient performance is not in itself enough to unlock the secrets of a subtle and interesting script; nor to invest an ordinary script with something over and above itself.

Many very ordinary scripts have been turned into great theatre by the "over and above" of the performer's art. Irving's performance of Mathias in *The Bells* is a conspicuous instance. Who now remembers that the script was adapted from Erckmann-Chatrian by Leopold Lewis? The script is of no significance, Irving's performance of Mathias legendary.

A week's rehearsal enables a company, if it works hard, to know the words and business of a play; but it does not give time for the gradual assimilation of character, the gradual ripening of ideas, an unhurried process of experiment.

Theoretically there is an optimum rehearsal period for every production. The same play will take longer if A directs than if B does, or if there are elderly people in the cast, because they have more trouble remembering the lines. You cannot in practice generalize; but there is an optimum period. In my experience, with one exception no production has had quite enough time spent on its preparation.

The exception was a play by J. B. Priestley called *Dangerous*

Corner. It is a highly ingenious piece of construction but has not very much content. Like the musical cigarette box which was one of the props whose use its plot requires, it was a beautiful but perhaps rather trivial mechanism. In the original production none of the actors were over forty and all were experienced and efficient people. In a week they knew the words backwards. In two weeks we all felt we had explored the play's rather narrow limits of characterization and philosophy. There was another week before we opened. For three more days we rehearsed, the performance, at each run-through becoming slicker but less interesting and more perfunctory. With the author's permission we knocked off until a dress rehearsal on the night before we opened.

I do not mean to imply my own and the actors' superiority to Mr. Priestley's play. It could have been, and subsequently has been, done better. But in less than the allotted span of three weeks we had reached the limit of what *we* could do with it. Three weeks, incidentally, seems to me about the optimum period for a fully efficient company to prepare a play, if it offers no exceptional technical or interpretative difficulties. It is not enough for a subtle, complex play.

Hamlet, oddly enough, is a play which can be rehearsed very quickly. There are few scenes involving more than two or three people; the big ensemble scenes are short—even the finale is shorter and far less difficult than, for instance, the great finales to *Twelfth Night, Measure for Measure* or *All's Well.* If the director and the actor who plays Hamlet are well prepared and in full agreement, the production can, in my opinion, be put together in two weeks. The reason for this is that none of Hamlet's scenes demand a very close rapport between the participants. Most of the psychological material is conveyed in soliloquy; to a unique degree the rapport is not between actor and actor, but between Hamlet and the audience.

It is a fact, and to the professional director not always a palatable one, that in every play the principal rapport is to some extent between the actors and their audience, rather than between themselves. Sometimes—the great scenes between Iago and Othello are a conspicuous instance—scenes simply have no meaning, and there can be no audience–actor rapport, unless the contact between the two actors is close and unselfish, each playing to, and for, the other, as much as, perhaps more than, for the audience.

Technically my range was being broadened, partly by the wide variety and style of the plays, partly by the design of the Festival Theatre. Mr. Gray had so reconstructed it that it was almost unworkable for a realistic play. We nearly killed ourselves to put on *The Cherry Orchard* with three different realistic sets and a multitude of props. But with its cyclorama, easily moved platforms and elaborate lighting equipment, it was possible to get showy and interesting effects with figures isolated in rather vague and unidentified "space."

This suited well for "expressionism," which was still fashionable. We were able to contrive a good *mise en scène* for *The Machine Wreckers* and for *Iphigenia*, or *Tobias and the Angel* —all the plays which permitted a rather abstract method of staging, where locality was either unimportant or could be implied in terms which were general rather than specific, atmospheric rather than literal.

After my years in Scotland, where nearly all our plays demanded rather boringly literal, interior box sets, this was extremely liberating. Moreover, Terence Gray had bequeathed to us the services of a really brilliant electrician, Mr. Steén, who taught me a great deal—not about electromechanics, wiring, fuse boxes, watts, ohms, earths, or short circuits; but I think I did absorb some common sense about how to light actors and sets, to make them look as I wanted them to look, without the time-wasting process of trial and error in which many excellent electricians bog down.

Experts in stage lighting, like experts in every other field, are seldom content to adopt a simple or easy way their wonders to perform. They like to surround their craft with a bit of mystery. Just as doctors prescribe bread pills in Latin and a handwriting totally baffling to every human eye except that of the particular pharmacist with whom they are hand in glove; just as musicians have to say *fortissimo* instead of "very loud," so stage-lighting experts like to make use of a highly technical vocabulary, to provide more equipment and to usurp more time than, in my opinion, their contribution to a production usually justifies.

In the United States, particularly, it is current practice to work with a tremendous number of quite low-powered lamps rather than a smaller number of greater power. This means that a great deal of time has to be allotted to the process of "focusing"—mere focus-pocus. It is also customary to filter the light through a number of different pale-colored mediums. I entirely see the advantages of colored light in certain contexts. But on Broadway hundreds, even thousands, of man-hours per season are spent setting up elaborate combinations of pale rose pinks, salmon pinks, "surprise" pinks, gold, pale gold, old gold, greeny-blue, pinky-blue, steel and gray-blue, in order to light very ordinary interior sets for very ordinary little comedies. I hate to think of the money all this costs; and I hate to look at the result, which is as if the stage were bathed in a weak solution of apricot jam.

Constantly, in my opinion, light is used to do a coloring job which a competent designer should have already achieved in the painting of the scenery and the choice of dress materials.

There is a theory quite widely held by actors that white light is "unbecoming." Aging leading ladies, who know nothing whatever about lighting but are accustomed to getting their own way, insist upon being lit in their own pet shade, usually of pink. This is nonsense. If white light makes a lady too pale, the answer is not to color the light but to color the lady. It is not the color which makes light "hard" or "unbecoming," it is the degree of intensity and the angle at which it strikes the face. In general, the American practice of using the first pipe almost directly above the actors' heads as a dominant source of light makes for extremely aging and unbecoming results. Lit from this source, even the tiniest, most retroussé button of a nose casts a shadow, endowing its wearer with the appearance of a moustache; eye sockets disappear in heavy shadow; fat faces appear fatter, craggy ones yet more craggy. Miss Ruth Gordon, a brilliant actress who makes no secret of her years, wisely includes in every contract a clause that footlights shall be used. She realizes that from a source below the eyes an actor can be lit more glamorously; also, that only so can the expression of the eyes be fully revealed.

During this Cambridge period I do not think I had begun to develop any particular philosophy of the theatre.

I had as yet scarcely any working contact with the commercial theatre, either in the West End of London or on tour. I regarded it with mixed and contradictory feelings. On the one hand was stage-struck shyness, a timid longing to be part of the highly paid, highly publicized world of successful stars, managers, writers, directors, about which I had read and heard gossip.

On the rare occasions when I had met any of these beings I had been snobbishly impressed. They seemed handsome, interesting, exciting, and all the rest of it—because I had expected them to be so. I had not really examined these creatures, partly, I suppose, because I half-consciously wanted to protect my illusions about them, partly because I was far too shy and flustered to think about *them;* I was concerned only that these great ones should not be vexed and bored by my insignificance, that they should not dash a foot against the stone of my dullness and provinciality.

On the other hand, I still had an obstinate conviction that metropolitan glamour was vulgar, that there was virtue and strength in provinciality. I heartily despised a good deal of the professional theatre for its blatant commerciality, its playing down to what I considered ignorance and bad taste.

Like most ardent young people, I was filled with missionary zeal. I thought it my duty to try to make people like what I liked, I even thought that if I tried hard enough the attempt would succeed. I still had the ambition—very secret and in no way practical; perhaps daydream is a more accurate description—to have a theatre of my own, which would make no concessions to popular vulgarity, which would be a Temple, but which would also—and only later did experience teach me how irreconcilable are these two aims—be extremely successful.

I had immature but not, I think, unsound ideas about what constituted a good play. I felt with due humility that classics were so because they had withstood the test of time. They were what respectable judgment had agreed over the years to admire. Therefore I too must try to admire and try to see wherein their merit lay. New work must have something interesting, not necessarily solemn, to say and must say it in theatrical terms, in terms which I could envisage on the stage. I was, and still am, a sucker for jokes and horseplay, and for great moments, however corny. I was, and still am, vehemently averse to political and social propaganda disguised in dramatic form.

This was a period when intellectual and pseudo-intellectual young people were greatly inclined to plays about the People. The People were young and handsome, except for a few wise father-figures and noble mother-figures. The People were oppressed by creatures called Capitalists, every one of whom was ugly and irredeemably wicked. In between were a lot of mean-spirited cravens called Bourgeois. The Bourgeois too would be terribly wicked, if they dared. And that always seemed the single respect in which these plays came within hailing distance of anything resembling life as I knew it. I am a bourgeois and so are almost all my friends; and we would all be not terribly but moderately wicked if we dared.

I have now lived long enough to see these same ideas trotted out with some small, technical concessions to prevailing fashions and with the names of the protagonists altered. The wicked Capitalist is often a Nazi Officer, a corrupt Trades Union Boss, a Roman Catholic Archbishop, a Teen-age Werewolf, a Communist or a Mother. The label is immaterial because it only conceals the same old dummy, constructed out of prejudice, inflated with gas.

As yet my own likes and dislikes seemed to derive from good reasons. At all events I was at pains to rationalize them. I tried not to be "prejudiced"; tried, with some hope of success, to "improve" my taste. I do not think it crossed my mind that my taste was being formed by factors over which I had no control whatever.

At this period I do not remember giving any thought at all to what the art, or arts, of the theatre might be. I accepted a vague jumble of ideas, often entirely contradictory, and believed that they might, by unremitting effort, be directed towards the development of better taste, conduce to the benefit of the human race.

I was not discontented with Cambridge, far from it, or anxious for more money; I felt I was being paid adequately. I was still self-consciously provincial. I rather despised myself for being stage-struck, for reading wistfully, and by now a little jealously, about first nights in the West End of London, about interesting goings-on in Paris, Berlin and New York. Yet at the same time I wanted my work to be noticed, longed for opportunity in a wider sphere, at once wanted and dreaded to step into a less sheltered, less "special" kind of theatre than our little tabernacle at Cambridge with its kind and generous patron, its pleasant but slightly restricted companionship.

I felt now that I had enough experience, enough technique to be regarded as a professional; but that I had not, as yet, worked in fully professional conditions. I had taken, as it were, quite a long course of swimming lessons. My strokes were reasonably proficient. I had made an adequate showing in a luxurious indoor pool. Now I was confronted with the sea. At any moment I must plunge.

6

Montreal

THE PLUNGE, however, was deferred. I received an offer from the Canadian National Railways.

It may seem odd that a railway company, however vast, should make offers of theatrical employment. However, in Canada at this period (1929) radio was operated by the two great railroads—the Canadian National and the Canadian Pacific. I think that in the Canadian National Railways radio was administered as a subsidiary activity of the Express Department; perhaps it was Telegraphs, it is not important.

The head man of the Canadian National Railways' Radio Department, Mr. Austin Weir, had decided to produce a series of scripts dealing in dramatic form with Canadian history. Merrill Dennison had been engaged as author. Since, to date, Canada had no indigenous radio drama, it was decided to import a director from Britain.

I never heard why the election lighted on me. My name was on a list and a representative of Mr. Weir came to look me over. He arrived at the Festival Theatre one Sunday morning in October and found me hunking scenery out of a loft, clad in little beside a pair of sneakers. To a Canadian, whose teeth were chattering in Britain's season of mists and mellow fruitfulness, perhaps I seemed a hardy, rugged, pioneering type.

Merrill Dennison and Mr. Weir met me at the dockside in New York. Winter was wintry then. Snow was piled up in great dark-gray mounds by the sidewalks. To give me a quick tourist's once-over of New York we went to the top of the brand-new Chrysler building, then the highest; and mighty splendid it seemed, with masses of chromium—still a novelty —and bright blue leatherette, and elevator men in bright blue uniforms who seemed to have strayed out of a bang-up production of The Prisoner of Zenda.

Then, to see how the other half lives, we went down into the subway at rush hour in Times Square. Walpurgis Night on the Brocken would by comparison have seemed like tea in a country vicarage. The fetid air was rent by oaths, by howls like the tormented damned in hell; a train already packed was attacked, fallen upon, by Maenads. I saw a colored man place his foot against the buttocks of a woman and boost her by main force through the choked doorway of a coach already bulging. In a gladiatorial, bullfighting way, and after staid old Cambridge, it was thrilling. I too screamed and cursed and pushed the face of a person much older and weaker than myself. What fun! And how different, how gloriously different, from the home life of our own dear Queen!

After that I remember little. Prohibition still reigned. There were knocks at sundry dark doorways, and faces peering through grilles. I remember two douce, demure Mr. Weirs and several gloriously amusing Merrill Dennisons. I remember the squealing consternation when I started to undress in the pullman without pulling the frowsty, sage-green curtain of my "lower" in the night train for Montreal.

Montreal—this was thirty years ago—seemed, to my untraveled eyes, everything that was romantic. I loved the intense cold out of doors and the intense heat indoors. Most British people find this trying; in my thick suits I certainly sweated, but the extravagant temperatures were all part of the exhilaration. It was Christmastime and the lit trees, the masses of Bermuda lilies, the snow, the policemen in fur hats, the incense-laden gaiety of a predominantly, very consciously, Catholic city . . . it was all very "foreign," and congenial.

I used to wander about the streets staring at the fascinating types, so very unlike the inhabitants of Glasgow or Belfast, Oxford, Cambridge or Kensington. I ate in a little Czech cafe and for the first time encountered peanut butter, bacon fried with bananas, and all sorts of things which were cheap and evidently commonplace, but were new to me. There was a Syrian bakery with a delivery van, which was a sleigh drawn by a coal-black pony, Syrian too no doubt, whose harness was hung with glittering brass bells; Greek fruit-shops, Chinese laundries, the cosmopolitanism which is so commonplace in the New World seemed to me wonderful.

In my spare time I walked on the Mountain—a real mountain, quite high, which sprouts up in the very center of the city and provides it with a glorious playground. I wandered through wintry cemeteries and read the names on the tombs —so many, like myself, Irish and Scottish—and felt a strong pleasure that, like them, I was bringing something of the Old Country with me and would, God willing, take something of the New World home. I read *Maria Chapdelaine*. I visited kind, dull cousins in Westmount, stronghold of well-off, Empire-minded, bourgeoisie. In Westmount they regard —or did then; no doubt they have reformed all that—the French-Canadians as "natives," make a point of mispronouncing French names . . . "Noter Dayme, Plass Darms, Saint Dennis" . . . and, in general, of acting as if Boney and his Frog-eaters were expected any moment to assail the white cliffs. The French-Canadians, on their part, much more French than the inhabitants of metropolitan France, much more Catholic than the Vatican, extravagantly exemplified the sort of ideas about "foreigners" which were current in Tunbridge Wells and Lemington Spa during the Boer War; were, in short, charming, volatile, unpunctual, "artistic" and inclined to smell of garlic.

I lived at the Y. It was very central, very cheap and very clean. Each Saturday there appeared in my room the weekly issue of the House Mag. Its tone was so extravagantly hearty and chummy, so muscularly Christian, that I could hardly credit it was not meant to be funny. It addressed its readers as though we were members of some surrealist English public school of the eighteen-fifties, furiously hearty, desperately sin-conscious, but thoroughbred. Yet the young fellows, whom I met in the showers, in the elevator or at breakfast in the canteen, did not seem unduly hearty, sin-conscious or thoroughbred. Who, I wondered, attends the Informal Mixed Socials, the Indian Pow-Wows, the Quiet Chats which each Saturday, with grisly relish, the House Mag reported?

Even in Canada the sty where our radio plays were produced was called a studio. It was decorated in a cabbage green and everything in sight was made of basketwork, also in green, splotched with gold. There were no windows; even at nine of a midsummer morning we worked by electric light, shaded with green basketwork; there was no ventilation, conveniences were few and remote. It was a rather sissy version of the salt mines.

But we had good fun there. My colleagues were all railway workers rather surprised to find themselves drafted into this newfangled nonsense of radio, and very much surprised to be mixed up with play-acting. *The Romance of Canada* must have been one of the earliest radio serials. It certainly was the first dramatic effort of any scale on the Canadian air.

For about twenty weeks we churned out a new historical episode every Tuesday, often with large casts and complicated effects.

In those days there was no professional theatre in Canada. The talkies, newly and triumphantly emerged, had swept all before them. A few amateur groups bore the torch of drama. My first job was to recruit a company. In this my mainstay was Rupert Caplan. He had acted professionally in New York but was now back home in Montreal assisting his uncle in a textile business. He is a very talented and enthusiastic man and I owe him a great debt for his help in launching this pioneer effort.

Caplan introduced me to most of the principal amateur actors in Montreal, Ottawa and Toronto. These formed a nucleus, to whom I added as occasion demanded Scots, where a Scottish accent was appropriate, Cockney, Irish, Yorkshire or Welsh. Dealing as they did with early days in Canada, the scripts demanded mostly people from the Old Country, with marked regional accents to differentiate each character from the rest.

We unearthed some splendid talent. A bellhop from the Windsor Hotel was a first-rate Irish character man. At the Y a young man newly immigrated from Fife was doing the night shift on the elevator; he became our resident Scotsman. From time to time we did hire professional actors for leading parts. But mostly the players were amateurs, who worked with great attention to duty and maintained a very creditable standard.

Our only excursion into the professional field was unfortunate. A stock company was playing in Ottawa that winter, and for one play I hired the two leading actors.

Mr. X was a handsome fellow, about forty, sharply and flashily turned out. His leading lady was handsome and even more flashy. He referred to her as "my sister" and so, maybe, she was, though they were of markedly different build and type, and even race. They rehearsed confidently and, while not outstandingly talented, they knew their business.

On *the* night, five minutes before the performance was due to begin, I was informed that policemen had arrived and wished, then and there, to place Mr. X under arrest. I explained the situation to the cops and persuaded them to wait till the end of the performance. The last word of the play had hardly been spoken when three policemen entered the studio and, in front of everybody, placed handcuffs upon the wrists of Mr. X.

Sympathy on his behalf was mingled with feverish curiosity as to the nature of his crime. Was it robbery, murder, rape or merely bigamy? In the circumstances no one quite liked to ask. In silence we admired the *sang-froid* with which he carried off the situation. He bade a courteous good night, showed his very white teeth in a smile that was only a little too jaunty, and swaggered out with the escorting cops. "My sister" behaved with equal composure. No emotion was shown, not even surprise.

Next day I took him his pay and handed him the notes through the bars of a sort of cage. As smartly groomed as ever, exuding a scent of expensive hair oil among the drunks and riffraff in the cage, he thanked me for coming, hoped we should meet again, showed his white teeth and said good-bye in a tone indicating that further conversation would not be welcome.

The Romance of Canada fell sick of a disease to which all serial undertakings are liable: the gradual exhaustion of the author. Merrill Dennison began with *Henry Hudson*—an excellent script for which I was able to find an excellent cast. We got off to a flying start.

But gradually the pace began to tell. Halfway through the series, with about ten more scripts to write, poor Merrill was in trouble. He would deliver the current script just in time for the first rehearsal and then, exhausted, with no ideas, no enthusiasm, he would have to sit right down and beat his brains afresh. Furthermore, after the first ten or twelve installments he had used up the most familiar, as well as the most obviously "radiogenic," episodes in Canada's rather brief history. Each week entailed more and more research.

More and more demands were placed, as is the way of weak radio writing, upon the effects department. The nadir was reached when we were asked to suggest, without benefit of dialogue or any descriptive build-up, that an elderly man was being gobbled up by rats.

In these latter days when radio serials and TV serials are routine procedure, the problem has been solved by reference to Homer. The soap operas, like the *Odyssey*, are the product not of one mind but a group.

At the end of my contract, and as a sort of tip in addition to my salary, Mr. Weir arranged that I should travel right across Canada as a guest of the Canadian National Railways. It was a wonderful present. I went right over from Montreal to Prince Rupert in the far Northwest, over to Vancouver Island where I have relatives, then back East, stopping here and there, to make contacts imaginatively arranged by Austin Weir.

This trip gave me a glimpse of Canada, an impression of its immensity and diversity, and the chance to meet many kind and congenial people who have become lifelong friends. I left Canada thrilled with what I had seen, eager to return and to be somehow, at some time and in some way a participant in the adventure of developing this land with its vast possibilities, so many of them still dormant, still undreamed—the romance of Canada.

The voyage from New York to Galway was blessed with golden midsummer sunshine and calm. But on the voyage an episode occurred which, although it has apparently nothing whatever to do with the subject of this book, has always seemed to me strange and dramatic.

It was about four in the afternoon. Tea was beginning and all the passengers had left the boat deck, where I was reading.

It was very quiet.

I glanced down at the deck, below and forward of where I was, and suddenly a woman who was standing at the rail clutched at her hair. Holding long strands of hair which fell about her shoulders, she sank down on her knees and seemed to be praying. It was still very quiet. Then the ship's hooter sounded the alarm signal—a long blast followed by short ones—and the ship keeled over in a very sharp turn. Now all hell broke loose among the passengers. We had struck a rock, an iceberg, a sea serpent; we were sinking; we were lost. Papa yelled for mama, mama yelled for sis and junior, life belts appeared, officers dashed about. A steward continued to proffer French pastries. Gradually word spread that a man was overboard, we were turning about in the hope of picking him up. Now somebody saw him— "There! Right there, don't you see?"

Again there was absolute silence. The ship's engines were still. Not a sound.

Then there arose the strangest noise. I can hear it still. Not a shout, not a groan, not a sigh, but something of all three; quite loud; the audible and collective reaction of several hundred people to what we all saw—a man, floating face downward in the water, in, of all things, a waterproof. It floated out and around him like gray ectoplasm. He seemed to be drifting past us quite fast, but of course it was we who were moving. Out of the pocket of the raincoat, floating on the surface of the sea, was a long narrow paper, still pink, easily recognizable. I had just such another; it was his return ticket.

Now a second collective impulse swept the crowd. Everyone wanted to do something, to help. They leaned over the rail and yelled encouragement, exhortation, to that down-faced thing as it floated past and away; people hurled deckchairs, lifebelts, anything handy; children hurled their toys; I saw an old gentleman, weeping and stamping with frustration, pelt the insensate ocean with egg sandwiches.

A boat was lowered. They picked him out. After artificial respiration he lived.

Among the pink lampshades, the stuffed olives and dry Martinis, the word passed around. The ship's doctor had told the second engineer, the second engineer the purser, the purser told Miss Reisinger; all, of course, in strict confidence, just between you and me. He had been unemployed. He had "gotten rather depressed." He had slashed his wrists and jumped into the sea.

Very sad, of course; oh dreadfully sad. Another Martini?

But hadn't the crew of the lifeboat been marvelous, especially that very handsome seaman in the bow? Another? Of course, when you come to think of it, it was rather an inconsiderate thing to do. I mean—depressed, that's one thing, but to jump right into the sea! I mean— Junior was so scared he couldn't finish his cookie. Another Martini? But the crew of the lifeboat! Let's all drink their health. I know, let's drink it in champagne.

7

Westminster Theatre

ON MY RETURN to Ireland I married Judith Brether-
ton. Her father was a lawyer of English North Country
family; her mother was of Guernsey stock. Our parents were
old friends, but I am five years older than she, which meant
that in childhood we saw very little of one another. Indeed,
we hardly met till we were both grown-up.

This book is a professional, not a personal, document; but
I think I may go so far as to say that we have lived happily
ever after.

In the following autumn Anmer Hall, our patron at Cambridge, converted a cinema, near Buckingham Palace Mews,
into the Westminster Theatre. Anmer Hall's idea was to use
the nucleus of his Cambridge company in a stock company
which, reinforced by actors of established reputation, should
present a series of interesting and serious plays. We opened
with the first production of a new play by James Bridie called
The Anatomist.

Henry Ainley, who had been ill for several years, made a
successful comeback in the leading part; Gillian Scaife and
Betty Hardy were excellent as two Edinburgh ladies; but it
was the low-life characters who really scored—Harry Hutchin-
son and James O'Rourke, ex-members of the Abbey Theatre,

played Burke and Hare, the murderers; Morland Graham from the Scottish National Theatre played a corrupt hospital official; Flora Robson made a most touching figure of an Edinburgh prostitute. Several productions followed at intervals of about six weeks, with a semipermanent company of which the nucleus was still the Cambridge contingent.

After the struggle to produce play after important play in a week, the schedule at the Westminster seemed very leisurely. Some of us younger people formed a play-reading society which was joined by other earnest professionals. We started to prepare Masefield's *Iseult the Fair:* I was to read King Mark, Margaret Webster was Iseult, and Esmé Church directed. However, the reading never took place because Miss Church and I both had to abandon it for more remunerative work in the West End production of *Dangerous Corner*. This was J. B. Priestley's first play, and I was very flattered to be asked to direct it.

Priestley and I had never met; he had liked my production of *Six Characters* at the Westminster and took a chance on that. I greatly admired the generosity and courage which would dare entrust his first theatrical venture to the hands of a young and unknown director. I liked working with him; he said what he thought in right plain terms; but plain speaking is fine when, as in Priestley's case, it is honest and kind.

The company was to be chosen by me, subject to Jack Priestley's approval. Marie Ney, Flora Robson, Esmé Church, Richard Bird, William Fox and that admirable actor, the late Frank Allenby, were all engaged. On Marie Ney's recommendation Murray MacDonald became stage manager. He was a Glasgow man whose brother, Dr. Honeyman, I had already known as a stalwart pillar of the theatre in Scotland.

The single disagreement between Priestley and myself was over the part of the young girl, a short but difficult role for which I wanted Diana Churchill. Priestley did not think Miss Churchill right and a young actress was chosen whose beauty did not, in my opinion, compensate for her lack of experience and technique.

In casting, managers are often too much influenced by the appearance of actors and actresses when they come to be interviewed. The face, figure and clothes simply cannot be judged out of the context of performance. It is my experience that all you can get from an interview is a rough and ready first impression. You can tell if *you* are attracted by a particular personality; but not if it is, in general, attractive. You can get a fairly accurate idea of stature; but that is not of prime importance. True, if your leading gentleman is a fascinating five feet eight inches, you will be wise to seek a short, rather than statuesque, lady to play love scenes with him. But, in general, it is not a good idea to buy actresses and actors by the yard or by the pound.

Yet this is the principle which inexperienced managements, especially in America, constantly adopt. A part is to be cast: agents are called; a stage is hired and onto it, merely to be looked at, troops a host of men and women. However courteously the manager and his assistants conduct this ceremony, it is still humiliating for the actors. They are being looked over like cattle, and they know it. To counter the embarrassment many of them develop a brassy, vulgarly confident manner, which is either pathetic or else alienating and makes it extremely hard to know what sort of a person it conceals.

If, as often happens, you have to engage someone whose work you do not know, whom perhaps you have never met, then I think the actor and director ought to have the chance to make acquaintance in the most relaxed and leisurely circumstances possible.

This problem of casting is particularly acute in New York, because it is the sole theatrical center for an entire continent. The theatre, so highly centralized, is a vast organization: every season hundreds of employers interview tens of thousands of prospective employees of whom the vast majority are total strangers; they have never met before and will quite likely never meet again. In casting a Broadway musical, I was present at auditions for more than a thousand people to fill six or seven vacancies in a chorus.

In London, Paris or Berlin, the theatre is a business on a far smaller scale. After you have been working for five or six years in the London theatre you know the work of nearly all the prominent actors and a considerable number of the less prominent. You know several hundred of them by sight and are on familiar and friendly terms with several score. Plays can be cast—and, in my view, can only thus be cast efficiently —almost entirely from a group with whose work and personalities the director is already acquainted.

In the smaller centers—Dublin, Copenhagen, Athens, for example—the number of actors is still more limited. Every professional knows virtually all the others. Of course, in such circumstances, the range of casting is more restricted. Quarts have occasionally to be poured into pint pots, square pegs to be squeezed into round holes.

On Broadway and to a lesser extent in London, it is usual to cast a play to "type." That is to say an actor is engaged for a particular part because his appearance, voice and mannerisms seem to resemble the management's conception of the part—or because he has recently played a precisely similar part.

Type-casting is certainly an insurance against the wilder flights of miscasting. But, by casting obviously to type, a manager tends to restrict any creative or imaginative contributions by the actor; such casting tends to create very obvious, dull stereotypes. Managements reading a script, often hurriedly and rarely imaginatively, jump to the mistaken conclusion that such a character conforms to the stereotype which is known as a John Smith part, because John Smith has successfully played a vaguely similar part.

More harm tends to come from metropolitan type-casting than from the occasional monstrous miscasting which occurs in smaller centers because there simply is no one else available.

After *Dangerous Corner* I returned to the Westminster to direct a play about Disraeli. Nobody thought that it was an

especially good play; but it was a marvelous vehicle for the
particular talents and qualities of Ernest Milton, who was to
play Disraeli. On the day of the first rehearsal Mr. Milton
had to go into hospital. The management was left with a
vehicle, but, so to say, no horse. There was a theatre to be
filled and a cast of fourteen to pay. It was decided that we
should do Shakespeare's *Love's Labour's Lost*, which fitted
the cast to the extent that there was an actor for each part
and a part for each actor.

I had seen the play not long before in a delightful production by Nugent Monck directing a semi-amateur cast in the
little Maddermarket Theatre in Norwich. In Monck's production a permanent set suggested no clearly identifiable locality;
there were no breaks between scenes; the comic episodes,
which in Shakespearian production then, even more than now,
were apt to be heavily overlaid with "vaudeville" business,
were treated simply, realistically and sympathetically. Most of
the good ideas in my production were culled from Monck's
at Norwich.

I have no shame in confessing this. No art is completely
original; there are always influences. The artist is rarely
conscious of the most important and significant influences.
But in matters of style, in the externals, artists, especially
young artists, invariably imitate what they admire. From
Monck I absorbed various points of style, and a point of
view about this particular play. It may not have been his
point of view; it was what I made of his point of view.
Equally, Monck was indebted to other directors—notably
William Poel. We all learn, borrow, steal, if you like, from
one another. But if this is theft, then all are thieves who have
the wit to profit from other people's experience. I look upon
this kind of theft as a compliment to the person whose ideas
are used: imitation is the sincerest form of flattery. I have
been sincerely flattered in this way more than once by other
and younger directors, and I am only grateful to them. And
now I confess my debt to Nugent Monck, not with a blush
but with pride that I had the sense to pick so good a model.

To a performance of *Love's Labour's* at the Westminster came Harcourt Williams. He had been director at the Old Vic for several seasons and now, although no one knew it at the time, he was looking for someone to recommend as his successor. He liked the production. He advised Miss Lilian Baylis, the boss of the Old Vic, to go see it.

We youngsters at the Westminster were very interested to see this legendary figure. She sat in the stage box, which at the Westminster is, like the seats reserved for young gallants in an Elizabethan playhouse, practically on the stage. We had no idea why she had come, but it was mighty interesting to get a close-up view of this thick-set, elderly person in glasses, who looked like a parish worker, who talked throughout the performance to her pretty young lady-chauffeur in a tone almost as loud as the actors and in the unmistakable accent of South London suburbia.

Not long after, I was summoned to the Old Vic for an interview.

I remember arriving at the stage door; I remember the doorkeeper; the stone steps up into a corridor and a woman cooking a whiting for Miss Baylis' lunch on a little gas ring behind a festoon of faded pink cotton, which was supposed to conceal the fact that the cooking area was in a public corridor. The office was densely crowded: here a "Hamlet" chair, there a rickety sofa, a pretty little marquetry chair—forlorn stray from some Edwardian drawing room. As I wait, the sapphire plush cover of a side table is violently agitated and two dogs rush snarling out—Scamp and Sue. They were quite nasty little dogs, spoiled and bad-tempered. Miss Baylis, someone once said, came to dogs too late in life. She loved them not wisely but too well. Beneath that table Scamp and Sue had a home from home—basket, water, bones and so on. The top of the table was covered with portfolios, sketches for sets and dresses.

But the room was dominated by The Desk; a large affair in oak with a roll top. It was densely covered with papers; on the top were knickknacks. Presents from Margate, Lucerne,

the Trossachs, a bowl of Benares brass full of rusty paper
clips and shriveled rubber bands; a bunch of flowers, a tray of
dirty tea things and three telephones. Tacked to the roll top
was a post-card reproduction of Dürer's *Praying Hands*. All
this I remember perfectly—and hearing Miss Baylis in the
corridor, asking the person with the whiting what the dogs
were getting for lunch. Of her entrance into the office, what
she looked like, or said, I have no recollection whatever. Nothing was concluded at that interview. I gathered later that she
had not liked me very much, and when eventually she did
engage me it was with no feeling of pleasure or confidence.
She did not, I'm afraid, regard me as one of those God-sent
shining ones, those saviors upon whom she liked to believe
her life and that of the Old Vic depended. There was a va-
cancy; I was willing to fill it. The salary being what it was, I
guess the queue of applicants did not stretch far.

Now, on the threshold, as it were, of the Old Vic, let us
do a little retrospective theatrical stock-taking.

It was now ten years since I had begun at the Oxford
Playhouse; not, I think, the most fruitful or important decade
in theatrical history. Perhaps the most significant event had
been the development of radio, quickly followed by the re-
placement of silent films by talkies. Against the competition
of these two the theatre was fighting a desperate rear-guard
action. In Britain as well as in America, road-company business was by the end of the decade in full retreat. The theatre
had lost its supremacy as a supplier of popular entertainment.
The habit of regular playgoing was disappearing. Metropolitan audiences consisted more and more of tourists and people
on a spree or in town on expense accounts. Such audiences
are not in general interested in the more serious offerings.
Most such people just want a night out. More and more the
theatre was dependent for survival upon prestige, upon a comparatively small wealthy or intellectual minority, upon its
value as a training ground for writers, directors and actors.
But more and more these were, in their turn, depending upon

the mass-distribution media to spread upon their bread the butter of a good income and popular recognition.

In the straight theatre I suppose Bernard Shaw has been the most important figure in the English-speaking world. Maybe Eugene O'Neill will seem to posterity a greater dramatist; in my opinion he is so. But posterity may find the bleakness of his manner, the small vocabulary, writing which is at once diffuse and inelegant an even greater barrier than it is today. On the other hand, while less intellectual and less well informed about affairs than Shaw, he knew far more about people. But neither his output nor his influence upon his contemporaries was as great as that of Shaw. The production in 1924 of *Saint Joan* by Bronson Albery and Lewis Casson, with Sybil Thorndike as Joan, was perhaps the outstanding single event.

During this decade, Harley Granville-Barker, the only great British director, was in retirement. The most successful director was Basil Dean, who excelled in the arrangement of minutely detailed realism. He had little poetic feeling. His production of Flecker's *Hassan* was one of the important events in the theatre of its time (1923); the play was at the time very highly regarded; the production was lavish, a full orchestra played the Delius score, the cast was illustrious; but, in my opinion, the evening was a hash; and so was Dean's production at Drury Lane, again in sumptuous style, of *A Midsummer Night's Dream*. But within the limits of a rather unaspiring naturalism he was a superb technician. Under Dean's direction an author could be sure that his play would be thoughtfully and cleverly cast, well mounted, and skillfully presented. He was the best exponent of prosaic naturalism in this period of the British theatre.

First among the London actors was Gerald du Maurier. He had unrivaled charm, economy and skill, confined within the limits of an unambitious view of his calling. He never attempted to enlarge his technical range, or to put his great popularity and prestige at the service of any altruistic cause other than the conventional public charities.

Henry Ainley, endowed by nature with the attributes of a great classical actor—Hyperion's curls, the front of Jove himself, an eye like Mars to threaten and command—for some reason never achieved what he seemed to promise. Like many gifted and beautiful creatures he never had to work quite hard enough. Then, later, the effort to learn the technical tricks of the trade seemed pedestrian as well as laborious. He died, prematurely aged, when normally the best years should still have been ahead. I was privileged to know and work with him near the end of his life; became fond of him, and admired greatly a generosity of spirit scaled to high physical magnificence. Only discipline was lacking.

Of the women, Sybil Thorndike and Edith Evans were unquestionably the leading serious actresses—Thorndike, noble and compelling in tragedy, but at her greatest in performances which require grotesque frenzy, madness, violence; Evans at her best where artifice reveals nature, where sophisticated simulation reveals simple truth—her Millamant in Congreve's *Way of the World* may possibly never be excelled. Outstanding also were two comediennes, who in this decade grew charmingly into old age—Irene Vanbrugh and Marie Tempest.

As to the lyric stage: the leading impresario was C. B. Cochran. Performers at their zenith were Leslie Henson, Jack Buchanan and Nelson Keys; and among the women, Beatrice Lillie and Gracie Fields. Fluttering between the "lyric" and the "legitimate" theatre were two fellow graduates from the grim ranks of child actors: Gertrude Lawrence and Noel Coward.

Coward's, I think, is an overpublicized but underestimated talent. Not only has he been a leading entertainer in the popular field for a great many years, he is the author of *Bitter Sweet*, the best musical of the decade we are considering; its composer and director as well. He is also the author of *Hay Fever*, an artificial comedy which, in my view, has as good a chance of immortality as any work of an author now living.

It is "minor" work, its pretensions are small; but as well as its author's typical glitter and sharp satiric sting there is an "over and above" of wholesome horse sense.

In most authors the over and above, the work of the unconscious self, is usually concerned with sensibility; the conscious part is common-sensible. In Coward, as in Wilde and Congreve and Swift—and, I suspect, all important satirists—the conscious aim is to be sharp and glittering, amusing; the over and above is tender, it speaks of a practical and rather feminine good sense. In *Hay Fever* one catches, between the lines, a glimpse of that aspect of Noel Coward which made him a good president of the Actors' Orphanage. Usually this position had gone to an eminent actor who made a dignified figurehead, gave a handsome subscription and saw to it that seven or eight of his well-off friends did the same. Coward did all this; but he also visited the orphanage, made sure that the beds were clean, that the slops were emptied, the stairs swept, the meals adequate and that the orphans felt that their president really stood *in loco parentis*.

During the decade my own playgoing had been fairly extensive. In Belfast I saw the road company of *Saint Joan*, with Dorothy Holmes-Gore magnificent in the lead. On the night when I was there, a small riot occurred. Some rabid Protestants made a demonstration when, in the cathedral scene, Miss Holmes-Gore entered carrying, on the author's instruction, a cross. There was a Catholic counterdemonstration; beer glasses flew about the auditorium, ladies ducked and squealed, and, for a time, the performance was suspended. However, it all blew over and the play ended with no more fuss. It always seems odd that for Irish Protestants the cross is not a Christian symbol, nor a symbol of love; it is a detested and specifically Roman Catholic sign. If you want to be nicely received in Belfast or Portadown, carry a crescent, carry a hammer and sickle; wear, if you will, a scarlet letter or a green carnation. People will still be their wonted, wholesome, civil selves. If, however, you want to be beaten, reviled and possibly stoned to death, display prominently that emblem which proclaims that the Son of Man died to save sinners.

Another good thing I saw in Belfast was Chalmers Mackey and his company in *The Shaughraun*, Boucicault's Victorian melodrama. Mr. Mackey was a charming old gentleman who had been touring "the smalls" in Ireland for well over half a century. His company were nearly all as old as their leader. The performance was a touching and impressive piece of bygone theatre which had somehow survived into the twentieth century. In the main, however, Belfast in the twenties was, as it is now, a theatrical Sahara.

In Glasgow I saw many of the London productions touring either before, or after, their London run; many of the successful musicals and most of the leading vaudeville personalities of the day. I also saw the Princess Panto. The Princess Theatre was in the Gorbals, a slum area south of the Clyde, one of the roughest, toughest districts in Europe. Its management annually presented a pantomime in the vernacular: an entertainment vaguely based on a fairy tale, *Jack and the Beanstalk*, say, or *Puss in Boots*, with constant interpolations of popular song, whatever was current at the time, with troops of child dancers—little girls of about twelve to fifteen, and with most of Scotland's best comedians in the cast. It is a tradition of British Panto that the Hero be played by a girl—a hefty, strapping lass with a good strong voice to lead a chorus; this is the Principal Boy. The Principal Girl is the Hero's sweetheart and is played by a small, very feminine, helpless, clinging type. Then there is The Dame, who is played by a low comedian dressed up as an Old Woman, with no attempt at feminine charm, but a good deal of rough-and-tumble business; it's a poor evening if, at some stage, the Dame's drawers don't come down, or she becomes the center of a china-smashing, egg-throwing or water-squirting act.

In my day the principal comedian of the Princess Panto was, and had been for many years, Tommy Lorne. He was now a tall, thin old man, well up his sixties. But in his outrageous female disguise he would hold that rough, excited audience in the hollow of his great bony paw. He was A One, too, for pathos. Many's the tear I've shed at Tommy Lorne, and many's the time I've gasped and ached, and gasped again, in an utter exhaustion of merriment.

The Panto is supposed to be a Christmas treat for children. But the Princess Panto was entirely, and even shamelessly, adult; the Christmas season began early in October and rarely finished before Easter.

Now the old Princess is no more and Tommy Lorne is no more. But the old house, now the Citizens' Theatre, still continues the policy of indigenous theatre; still offers an uproarious, though now slightly purified, Christmas show.

My experience of the classics was limited. Unless you lived in London, that was bound to be so. As a child I had seen and loathed the Ben Greet Shakespeare Company, who gave what were called "Pastoral" performances—a euphemism for playing in the waterlogged gardens of artistic hostesses. For Ben Greet no rent to pay and a free supper for the company; for the audience, the torture of being eaten alive by midges.

At Oxford I saw the Benson Shakespeare Company. This company was regarded as a great nursery of talent, and Benson had done a great deal in keeping Shakespeare's plays continuously before the public. But when I saw the company it was not very good. The productions, by then extremely old-fashioned and also dilapidated by long and continuous touring, were in a style which I assume derived from Irving.

It all seemed very dowdy. I suppose the twenty-year-olds of to-day must be thinking exactly the same of my generation and our work. And yet I suspect that the Benson company at this epoch was *not* making an illuminating contribution. Sir Frank Benson, nearing seventy, was still playing young leading roles. He had been a very handsome, athletic man and proud of his physique. But now he was faded and gaunt, and the spectacle of rouged and ruined masculine beauty was a sad one. In the part of Caliban he turned a few creaky handsprings and, at one point of the play—I forget the precise context—a pair of parallel bars appeared on the Magic Island and Caliban, gravely and to the embarrassment of a respectful audience, hung upside down.

Hamlet was better. Benson was, of course, distressingly old for the part and acted without any fire. But it was an intelligent performance and, for the first time, I began to see why these plays were considered masterpieces, to realize what great elaborate pieces of structure they were—dramatic cathedrals; to see how interesting they were as narrative, how, over and above and through the narrative were implicit meanings, like the echoes in a cathedral. I began to feel what richness of character was there, to hear what melody was in the lines.

Like thousands of others, I am grateful to Sir Frank Benson and his company. They threw open windows which would otherwise have remained shut. They may have been rather dusty, grubby old casements which creaked open, but they gave onto the foam of perilous seas in faery lands forlorn.

After that, for some years, I saw no Shakespeare on the stage. No disappointment. I was now involved in folk plays, written in naturalistic prose and thick dialect. In Belfast and Glasgow we were apt to regard Shakespeare as far too highfalutin and "fancy" for us. As for Shakespearean acting, or what we took to be such on the evidence of what we had seen, I cannot begin to describe the contempt in which we held it. We saw nothing in it but empty ranting and roaring.

Two productions taught me better. First, Lewis Casson's nobly rhetorical *Henry VIII*, with splendiferous decor by Charles Ricketts and a powerful, astringent Katherine by Sybil Thorndike. Then, a year or two later, indeed just around the time when I was being considered by Miss Baylis for the Old Vic, John Gielgud did an exquisite production there of *The Merchant of Venice*. Here, for the first time in my limited experience, was a Shakespeare comedy which was not heavily and boringly trying to be funny, but was instead elegant and witty, light as a feather, and so gaily sophisticated that beside it Maugham and Coward seemed like two nonconformist pastors from the Midlands.

Gielgud had, I suspect, in this production been influenced by Michel Saint-Denis and the productions of *Noë*, *Loire*, *Marne*, and *Lucrèce* by the Compagnie des Quinze. These had been seen recently in two London seasons presented in successive years by Bronson Albery. All of us who went were enchanted by their style, the elegance and simplicity of the setting, the choreography, the music of the speech, and especially by the complete break with a naturalism which was already becoming irksome. Of course the Compagnie des Quinze were playing in London in French. The audience knew just enough French to get the general hang of what was going on, and no more. It was like a delightful spoken opera except that the performers were shapely and agile and imaginative . . . no, it was like a delightful ballet, only that it had fifty times more content than any ballet ever seen, and the performers were mature and intelligent.

The odd thing is that I have had just the same enchantment from the Habimah in Hebrew, from plays in Finnish and in Swedish, Yugoslav, Irish, Danish, Greek and Russian. I had just the same experience from Maurice Schwarz and his company at the Yiddish Art Theater in New York.

Newspaper critics are always praising foreign actors because they are interesting *in spite of* linguistic barriers; but could it possibly be that they are interesting just *because* of this barrier? You know in general what the acting is about, but not in detail; therefore you are not vexed by small deficiencies, not aware of little oddities and vulgarities of pronunciation or fretted by prolixity or inadequacy in the text.

When a year or two later Saint-Denis directed *Noë* in an English translation, with Gielgud and a very good company, the magic was gone. I do not believe the French production had been so much better. It had the glamour of something half-intelligible; what was merely guessed at got the benefit of any doubt. It was like a glamorous but rather passée woman in a big shady hat and heaps of tulle. The English production was the same lady in a cold, hard northeast light, a raincoat and no hat.

Needless to say the two seasons of the Compagnie des Quinze cost their sponsor a great deal of money. But they were fruitful all the same. Gielgud, Byam Shaw, George Devine, Olivier, myself and many others were all heavily influenced by Saint-Denis, who was himself the product of Le Vieux Colombier, Paris, where he trained under his uncle Jacques Copeau.

When I went to the Vic I was somewhat out of love with naturalism. I had had my fill of it in Scotland. Almost all that I had admired in the theatre recently was non-naturalistic, attempting to express the truth of a character, a story or a situation by means other than literal imitation. Partly this was fashion. In all the arts naturalism, or realism, was out of fashion. This, I suppose, in painting was inevitable when the camera could give such marvelously recognizable impressions. Henceforth painting was less concerned with imitation than with comment. In the theatre the movies had a similar effect. Even by 1933 the movies could tell a naturalistic story better in most ways than it could be told on the stage.

I did not know what I wanted to try to do at the Vic. I had seen several productions there. But, with the exception of Gielgud's *Merchant*, I had not enjoyed them very much. The scenery and dresses were obsessingly cheap and dowdy; the acting and the production tended to be "Bensonian"—full sets, which one felt would have been realistic had there been more money, alternated with front scenes before curtains. The senior actors spoke good and loud and gave vigorous stereotypes of Hero, Villainous Duke, Honest Warrior, "Character" Scrivener and so on. The junior actors were obviously beginners. There was an air of making-do, of depending upon the extreme cheapness of the tickets and upon the magic name of Shakespeare to obliterate the stigma of hasty and overfrugal preparation.

I think my strongest feeling was that I must try to make the productions *look* handsomer, and try to make the plays seem more like something which I myself would enjoy if I were in the audience, less like animated pictures in a Shakespearean lesson book. I was conscious that this was a great opportunity, but felt that the opportunity lay rather more in the field of social service than of Shakespearean production. To explain why this was so, I must briefly summarize the history of the Old Vic.

8

Old Vic:
First Century

IN 1817, two years after the defeat of Napoleon Bonaparte, a new bridge was built across the Thames. The opening ceremony was attended by the Prince Regent and the Duke of Wellington. They rode in state across the new bridge, named Waterloo in commemoration of the recent victory.

The new bridge provided a link between central London and the south, or Surrey, side of the Thames. Great housing developments followed in south London. These districts— Lambeth, Southwark, Bermondsey, Kennington, Camberwell —have been for about a hundred years predominantly industrial, factories, warehouses and so on, with a very poor, crowded, residential population, which only now, in the middle of the twentieth century, is being rescued from slum squalor and rehoused in a manner more in conformity with modern ideas of what is owed to every member of a selfrespecting community. But at this time the new districts south of the river were being hopefully developed as pleasant and even elegant residential property. Many fine old terraces and squares bear witness to the respectable aspiration and excellent taste of their builders.

To cater for the entertainment of this rapidly expanding

population, at the intersection of Waterloo Road, leading south from the bridge, with two other busy streets, the Lower Marsh and the New Cut, a new theatre was built. In 1818 the Royal Coburg Theatre opened its doors. It was named Coburg because it was "under the immediate patronage of His Royal Highness Prince Leopold of Saxe-Coburg," the young husband of Charlotte, the Prince Regent's daughter, and heir presumptive. The theatre's curtain was painted with a view of Claremont House, the home of Leopold and Charlotte. But a few months before the opening of the new theatre, Charlotte died in childbirth. Not long after, Leopold left England, never to return. And so the theatre was deprived of its patron and saddled with a rather pointless name. In 1833, in compliment to the new heiress to the throne, it was renamed the Royal Victoria.

The grand opening of the Royal Coburg in 1818 was a splendid affair. The theatre was elegantly decorated; it boasted a "Grand Panoramic Marine Saloon" designed and executed by Mr. Serres (Marine Painter to His Majesty), and "A Superb Central Lustre" which reflected the light of a thousand wax candles; the proudest boast of all was a curtain which filled the proscenium arch and was made entirely of looking glass. This gave the illusion of a gigantic circular auditorium. Ladies and gentlemen, melting like the thousand wax candles in suffocating heat, beheld amazingly similar ladies and gentlemen melting in the illusionary heat of a thousand reflected wax candles.

A yet further attraction is mentioned on the playbill. "Extra patroles are engaged for the Bridge and Roads leading to the theatre, and particular attention will be paid to lighting the same." The patrols and extra lights were a much-needed protection for persons venturing into a district still marshy, intersected by frequent and filthy ditches (the street names Lower Marsh and New Cut indicate clearly the terrain), still infested by rats the size of terrier dogs, by pickpockets and the dreaded garrotters.

For a time the theatre had quite a distinguished history.

Among other important actors, Kean played there, Macready, Barry Sullivan, Sheridan Knowles and Phelps; Vestris danced there; Paganini played the violin; the Vic stage knew Joey Grimaldi, the great clown.

Hazlitt attended a performance at the Coburg in 1820 and saw Booth as Brutus. He was disappointed in the acting and declared that the audience was largely composed of "pickpockets, prostitutes and mountebanks."

Kean's appearances at the Coburg were in 1831, not long before his death. He was hired to give six performances—in five of his most celebrated roles—Richard III, King Lear, Othello, Macbeth and Sir Giles Overreach in A *New Way to Pay Old Debts*. The salary was £50 a night.

The opening performance was of *Richard III* and went well to a crowded house. The next night Kean played Othello. Iago was played by Mr. Cobham, an extremely popular member of the Coburg's stock company. The locals turned out in force, determined that their favorite should show to advantage against an aging, overpraised and hideously overpaid star. Othello's best effects were marred by popping corks; great speeches were "frequently interrupted or freely commented on, as was the fashion of this house." Iago's efforts, on the contrary, were received with great applause and cries of "Bravo, Cobham, Bravo!" "At this want of judgment," I quote from Molloy's *Life of Edmund Kean*, "Kean's indignation, which had been inflamed by liberal potions of brandy and water, overflowed and when called before the curtain at the conclusion of the tragedy, he hesitated to obey. But the clamour continuing he walked forward to the centre of the stage, his eyes flashing with anger, the paint but half rubbed from his cheeks, a cloak wrapped round him, and abruptly demanded 'What do you want?' "

Here I must interject that this was not a curtain call in the sense which we now understand—a polite and, through habit, often perfunctory matter of handclapping and bows. The audience was summoning Kean to come before it and receive "the bird." The summons was clearly unexpected, since he had started to undress and take off his make-up.

" 'What do you want?' Kean abruptly demanded.

"This question, so suddenly asked, caused momentary surprise, but soon a volley of voices shouted in reply 'You, you, you!' 'Well, then, here I am,' answered Kean. 'I have acted in every theatre in the United Kingdom of Great Britain and in Ireland, and in all the principal towns throughout the United States of America, but in my life I never acted to such a set of ignorant, unmitigated brutes as I now see before me,' saying which, he flung a corner of his cloak over one shoulder and slowly made his exit.

"The manager and his company who had crowded to the wings . . . could scarcely believe they heard aright and now expected the house would be torn down and left a blackened ruin, to mark the indignation of the offended Gods.

"As it was, the Gods were momentarily stupefied with amazement and watched his slow exit in 'a frightful silence, such as precedes the roaring of thunder.' "

When the thunder burst it came as a cry for Cobham— "a cry that was taken up and repeated until the theatre shook; a show of enthusiasm for their old favourite being considered their best way of punishing the great actor. Mr. Cobham appeared bowing and smiling, and went through pantomimical expressions of gratitude and emotion until silence was granted, when he said: 'Ladies and Gentlemen, this is unquestionably the proudest moment of my life. I cannot give utterance to my feelings; but to the latest hour of my existence I shall cherish the remembrance of the honour conferred on me by one of the most distinguished, liberal and enlightened audiences I ever had the pleasure of addressing.' "

At this period, in 1831, the neighborhood was already beginning to go down. The elegant terraces and squares were discovered to be damp and ratty; the low-lying district was foggy, the upper-middle and middle-class people were moving out onto higher ground farther south; house after house was turned into tenements. The process of decay was enormously accelerated by the coming of the railway. The main lines from the south and southeast of England were carried over the low-lying districts on great viaducts which dominated and darkened the houses under and beside them, and filled them with smoke and noise.

As the district declined, so did the fortunes of the Royal Victoria Theatre. Fewer and fewer patrons came over the bridge from central London into what was now a really squalid slum. It was around this period that the name Royal Victoria became abbreviated to The Vic, and gradually, affectionately, The Old Vic.

The taste of the locals was for blood and thunder, washed down with plenty of beer. Here is a description by John Hollingshead of the Vic in its melodrama days: "In the dramatic version of *Oliver Twist* the murder of Nancy was the great scene. Nancy was always dragged round the stage by her hair, and after this effort Bill Sikes always looked up defiantly at the Gallery, as he was doubtless told to do in the marked prompt copy. He was always answered by one loud and fearful curse, yelled by the whole mass like a Handel Festival chorus. The curse was answered by Sikes dragging Nancy twice round the stage and then, like Ajax, defying the lightning. The simultaneous yell then became louder and more blasphemous. Finally, when Sikes working up to a well-rehearsed climax, smeared Nancy with red ochre and taking her by the hair (a most powerful wig) seemed to dash her brains out on the stage, no explosion of dynamite invented by the modern anarchist, no language undreamed of in Bedlam could equal the outburst."

The gallery at the Old Vic "contained about fifteen hundred perspiring creatures; most of the men in shirt-sleeves and most of the women bare-headed, with coloured handkerchiefs round their shoulders, called 'Bandana Wipes' in the slang of the district, and probably stolen from gentlemen who were given to snuff-taking. This 'chickaleary' audience was always thirsty—and not ashamed. It tied handkerchiefs

—of which it always seemed to have plenty—together until they formed a rope which was used to haul up large stone bottles of beer from the pit, and occasionally hats that had been dropped below."

I have always thought that this sounded enormously exciting and lively, and have often wished that the theatre had not become so genteel. But doubtless that is the *nostalgie de la boue* engendered by an upper-middle-class education and careful protection from all but the more "picturesque" aspects of squalor, enjoyed as well-off foreigners enjoy a conducted tour through the slums of Naples, Marseilles or Cairo.

The period of the Vic's degradation lasted almost fifty years. It was not till 1880 that any change for the better occurred.

Two remarkable women—aunt and niece, both spinsters —were responsible for the extraordinary transformation which occurred at the Old Vic, and through the Old Vic have exercised an important influence upon the British theatre of our time.

The first was Emma Cons, who was born in 1838. She studied as an artist; one of her teachers was Mrs. Hill, the mother of the famous Octavia Hill, one of the great pioneers of social reform in mid-Victorian England and one of the earliest women to become prominent in the public life of the country, a precursor of "female emancipation," the movement which about fifty years later culminated in the granting by Parliament of political equality between men and women.

Emma Cons began her career as what I think we should now describe as a commercial artist—she had been by turns a metal engraver, illuminator (in this capacity her skill attracted the attention of John Ruskin) and designer of stained-glass windows. During this period (late fifties and early sixties) there was growing around her a movement which was to influence her life; an effort was being made to ameliorate the poverty and squalor of the London slums. Areas of slum property were purchased by philanthropists who felt that their ownership involved some responsibility for the well-being of their tenants. John Ruskin, for instance, bought some dilapidated property in the neighborhood of Cavendish Square and installed Octavia Hill as his manager, with Emma Cons as one of her assistants. Miss Hill in one of her letters describes this place as it was when she was first appointed: the contrast between the smashed windows, filthy stairs, leaky roofs and bad sanitation of the alley and Cavendish Square, just round the corner, with its elegant, fashionable inhabitants, troops of servants and handsome equipages. The alley was named Paradise Place.

By degrees other properties came under the control of the Trust which Miss Hill managed. Emma Cons, who had served an apprenticeship under her friend Octavia in Paradise Place, was put in charge of Barrett's Court, another mass of degraded squalor, near Oxford Street.

Gradually her social work superseded her work as an artist, and a few years later Emma Cons decided to part company with Miss Hill and work on her own in Lambeth, a very poor district on the south bank of the Thames. With the help of friends (she clearly had a remarkable gift for enlisting the help of rich and influential people) she bought a considerable area of property; with a board of distinguished and titled persons, and herself as managing director, she formed the South London Dwellings Company and threw herself with enormous energy into the task of building "Model dwellings for Working Folk." The phraseology is typical.

It did not take Miss Cons long to discover that the principal, immediate cause of misery and squalor in her district was intemperance; or that the principal focus of intemperance and vice was the rough, tough establishment at the intersection of Waterloo Road with the New Cut. She went to the Old Vic and was horrified with what she found there. The entertainment on the stage was degraded and rowdy, but the theatrical activities of the Vic were not much more than a cover-up for the far more profitable trade of its saloon.

The theatre was living upon "wet money"; its saloon was not merely a drinking-place, but was also the principal "place of assignation" in the district. It was here that the prostitutes were picked up.

We are accustomed to think of the English Victorian spinster as a mousy little person, who pressed wild flowers, embroidered smoking-caps for the curate, filled his pipe and made cups of tea for dear papa and was much given to fits of the vapours. Miss Cons was a very mousy little person indeed and was terribly shocked by the goings-on at the Old Vic. But she did not throw up her tiny mittened hands and take the vapours; she took action. She did not run away from the horrid, wicked Old Vic; she bought it, lock, stock and barrel —more particularly barrel.

Following the pattern of her housing project, she formed a committee. Lord Mount Temple was its president; its members were rich and influential and this time included various distinguished figures of the musical world—Arthur Sullivan, Julius Benedict, Carl Rosa. These people provided the money and dressed the window. Miss Cons was the honorary secretary and did the work.

In 1880 the Old Vic closed and on Boxing Day reopened with the formidable title of The Royal Victoria Coffee Music Hall and a policy which stated that "a purified entertainment shall be given and no intoxicant drinks be sold." It need hardly be stated that this enterprise got almost immediately into financial difficulties. Old patrons went elsewhere in search of booze and a less purified entertainment. New patrons were chary of a neighborhood and a building whose reputation had for more than a generation been unsavory.

At the end of eight months the committee, faced with an alarming balance sheet, was for cutting down and subletting its white elephant. Miss Cons, who knew that any tenant would certainly return to the old policy of "wet money" and assignation in the saloon, argued that the work was only a financial, not a moral, failure—no mention was made of artistic success or failure—that the committee was responsible

for a charitable, not a business, project, and that its clear
duty was to put its hand into its pocket and keep right on
losing money. Miss Cons carried the day; her evangelical
peers pouted but coughed up.

The financial difficulties naturally persisted. The purified
entertainment was received with daunting apathy; every committee meeting was a battle and poor Miss Cons must have
often wished she had never waded into the treacherous waters
of theatrical management. When things were at their worst
she wrote to Samuel Morley, an extremely wealthy textile
manufacturer. Morley, passionately interested in temperance
reform, gave her substantial financial help and moral support. The new Old Vic had survived the first great crisis.

At this period the program was exceedingly varied. Vaudeville, music, temperance meetings and science lectures had
their special nights in the course of a week.

The science lectures (admission one penny) drew an audience. "The men of science who found their way to the theatre
and addressed its audience on the Movements of the Stars
or the Wonders of the Telephone may have been taken
aback now and then by the manners of the Vic habitués;
playgoers accustomed to exchanging back-chat with red-nosed
comedians saw no reason why they should not also exchange
back-chat with professors. One eminent scientist paused to
arrange his mechanical apparatus. The pause was mistaken
for a dry-up. From the upper regions came a shout "Go
'ome and learn yer lessons."

Two young lads who had attended a science lecture came
round to ask Miss Cons for further help in their studies.
She was impressed by their intelligence and earnestness. Yet
another committee was formed to deal with this new development. Teachers were hired, the theatre's dressing rooms and
paint shop became classrooms. As a result of these classes,
Mr. John Booth in a history of the Old Vic states, "a plas-
terer's labourer gained a scholarship at Cambridge and a rag
and paper sorter is now (1915) a Chief Engineer on a P.
and O. Liner." Perhaps an even more important result was

that the informal classes in holes and corners of the old theatre were the beginning of what became in a few years the Samuel Morley Memorial College. Morley College now has its own buildings, its own charter, an existence quite separate from that of the Old Vic. It is one of the most important centers of higher education in South London. From little acorns great oaks grow. Miss Cons has an honored niche in the little-acorn department of history.

It was not easy to find a manager capable of running the Vic. Knowledge of theatrical business in itself was not enough; the Vic's activities, many and varied, demanded a many-sided leader, someone interested in science as well as in art, in music-hall songs and dances, in temperance and uplift; and all these multifarious bricks must be made with the very meagerest allowance of straw. A succession of managers came and went. It is noteworthy that the one who stuck it longest was no less a personage than William Poel, whose influence upon Shakespearean production has been as important on the technical side as was that of Miss Cons on the administrative. Poel's period of management was long, long before the Old Vic had anything to do with Shakespeare. He was concerned with the temperance meetings, science classes, lantern lectures and, of course, the purified variety shows.

Eventually, in despair of finding the right person, Miss Cons herself took the reins and continued as honorary manager until she was able to devolve this responsibility upon her niece.

Miss Cons' younger sister Liebe was a soprano. She married a baritone called Newton Baylis. Neither of them sang quite well enough to make a satisfactory living and their union was alarmingly fertile. It was not only the finance of the Old Vic which was a cause of anxiety to Emma Cons.

Eventually it was decided that Mr. and Mrs. Baylis and their troop of youngsters might do better in South Africa. Relatives clubbed together to provide the fare (one-way). The early eighteen-nineties saw them wandering about the veldt in a bullock cart offering their vaudeville act, "The Musical Baylises," to all comers, Quaggas, Kaffirs, Boers, giraffes, whatever lives on the veldt. Eventually they fetched up in Johannesburg, then an immensely tough mining city. Here the vaudeville act seems to have folded. The Musical Baylises quit the boards forever and the financial mainstay of the family became the eldest girl, Lilian, now about seventeen, who earned an excellent living by teaching dancing. An amusing passage in Mark Twain's *Journal* describes his meeting with a lively English girl who was giving lessons in the polka to miners, providing the music herself upon the mandolin.

Lilian, however, was overworking. She became gravely ill and Aunt Emmie in London wired to Johannesburg offering to Lilian her return fare, if the sea voyage, the rest and change, and a glimpse of home, would do her good.

What followed can be told in Lilian's own words: "I came home and found my Aunt very overworked and ill; and when I was convalescent, Aunt Ellen, Miss Martineau and Miss Everest [sister and intimate friends of Miss Cons] all urged me to take over the management of the Vic, as the much sought-after 'Right Person' had never yet materialized. They felt that my experience in organizing concerts in England and South Africa would be a valuable asset to the Vic; and after much consideration, I consented. I had intended to return to my parents and take up again my very profitable teaching on the Rand; but when I saw how things stood, I felt it my duty to stay and be of help to Emmie. From that time forward I made my home with my Aunts (Emma and Ellen Cons); I started work, as Manager of the Vic, at a salary of £1 a week."

If ever a round peg stepped into a round hole it was Lilian Baylis when she accepted Aunt Emma's offer of that job.

Things at the Vic began to hum. Young Miss Baylis hotted up the coffee and took a shot at hotting up the purified entertainment. Here she reckoned without her governors. The evangelical peers, the do-good ladies, the representatives of charitable trusts which formed the governing body had been staunch adherents. Again and again they had plunged their hands into their pockets and bailed the Old Vic out of Queer Street. But they were doing this because they conceived it their duty to uplift the masses and, more particularly, to scotch the demon rum. And now here was a young person, with great energy and a domineering manner, who was insisting that the programs were dull, that clergymen giving chats about the Holy Land, illustrated with magic lantern slides, were *dull*; that dear old Sir Fudley-Dudley's lecture on electro-magnetism, with a machine which gave deserving lads a tiny shock, was *dull*. That the weekly temperance meeting was *dull*.

She got into hot water by permitting a too-secular concert on the Lord's day—and hotter water by engaging for the variety program A Man with a Goat whose act was, so several governors who had seen it declared, reprehensibly vulgar. Paragraphs about the Man with a Goat appear and reappear in the minutes of the governors' meetings of this period with almost incredible frequency. It is clear that the Goat had acquired a symbolic significance. It represented this rather terrible, energetic young person from the colonies.

Miss Baylis was not the type to be daunted by a little opposition. Besides, she had an important ally—Almighty God. It was hard for those who did not share her kind of simple and fundamental belief to understand it. It was hard at times not to be exasperated, and sometimes hard not to be amused, at the way she seemed to have God in her pocket. But no one with any sensibility could fail to be moved with reverence and respect for her faith; and no one but a fool would underestimate its formidable power.

When I came to know this remarkable woman, she was already getting on in years and her extraordinary force of personality as well as her physical energy were beginning to decline. But she was already A Legend. Around her there had already collected an aura of greatness, a great body of anecdote, part true, part myth, a troop of uncritical adorers of both sexes.

She was a thick-set, dumpy person. I do not think she ever had been a pretty woman; in latter years her features had been twisted a little, the effect, I believe, of a slight stroke induced by a swimming accident in which she had nearly been drowned. As a result she spoke out of the side of her mouth; this, with a marked Cockney accent and an extremely individual turn of phrase, made her an all-too-easy mark for impersonation. Many are the actors, from Dame Sybil Thorndike down, who, pushing their mouths to one side, assuming an outrageous accent and a frightful parody of her idiom, reincarnate her with irreverent amusement but not without affection or respect.

When she came to the Vic, the most popular and successful programs were the concerts of operatic music. Ladies and gentlemen in semi-evening dress stood around a semi-grand piano and fired off the better-known "gems." Miss Baylis wished to develop these concerts into proper operatic performances. She believed that if people were given *the best* they would like it, not perhaps at first, but eventually. It was part of her remarkable character that she never was seriously troubled about discovering what was the best, or why it was so, in art or human nature or anything else. She believed it would be made known by Divine Revelation. I don't think it ever occurred to her that the best, as revealed by her God to Lilian Baylis, could possibly differ from any revelation by any other God to anyone else; if so, her revelation would certainly be the true one. It was the key to her greatness.

God told Miss Baylis that the best in music was grand opera —hardly the orthodox view, but there it was. "My people" —her customers were always called "my people," an assumption half motherly, half royal—"my people," she decided, "must have The Best. God tells me The Best in music is grand opera. Therefore my people must have grand opera."

Quite undaunted by the staggering expense and difficulty

involved, she proposed to her governors the formation of an opera company. The governors would not hear of it; they regarded it as highly dangerous and immoral. Eventually a compromise was reached: the performers might dress up, they might even paint their faces; the opera would be given as written; but there must be *no actions*. After a year or two, actions began to creep in; gradually the story of the opera would be quite fully mimed. The governors appear to have closed their eyes to this, influenced perhaps by the striking box-office success of the experiment; or perhaps, when they beheld them, the actions did not seem quite as licentious as they had feared.

With the passing of the years, gradually but steadily, the opera performances became more frequent and more accomplished. At first only noncopyright works were performed, for the excellent reason that there was no money to pay copyright fees. Gradually the expanding business justified expansion of the repertoire, the orchestra and the corps of singers. The chorus still consisted of clerks and shopworkers and students who came on to the Vic after their day's work; a few were rewarded with a very tiny wage; most had to be content with lemonade and a sandwich.

Miss Cons, although herself an artist and a person of considerable culture, does not seem to have been at all interested in the artistic quality of the Old Vic's program. Her attention was entirely focused on the social and moral aspects of her work. It does not seem to have struck her forcibly that her Coffee Music Hall lacked an artistic policy, that purity and temperance are not perhaps best served by a program whose chief merit is the negative one of avoiding impurity and intemperance.

Lilian Baylis was not such a well-educated or cultured woman as her aunt. Her schooling had been scrappy and brief. Although as a member of the Musical Baylises she had some training in musicianship and some experience as a performer, no one could say that she was either a very gifted or a cultured musician. Indeed, she was not in any sense a highly cultivated person. But, call it revelation or intuition or just plain good sense, she saw, as Miss Cons had never seen, that, if the Old Vic were to be useful, a positive artistic approach was as necessary as positive convictions about moral and social reform.

With the Opera developing gradually but steadily, Miss Baylis felt it was time to make another positive move. In the weekly vaudeville program a dramatic sketch was occasionally presented. She was struck by the great talent of some of the actors, and by its superiority to the dramatic material of the sketches. The thought occurred that my people were certainly getting the best in music, but not so certainly in drama.

She took the problem to God. The answer came that Shakespeare was the best in drama.

This time the governors had no objection. By now they probably realized that, once God had told Miss Baylis what to do, there really was no point in opposing their joint will; also Shakespeare, though expensive to produce, is unassailably respectable.

In 1914, with the clouds of war already darkening the sky, Miss Baylis launched the Old Vic Shakespeare Company. The war years 1914–1918 were difficult, with shortage of material, with air raids, with almost no young men available. Sybil Thorndike played not only female leads but also Prince Hal, and the Fool in *Lear*. At the end of the war, however, a group of young actors, including Russell Thorndike, Sybil's brother, realized that a season at the Vic offered an opportunity, then unique, to play five or six varied parts in as many masterpieces. An interesting group collected and a series of productions followed which received remarkable critical notice at the time, but now seem forgotten. Their director, Robert Atkins, has now, thirty-five years later, rather dropped out of the front rank. But it was largely due to his great talent that the Old Vic Shakespeare Company found its feet, so to say; by the early nineteen-twenties every play in the First Folio had been given, including *Pericles* and *Titus Andronicus*, an achievement which hitherto no other theatre had even attempted and which none has attempted since except the Old Vic again, when, as a "Five-Year Plan" (1953–1958), the whole canon was once again produced.

In 1921 the Company played its first foreign engagement, in Brussels.

During the decade 1914–1924 the wonderful Old Vic audience was created. This, in my opinion, rather than any of the many excellent happenings upon the stage, was the Vic's greatest achievement. It was not quite the audience which Emma Cons and her evangelical peers had in mind when they opened The Royal Victoria Coffee Music Hall. It no longer consisted of the neighbors. There was certainly always a sprinkling of locals; but for the most part the audience consisted of serious and predominantly young working people from all over London. Most of them traveled considerable distances—one of the assets of the Vic's position has always been its accessibility by public transport, the rail and bus services are both excellent—so that, with far lower ground rent and rateable value, it is just as easily reached as the theatres in central London.

The Vic audience was attracted by the combination of a serious classical program with low prices. It was intelligent but poor and consequently unspoiled. It had youthful enthusiasm and earnestness; it was intensely aware and proud of its responsibility as an audience; intensely identified with its favorite players and the theatre of its choice.

In 1926 John Gielgud emerged as the first important actor who had been trained and developed at the Vic. He had carried spears, screamed "Long live the King" from the rear rank of milling crowds and worked steadily up the ladder to his first, very youthful, thrilling *Hamlet*. In 1927 Edith Evans was the first established "star" actress to join the Old Vic. Stars had made special guest appearances at gala performances on Shakespeare's birthday, Twelfth Night and so on. But this was the first occasion when a top-flight performer had undertaken the risks and rigors of a full season for the negligible financial reward which this theatre could offer.

From now on the Vic became an important center of theatrical production, not as yet recognized as such, except by its limited but growing audience and by the more intelligent and serious members of the profession. But the impetus was there; from about this date ultimate recognition was inevitable.

Meantime the opera company too was on the upgrade; both audiences and the size of the company were increasing steadily. About this time the British National Opera Company, after years of gallant achievement, was forced by financial difficulty to curtail and finally discontinue its activity. Each summer there would be a brief, star-spangled, outrageously expensive International Season at Covent Garden, which did not quite compensate by glamour what was lacking in serious purpose and artistic cohesion. For most of the year Miss Baylis' opera company at the Vic had sole possession of the field and began to cultivate an audience for opera in English, which, like the Shakespeare audience, did not consist of fashionable, conspicuous or wealthy people, but was, on the other hand, intelligently, freshly critical and lively.

Finance was a perennial anxiety. The Old Vic is constituted as a charity. It is legally incorporated under a charter from the Charity Commissioners; a board of governors is entrusted with the responsibility of seeing that the terms of the charter are carried out. Some of the governors are elected by various public bodies, the Borough of Lambeth, for instance, the London County Council, and the University of London, and by various charitable trusts—the City Parochial Foundation, for instance, and the Carnegie Trust. These governors have power to co-opt others.

The Old Vic Charter states that "The Theatre shall be used primarily for the performance of high-class drama, especially of the plays of Shakespeare, and of high-class opera, or the holding therein of public lectures and musical and other entertainments and exhibitions suited for the recreation and instruction of the poorer classes.

"Admission to the performances, lectures, entertainments and exhibitions shall not be gratuitous, but shall be at such prices as will make them available for artisans and labourers."

In practical terms this has always been interpreted by the governors as meaning that the cheapest seats shall cost no more than a few cigarettes or a glass of beer, and the expensive seats shall cost considerably less than the current price for similar seats in the West End of London.

At such prices, and having to maintain the resources necessary for even the most stringently economical productions of opera or Shakespeare, the business could never be profitable, even if the house were, and it nearly always was, very full. Year after year Miss Baylis' companies played to a percentage of capacity which was the envy of other theatres; but year after year expenditure exceeded the takings, and usually exceeded also various charitable gifts and allowances. Miss Baylis was forced to maintain an unceasing vigilance upon her staff, growling like a bulldog at the expenditure of every halfpenny; while at the same time, like the curate of a poor parish, she had to do the humiliating and monotonous routine of begging for the charity of those who could afford it, while with jumble sales and the like she wrung a few extra pence out of the faithful.

By the end of the nineteen-twenties she was faced with a further problem created by the very success of her companies. No activity can stand still; movement must either be forward or backward. The opera and drama companies had now expanded beyond the limits of a single building.

At this period they shared the week's bill. The opera played about five performances a week, the drama about three. It was felt that each now commanded an audience large enough to play eight performances weekly; not to do so was therefore wildly uneconomic. Moreover, each company was now considerably larger than the theatre could conveniently contain. The overcrowding and confusion were calamitous.

Miss Baylis took this new dilemma to God; and God, as usual, took it by the horns and commanded her to buy another theatre. He did not, however, reveal a source of capital. Sadler's Wells was empty, in fact derelict. Members of the board of governors, bemusedly following Miss Baylis on a whirlwind tour of the building, got their feet soaked as they waded across the ruined stage; Evelyn Williams, Miss Baylis' secretary, like myself a truth-telling no-nonsense denizen of Ireland's intractable north, assures me that on this occasion she picked a bunch of mimulus and purple loosestrife (Ophelia's long purples) which were sprouting up between the boards where Phelps had trod. These are marsh plants; their roots were in London's New River, which flows under the building from the nearby New River Reservoir on its way to join the Thames.

Like the Old Vic, Sadler's Wells stands in a poor district —Islington, near the Angel. Like the Old Vic it has had an interesting and even intermittently distinguished history. Originally it had been a sort of spa. The waters hereabouts are reputed to be chalybeate. On the banks of the New River the Dibdin family, whose most famous member wrote *Tom Bowling* and other minor classics, operated a pub and gave sort of *café chantants* out of doors in summer. The district was countrified then and people came up from town to take the air, the waters—chalybeate and maybe something stronger and pleasanter—and a light alfresco entertainment. This was in the late eighteenth century. Later, as the city spread outwards, the spa ceased to be attractive and a theatre was built in its place. This reached the apex of its career when it was taken by Samuel Phelps in 1844. From then until he relinquished his tenancy in 1862 Phelps produced thirty-four Shakespeare plays, made his theatre one of the most distinguished in London and performed a valuable and recognizable service to the enlightenment and education of the public. It was Phelps' productions at The Wells which inspired young John Henry Brodribb, a clerk in the city, to embark upon the career which made him world-famous as Sir Henry Irving.

After Phelps' tenancy the theatre declined in distinction. So did the surrounding neighborhood, which lapsed from a genteel to a shabby-genteel condition and thence to near-squalor. The theatre changed hands frequently and was by turns music hall, then, latterly, movie house and finally roller-skating rink, getting ever more dilapidated.

Miss Baylis bought it for a song but was faced with large expenditure in putting it back into workable condition. In 1930 it reopened with a gala performance of *Twelfth Night* and a crippling load of debt.

The opening of the Sadler's Wells Theatre made it physically possible for the opera and Shakespearean companies to expand; it also made possible the realization of yet another of Miss Baylis' projects.

In 1926 a young Irishwoman called Edris Stannus, who had an introduction to Miss Baylis, crossed the Waterloo Bridge to keep her appointment. The interview has been delightfully described by Edris Stannus in her book *Come Dance with Me*; its upshot was her engagement at one pound a week for teaching "movement" to the drama students; plus a fee of two pounds for arranging any choreography required in a Shakespeare production. In addition she was to "lead a host of 'expenses only' dances in the Christmas Ballet production, supervise the Voluntary Office Workers (who danced in those works of the operatic repertoire which required a Corps de Ballet), and guarantee student-angels galore for *Hansel and Gretel*. . . ."

"I then visited," continues Ninette de Valois, the stage name of Edris Stannus, "her voluntary Opera Corps de Ballet. One girl had a wooden hand, but Miss Baylis informed me that an excellent kid glove was provided for her special use. . . . Thus, briefly, did Lilian Baylis contract me to the services of the Old Vic for four years, ever dangling in front of my eyes the rebuilding of Sadler's Wells in the dim future. I earned, on the average, about forty pounds per annum."

With the opening of The Wells, Miss Baylis could no longer refuse to de Valois the opportunity to develop a fully professional ballet company. This was the genesis of the Sadler's Wells Ballet, or, as it is now at its zenith entitled, The Royal Ballet.

The ballet was at first a further drop of expense and anxiety in the now formidable torrent of Lilian Baylis' expenses and anxieties. But this was a debt she owed, the payment of which could no longer honorably be postponed. Besides, Miss Baylis was no fool. She knew that in de Valois she had picked a winner. My people must have the best.

When I joined the organization, Sadler's Wells had been open for two years and was losing money heavily. No one, not even taxi-drivers, knew where it was. Habitués of the Old Vic regarded it as an impudent cuckoo in their crowded, but cosy, old nest.

Debts were enormous, the mere interest was a crippling financial load. Prospects were thoroughly gloomy. But somehow, Miss Baylis and the Old Vic had a confused way of muddling, paddling, struggling along to some state which might ultimately appear to symbolize, though never in a conventional manner, victory.

9

Old Vic &
Charles Laughton

IT WAS MY DUTY to propose a program and a cast
for the season of 1933–1934, which Miss Baylis would submit
for the approval of the governors.

Clearly it is no good deciding upon a program of plays
until you also know who is available to act them. However
much you may want to include *Macbeth*, say, or *King Lear*,
it is not a good idea to announce them till you are sure you
have someone for the all-important leading parts. Program
and cast must be assembled by a gradual process of fitting
together, rather like a jigsaw puzzle.

My first move was to approach Flora Robson. This shows
my inexperience. Now I realize that a Shakespeare company
cannot be centered upon a woman. All the great parts demand
men. I have also learned that, in forming a company, the
initial approach should be to the person who is going to play
the most responsible parts. It is, for instance, unwise to engage a man who will be ideally cast for Malcolm, if his presence in the cast, as for some reason it perfectly well may,
precludes the engagement of the best available Macbeth.

However, in this case luck was with us. Miss Robson mentioned the fact that she had been invited to play at the Old
Vic to Charles Laughton. Laughton, who admired her act-

ing as much as I did, was much interested in the possibility of being associated with the season. Though still only in his early thirties, he was at this time the most talked-of actor in London. He had had sensational success in three or four plays and now a film called *The Private Life of Henry VIII* had just been issued and his performance as Henry Tudor was being acclaimed all over the world.

Charles and I met at Flora's for dinner. We talked far into the night and agreed on all essential points but one. I found him a bit inclined to underestimate Miss Baylis. He had been obsessed by the dowdiness and tattiness of productions he had seen at the Old Vic, and had concluded that the Vic's main handicap was not poverty but what he took to be a willful determination on the part of Miss Baylis to run it on a parochial basis.

The next day I laid my cards upon Miss Baylis' table, like a poker player laying down a royal flush. There was a pause.

"Miss Robson's quite a nice girl, I'm sure. You've worked with her before, dear, haven't you?" said Miss Baylis.

I held my peace. This was clearly only an introductory chord.

A pause, then: "I saw Charles Laughton in that film. And in that play about a gangster in Chicago. Very clever, dear, of course. But I don't think my people would like him at the Vic."

"Why not, Miss Baylis?"

"I just don't think so, that's why."

Another pause. Then: "He's never played in Shakespeare, has he, dear?"

I argued a bit; she was good-tempered, reasonable and shrewd. Charles would be "West-endy," he and my people would never understand each other. I suggested that people had understood and liked him well enough in *Henry VIII*. He didn't seem to be A Nice Man. He was always playing horrid parts like gangsters.

"Does he go to Church, dear?"

The accusation recurred: "He's never played in Shakespeare." He would want her to spend a lot of money. I admitted that yes, he would; and so would I, whether she engaged Charles or not. If she did engage him, however, there was a good chance of money coming *in*. She admitted the truth of this, but balked at his salary. "Why should I pay twenty pounds a week to a man who's never acted in Shakespeare?" I reminded her that his film salary was fully twenty times as large. In that case, she snapped back, he ought to help the Vic—acting there was always called "helping the Vic"—for nothing.

The interview came to an inconclusive end. She must consult her governors. The governors evidently over-rode her scruples. A day or two later I got the green light.

Athene Seyler joined us, bribed with the promise of Madame Ranevsky in *The Cherry Orchard*; Ursula Jeans was to play the young girls; she was very lovely and had a great deal of character and good sense. Like Charles, she had never played in Shakespeare, but she was accounted one of the best of the young West End actresses. Leon Quartermaine, a little older than the rest of the team, had a fine record as a serious and poetic actor. From the Old Vic Company of the previous season, Roger Livesey was retained, Morland Graham, an old friend from the Scottish National Players, and Marius Goring, an ardent, gifted student with flaming hair. On the strength of his good looks and sturdily independent Yorkshire manner, I also engaged for small parts a young man called James Mason.

Charles Laughton, still very nervous lest the season be marred by the narrow economy of the Vic, persuaded The Pilgrim Trust to make some money available and, so that it did not just go into the general pool of Old Vic and Sadler's Wells funds, to earmark it for the specific purpose of mounting the Shakespeare productions. The money was immensely welcome, but it precipitated a crisis which very nearly wrecked the season.

Miss Baylis had for years been suing for the bounty of The Pilgrim Trust. She had wooed, wheedled, bullied, and wept. She had pulled every string to no avail. Now, suddenly at the request of a film star who had never played in Shakespeare, money was available. It was galling; and the fact that it was typical of the apparent frivolity and caprice of responsible, well-meaning public bodies did not sweeten the gall. To make matters worse, the string attached to the gift implied a criticism of Miss Baylis' powers of management; even, almost, of her integrity. There wanted not buzzers to infect her ear; many of her counselors, who should have had more sense, pandered to her vanity, applied the salve of flattery to her wounded pride, fed with gossip her incensement against Laughton and urged her to throw at the feet of The Pilgrim Trust its thirty pieces of silver.

To her great credit, Lilian Baylis pocketed her pride and with it the money. But the episode deepened her distrust of Laughton. She felt instinctively that he thought little of her achievements, did not share her ideals or her conception, despised her managerial capacity and derided her parochialism. She felt he did not understand the work and could only be "using" the Vic as a steppingstone in his own career. She treated him with an icy, rather naïve hauteur. To this, naturally, he reacted by imagining her to be a scheming, small-minded, mean-spirited old shrew, whose one idea was to keep the reins of theatrical power in her own incompetent hands.

I felt that a bad situation could be made ten times worse by clumsy diplomacy, so made no attempt either to mediate or to take sides. I felt sure that, in long term, each was generous enough to appreciate the good qualities of a rival heavyweight; and that, in short term, each was shrewd enough to see that their mutual interest would not be served by open warfare.

I had read Granville-Barker's Prefaces to Shakespeare, was familiar with the theories of William Poel, was in full reaction against naturalism, and had always disliked the Bensonian manner of presenting Shakespeare, which was, I suppose, based on Irving's presentations. The sets at the Lyceum were magnificently painted and lit; Benson's road-company equipment was inevitably battered and drab. But the principle was the same: "full sets," elaborate and careful pieces of antiquarian reconstruction, hovering uneasily between the realistic and the portable, alternating with "front scenes" played against curtains, or else pseudo-realistically painted drop-scenes as in vaudeville.

We would follow Poel and Barker and Shaw, make no cuts merely to suit the exigencies of stage carpenters, have no scenery except a "structure," which would offer the facilities usually supposed to have been available in the Elizabethan theatres: stairs, leading to a balcony; underneath, a cubbyhole in which intimate scenes can occur and where, concealed behind a curtain, thrones, beds and so on may be stored.

This structure would serve as a permanent background throughout the play, thereby eliminating tiresome pauses while scenery was changed, eliminating the "front scenes" with the actors standing in a line like ornaments on a chimney-piece, and most important, eliminating the cost of scenery. The money so saved was to go into costumes. The costumes would be of considerably better quality than the existing Old Vic wardrobe because of the grant from The Pilgrim Trust and would be invaluable as future stock.

Miss Baylis thought the idea of having no scenery rather dreary but appreciated that it was economical. When I suggested better dresses, resentment at implied disparagement of her wardrobe changed quickly at the thought of the new dresses going into stock. As in lightning calculation she rigged out the opera choristers for *Rigoletto* in the dresses which The Pilgrim Trust would provide for *Measure for Measure*, she gave consent to the plan for a permanent set.

The set was designed by Wells Coates, an architect whose work was then considered rather daringly modern. The aim of the set was to provide the necessary facilities, to avoid any precise suggestion of period, especially to avoid all fussy and irrelevant decoration. There was, I recall, plenty of talk about "good clean lines."

The result was, in my opinion, distinctly handsome; but, far from avoiding any precise suggestion of period, it proclaimed itself, almost impertinently, to be modern. It was also a little heavy to manipulate and wildly obtrusive. Whatever color it was painted, however it was lit, it appeared not as a merely functional background to the play but also as a powerful, stridently irrelevant competitor for the audiences' attention. I do not blame Wells Coates, but myself. He had had no previous theatrical experience; I was too inexperienced to guide him. It was a mistake to employ an architect, however brilliant, to undertake so important a piece of theatrical design without some sound theatrical craftsman at his elbow. Painted pinky-gray for *Twelfth Night*, our opening production, it completely dominated the evening and suggested not Illyria but a fancy dress ball on a pink battleship.

Our next Shakespearean production was *Henry VIII*, for which we were lent the Ricketts costumes and scenery of Lewis Casson's production nine years earlier. By the time we reached *Measure for Measure* and *Macbeth* I had learned a little better how to light and use the Wells Coates set and it became less obtrusive.

Measure for Measure was the best production of the season. Laughton and Robson were, as I now think, oddly and wrongly cast as Angelo and Isabella, but their scenes together were extremely powerful and interesting. Laughton was not angelic, but a cunning oleaginous monster, whose cruelty and lubricity could have surprised no one, least of all himself. Miss Robson suggested an uncompromising and splendid young Scotswoman in difficulties on the Continent. It was extraordinarily moving but far, far removed from the highly spiced mixture which I believe Shakespeare had in mind—incense-laden sexuality. Roger Livesey made a glittering and commanding Duke, a most interesting assumption of royalty, suggesting both the glamour and the sinister power of absolute authority.

Macbeth was to have been the high peak of the season. Laughton was longing to play it and full of interesting ideas. At the dress rehearsal his performance was electrifying. He and Miss Robson worked up an extraordinary tension in the sequence of Duncan's murder. His scenes with Banquo and the three murderers, his visit to the Witches, the desperation of the end, were all felt and transmitted with the utmost power and assurance. His acting that night bore the unmistakable stamp of genius. Alas, he never again, except momentarily, fitfully, recovered this greatness.

I think Charles Laughton did lack technique; when inspiration failed, as fail it often must, he had very little resource either of voice or movement. This often happens when actors, even actors of the greatest talent, whose experience has chiefly been in films, attempt great parts on the stage.

The technique of the film demands of an actor little sustained flight of imagination and makes only small demands upon his technical equipment. In the film studio it is possible to create an environment favorable for the inspiration which will carry an actor through the two or three minutes of a critical "take." Absolute silence, the concentrated will-to-win of a whole staff, a feeling of "occasion" the more intense because it does not have to be sustained.

In the theatre, inevitably there is more distraction. In a large audience there are always some stupids incapable of concentration; on a first night, and especially a fashionable first night, a proportion of the audience has come to be seen, rather than to see the play; there is a high proportion of inattention, the mere presence of the professional critics can be a distraction, and an intelligent actor is aware that most of them are there not to write a serious and informed critique so much as a gossipy and readable "report." Also, in the theatre there is no second chance. The least slip of memory, a single clumsy or mistimed movement can throw the whole machine out of gear. In the film studio, if a mistake is made, the shot is retaken.

It is nothing to make six or seven attempts at a critical shot. This relieves the actor of a great deal of anxiety and permits his concentration to be far more completely focused upon the mood and emotion of the moment, rather than upon technical details of rhythm and pace, position in relation to partners or lights, breathing and so on. Also, in the film studio full physical and imaginative energy can be expended on a brief moment. In the theatre this cannot be so.

It is not perhaps generally realized what a great physical, as well as intellectual and imaginative, effort is involved in the performance of a great role like Macbeth, Lear or Othello. A series of "arias" have to be performed which, if they are to be adequate, make elaborate demands on the breathing apparatus, upon the full resources of the voice from top to bottom. At some stage of the evening, athletic demands will be made—Lear must carry Cordelia, Hamlet must carry the body of Polonius; there are duels, battles. Othello must, after a violent struggle with Iago, feign epilepsy. In mere casual movement hither and yon upon the stage an actor will walk several miles in the performance of a big part, often in armor or dragging a great cloak; there will be several changes of costume, all of which have to be accomplished under the strain of very limited time. An important thing to learn in the course of rehearsal is where and how to rest, how to eke out limited resources of energy so that there will still be enough in reserve for the critical last lap. All these are problems which do not arise in the film studio.

A year or two after *Macbeth* I was forcibly reminded of all this; and realized how dependent Charles Laughton was—and I quote him as a conspicuous instance of the "inspirational" as opposed to the "technical" actor—upon the possibility, which filming offers, of waiting for the unpredictable moment when the angel troubles the waters.

I and the late Robert Newton were acting with Laughton in *The Beachcomber* a short scene which seemed to me fairly plain sailing. It must also have seemed so to our director,

Erich Pommer, for it was scheduled to take only a few minutes before lunch.

We rehearsed the scene carefully and then shot it. I had little to do. Somewhere near the beginning of the scene I had to say "good-bye" with a little emotional catch in the voice, rush to a door, open it and disappear, closing the door behind me. Newton had then to embark upon a tirade, to which Laughton replied in grunts and monosyllables. The whole thing took about two minutes.

The first take was technically satisfactory, but Laughton felt that his performance was not good. He felt that this scene was crucial to his whole interpretation of the character, and I expect he was quite right. His instinct in these matters is extraordinary. He requested the director to shoot it again, gave his reasons most pleasantly, clearly and intelligently, and Mr. Pommer of course agreed. We would break for lunch and at two o'clock the retake would be made.

At eight that night we were still at it. Newton, who had to work really hard, was behaving beautifully, but the effort to do so was making his performance quite meaningless. He was speaking like one in a dream. I had spoiled two takes by pulling my door too hard. Pommer looked agonized but grimly determined, like Prometheus after the eagle had pecked out his gizzard for the millionth time; electricians were whispering, grips inclined to snigger; Laughton, with the single-minded, total absorption of genius, was lost in his role. We called it a day.

The next day the ordeal continued. By lunch time the angel had still not troubled the waters, so Mr. Pommer decided to print the first take.

Those were the palmy days of filming, when almost limitless money was available for something which looked like a hot proposition; and when no proposition was hotter than Charles Laughton. I think Pommer was absolutely right to wait as he did; and so was Laughton. But it was with relief that I returned to the "live" theatre where, for better or worse, once the audience is in front the show must go on and, if inspiration is not functioning, one must make do with technique, trusting with some confidence that people out front won't know one from the other.

In addition to the Shakespeare plays that season we did *The Cherry Orchard* and *The Importance of Being Earnest* and Congreve's *Love for Love.*

The Cherry Orchard had been done in London by Fagan about ten years earlier, when it had met with some artistic appreciation and done no business. Our production was the first time that an English version of the play met with a large popular audience. Our sets suffered from the inevitably restricted budget, but I think in other respects it was a good production. We rejected the standard translation by Constance Garnett in favor of a new version by Hubert Butler which was much less "quaint"; the characters emerged as far more human and normal, and the actors were encouraged to regard it as a comedy rather than a prose-poem. The humor of the play was greatly helped by Athene Seyler's impersonation of Madame Ranevsky. It was a witty, wise and exquisitely skillful piece of work, falling short of perfection because this wonderful actress has no lyric quality. She looked, she moved, she felt so truly and sensitively; the gaiety, elegance, and poignancy were all hers; but not the power to delight by the sheer sensuous quality of the voice. Laughton was extremely subtle and interesting as Lopahin; Miss Robson brought her unique quality of poignancy to Varya; Morland Graham was Firs; Elsa Lanchester, as the eccentric little governess, made a haunting impression of loneliness; Livesey was Pistchik, James Mason Yasha the Valet, a devastating sketch of Don Juan below stairs; perhaps best of all in a notable group of performances was Leon Quartermaine as Gaev, the charming, futile, poetic, elderly bachelor.

The play ran for twice the number of weeks then customary at the Old Vic and could easily have run for many months. More important, it presented Chekhov not as the arch-exponent of Russian gloom but as a charming and easily intelligible humorist.

The Importance was not a wise choice. Nobody was really well suited. My direction was galumphing and uninteresting. The revival must be unique in that Canon Chasuble (Charles Laughton in a devastating, brilliant and outrageous lampoon) appeared to be the leading part. Business was good, but all memories of the production fortunately suffered a total eclipse by John Gielgud's glittering revival a few years later. This, by virtue of Gielgud's direction, his own performance as John Worthing, Edith Evans as Lady Bracknell, Peggy Ashcroft as Cicely and Gwen ffrangcon-Davies as Gwendoline, was as wonderfully successful in New York as in London, and in my opinion establishes the high-water mark in the production of artificial comedy in our epoch.

Love for Love was good fun. It suited the company; I felt more at home in this more vehement, hard-hitting milieu than in the elegance of *The Importance*; the uproarious enjoyment of packed houses buttressed Miss Baylis against the disapproval of some of her governors, who made strong objections to what they considered a licentious play.

Our season came to an end with what I think must be the worst production of *The Tempest* ever achieved. John Armstrong, who had designed wonderful clothes for *Measure for Measure* and *Macbeth*, succeeded in making the handsome actors look ugly and the ugly actors look funny; my direction was at once feeble and confused. The only good thing was Elsa Lanchester's Ariel, weird and lyrical in a balletic style which was at odds with everything else in the production and which better direction would never have permitted.

Charles and Miss Baylis ended up on speaking terms, but only just. At one time there seemed a chance that they would become quite friendly. Then came *Macbeth*. At the end of the first performance round to the dressing rooms comes Miss Baylis, aware of a need to administer cheerful but honest consolation to My Boys and Girls. Charles is in his room aware that the evening has not been a success, painfully aware

that his own performance has fallen short of the promise of
the dress rehearsal. If ever a human creature is vulnerable it
is a leading man at the end of a long exhausting performance
which he knows has been a disappointment.

Charles is at his dressing table, still made up as Macbeth.
To him comes Miss Baylis in the full academic robes to
which as an Honorary M.A. of Oxford she was entitled,
and which she very sensibly put on for first nights: beaming
benignly through her glasses upon the dejected actor, she
gave what I knew was a laugh of embarrassment. Anyone who
has been to a dressing room after a difficult first night will
know that embarrassment. Charles declares it was a hyena's
yell of triumph. She then caught him a smart crack across
the shoulder blades.

"Never mind, dear," she said, "I'm sure you did your best.
And I'm sure that one day you may be quite a good Macbeth."

He never forgave her. He believed it was her vengeance
for the affair of The Pilgrim Trust. In that I am sure he is
wrong. She was not a petty person. Had she wished for
vengeance she would not have sought it by being catty in a
dressing room. She would have invoked the Lord of Hosts.
Riding in fiery chariots, with tongues like swords, in thunder
and in whirlwind, His Messengers would have streamed the
firmament. Her foes would be crumbled to impalpable dust.
The dogs would lick their blood.

At the end of that season at the Old Vic I felt that I had
not quite fitted into the pattern expected of a member of
Miss Baylis' staff. My work on the whole had been acceptable
to the public at large but had been bitterly resented by some
of the old guard of Old Vic supporters. The burden of their
song was "This may be clever but it's not our Shakespeare,"
and indeed it was not. What they wanted was, quite reasonably, more of what they had liked in the past.

They did not, I suspect, analyze too carefully the reasons
for their dislike of what they regarded as wanton and im-
pertinent innovation. It did not occur to them that tradition

is not a stagnant pond but a river, or that their resentment might be a reflection not of the violent iconoclasm in the goings-on but of a violent change from what had become exceedingly old-fashioned. I think they would have resented the notion that the interpretation of anything so godlike as "their" Shakespeare could be subject to something so trivial as fashion.

The history of all the arts is full of endless variations upon the same theme: elderly persons denouncing innovation for no better reason than that it is new, young persons denouncing what is old-fashioned for no better reason than that it is old. The odd thing is that few people seem to recognize that the disease is chronic, and that invariably some innovation, not necessarily the best, will gain a footing and pass into the stream of tradition, refreshing, not polluting it. The question of good or bad seems irrelevant. No sensible person says that the internal-combustion engine supplanted the horse because it was "better." It was better in some respects which, at a given moment in time, seemed so important that the horse was displaced. In many respects the horse is a more satisfactory means of locomotion.

Innovations in art succeed or fail in being accepted, and then imitated, and eventually in becoming traditional for the same complex reasons which made the car replace the horse, made electric light replace wax candles and so on—all concerned far, far more with the social, political, economic and physical context than with any absolute merit in a particular innovation.

I do not mean to imply that the old guard at the Vic were particularly stupid people; on the contrary, they were intelligent and much of their criticism was reasonable, many of their strictures were deserved. But it was not reasonable or wise of them to focus, as they did, so much of their unfavorable attention upon *my* work at the Vic. Innovation was inevitable, if a young director were engaged. Young directors simply must from time to time be hired by a theatrical institution, if only to correct its inevitable tendency to fossilize.

For my part I was at fault in regarding criticism of my work and professional attitude as being personal. I had been too much influenced by a very unpleasant letter to Miss Baylis from two of her old guard—two elderly retired schoolmistresses—begging her to get rid of me at once, before I laid her life's work in ruins.

I think Miss Baylis showed me the letter in all good faith. She made it clear—and I am sure this was true—that she had no intention of taking the side of the writers; that, so long as I was employed by her, I should have her public support. But she felt I ought to know that such criticism was being widely expressed and that she did not regard it as entirely unfounded.

Fair enough. What I think she did not realize was how much I admired her achievement; how desperately anxious I was that it should not come to harm through my fault, and, consequently, how undermining to my confidence it was to find that she too was inclined to regard me as an irresponsible iconoclast.

I was able to explain that, in my humble but still firm opinion, the Old Vic stood in greater jeopardy through being dowdily and stodgily traditional than through being experimental, and even occasionally a little ostentatiously "modern." She let me have my say; she was reasonable and pleasant. But the episode did not draw us together. I felt that she did not entirely trust me, did not believe that I was sincerely putting the advancement of the Old Vic before that of my own career.

Even if this episode had not occurred, I am not sure that I still should have wanted to be, so to say, one of the generals of her staff. I was irritated and made suspicious by the many adorers of Miss Baylis. A great personality, as she undoubtedly was, inevitably magnetizes a quantity of satellites. Miss Baylis seemed to have more than her share; and, while in most respects so shrewd and sharp, she seemed oddly susceptible to flattery.

I see now that this was extremely pathetic. She was an intensely affectionate and enthusiastic creature; she had never married; her position as head lady made her isolated. The incense of the adorers was her only substitute for a love and companionship which her eminent, even noble, career had precluded.

But, whatever the explanation, her surrounding cloud of incense was an obstructive, suffocating bore. I was convinced that many members of her staff were incompetent and that several of them were rogues. I felt that Charles Laughton was not entirely unjust in his strictures on the organization. Miss Baylis' penny-wise policy meant that she bought everything as cheaply as she could. Her wardrobe materials came from the remnant sales of the department stores; her employees tended to come from the equivalent in the labor market.

It could be argued that this did, at least, mean that she was not employing people who were more interested in their wages than their work. On the artistic side this was often true. Actors and singers went to the Vic because it offered interesting opportunity, with a vocational rather than a greedy purpose. But in some of the technical and administrative departments it was otherwise. Men, hired at the lowest possible rate of pay to do routine tasks, did not always take an idealistic view of their responsibilities to the Old Vic.

In a business with a large turnover there are always "little pickings," always opportunities to "fiddle." The fact that they were so poorly paid allowed some of the staff to feel that little pickings and little fiddles were legitimate compensation. The very fact that Miss Baylis had a tight fist and an eagle eye only added zest to the game. Considerable pickings were had, the fiddling was loud and long.

It was my opinion that by paying better wages for more competent and reliable men; by parting with some of those who made the most sentimental and endearing protestations of zeal and loyalty, Miss Baylis would increase her annual expenditure but would also save money. Just trying to keep solvent was no longer, if it had ever been, the right way to operate. A large deficit would not be a disaster if, by incurring it, the results were artistically impressive. The time had come,

I felt, when it was more dangerous to struggle along on an inadequate budget and, by disappointing work, to risk the melting away of that wonderful and apparently so loyal audience, than to put its loyalty to the test, to risk spectacular insolvency against a no less spectacular improvement of standard.

Mine was a youthful and possibly immature view. Hers was mature, but perhaps tired and a little discouraged. She had for so many years borne the burden and heat of the day. She had become fixed in the groove of a narrow economy.

But, right or wrong, one thing seemed clear. At the end of the Laughton season neither my prestige nor my personal influence with Miss Baylis was weighty enough for any drastic counsel of mine to prevail. It seemed better to part on friendly, if not affectionate, terms; and perhaps to return later on, if wanted, and if it seemed we could pull enthusiastically together.

To balance the criticism of this season, offered so freely, and with undoubted honesty, by the Vic's neighbors, it may be recalled that the American critic Robert Benchley said that at this time the Old Vic was interesting at its worst, and at its best the most important experimental theatre in the world. But *The New Yorker* was not widely read in the environs of the New Cut.

The season at the Old Vic had put me in a good professional position. Plenty of work was coming in.

10

The Director

THE PROFESSIONAL DIRECTOR, or as he is no less incorrectly called in Britain, producer, is a recent phenomenon. The French, as usual more accurate, have words which define the duties and position of such a person; they call him either *régisseur* or else by the humbler, but I think more sensible, name of *metteur en scène*.

Until some fifty years ago it was usual for plays to be directed by the leading actor, or by some experienced member of the cast, or even by that lowly functionary, the author. Of course, someone had to conduct the rehearsals, arrange positions for the actors, supervise the settings, lighting and "effects." As in any cooperative activity there must be some direction and organization of effort, in any artistic creation there must be one dominant impulse.

The director's power in the theatre has increased partly because theatrical business has become enormously more complicated and costly. To take but two instances: sixty years ago neither income tax nor an employer's liability for the insurance of his staff was a serious financial or administrative burden; nor did an employer have to reckon with the complex regulations and demands of the unions to which different members of his staff might belong. Now it is no longer possible for one man to administer a theatre, to supervise a large company of actors, a stage staff, box office, catering, cleaning, advertising, heating, insurance and a hundred and one other arrangements; and also to be responsible for his theatre's artistic policy, to choose and cast the plays, to direct the rehearsals—keeping an eye on the minutest details of interpretation—while at the same time playing most of the leading roles.

Irving did this at the Lyceum in London for nineteen years. Before him, in a rougher and readier way, Phelps had done it at Sadler's Wells for eighteen years. Booth did it in America, and various great actors on the continent. No one, so far as I know, has attempted it successfully since 1914.

Laurence Olivier, at a height of world celebrity and popularity such as Irving never attained, attempted to operate as an actor-manager at the Saint James's Theatre in London. Although the policy and operations at the Saint James's were far less ambitious than those of Irving at the Lyceum seventy years before, the experiment proved quite beyond the powers of a single man to sustain. This is not to say that Olivier was an ill-qualified man; far from it. He is a shrewd and capable man of prodigious energy; probably as good a businessman and a no less dedicated artist than Irving. But in the time between the two experiments the whole social, political, artistic, and financial context had changed. In almost every respect the changes have made individual enterprise, whether artistic or financial, more difficult. The day of the actor-manager has passed away, not because there is no one fit to wear the mantle of Irving, Phelps or Booth but because, with the passing of the years, the garment has become unwearable.

A general devolution of tasks has taken place. The production of a play is now undertaken by a corps of specialists. Broadly speaking, there is a business or administrative side, with a producer—in British parlance, manager—in charge; and an artistic side, headed no longer by a leading actor but by a director.

In the re-shuffle the artistic status of the actor has suffered somewhat. The leading player is the figurehead of a production; he is the most publicized and probably the highest paid of the group of collaborators. But, in theory at all events, he is artistically under the thrall of the director and ranks in the administrative hierarchy as an employee, a paid hand of the producer. Naturally, in practice, no one with any sense insists upon theoretic rights or status. Actors working under the direction of Kazan or Peter Brook, Olaf Molander, Jean Vilar, Visconti, or any of the top directors, are content to trade some independence of thought and action to become part of the pattern of an important production. Conversely, young Mr. X, not long from college, entrusted with his first directorial job, is unlikely to say *Boo* too loudly to Mr. and Mrs. Lunt. Yet they will know that to him as director is owed at least that degree of subjection which will make him responsible for technical and organizational matters, with which they themselves have neither time nor energy to bother. And equally, Kazan or Visconti will certainly not ride roughshod over the dignity and creative contribution of senior actors, or indeed of any of their troupe. The theoretic hierarchy could never be made to work without the lubrication of common sense and tact.

The actors' status has further declined, and that of the director advanced, because in the mass media of movies, radio and television the contribution of an army of technicians is indispensable. These cohorts work under the director. Their importance adds to his. The actor's contribution, made for the most part in tiny snippets, under rigid limitations imposed by such technical items as camera, microphone and lights, is comparatively unimportant. Again and again it has been demonstrated that to be a movie star acting talent, or accomplishment, is almost completely irrelevant. Beautiful dimwits, of assorted size, shape and sex, command tremendous salaries, are extravagantly publicized, accorded the rather perfunctory and ambivalent worship, half admiration, half envious contempt, which fans offer to stars. But they are

readily expendable. All of a sudden, head office will decide
that they have had their day. They are heard of no more. Another assortment of beautiful dimwits reigns in their stead.
This is not to say that movie actors are without talent. We
often see sterling performances in support of the dimwits.
Now and again we even see a talented "star." But talent is
not necessary for stardom; is not even necessary to make an
actor vendible to a public primarily interested in moving
photographs of handsome men and women, only secondarily
in the dramatic aspect of these photographs.

Some part of the advance in the director's status has also
been made over the dead body of the author.

In the movies the author, often a composite of semi-
anonymous creatures maintained in luxurious captivity like
Strasbourg geese, rarely commands the making of a picture.
Directors cut, expand and distort scripts to suit their purposes.
In the theatre things have never come quite to this pass. But
it is true that movie practice has to some modified extent
affected the production of plays.

In my opinion, it is not wise for authors to direct their
own work. An interpreter with a fresh eye and ear, and without an author's overtenderness toward his own brain child, is
a valuable intermediary between a script and an audience. I
learned this painfully when, having directed my own play *Top
of the Ladder*, under Laurence Olivier's management at the
St. James's Theatre, London, in 1950, I was assured by many
discriminating friends that I had spoiled the play by failing
to cut obvious and repetitious passages. The best plan is for
the author to be present at rehearsals, provided, and in my
experience this is not too hard, both author and director behave themselves with reasonable forbearance and common
sense.

It is customary to suppose that the texts of classical plays
are as their authors wrote them. In fact, however, most of the
printed versions incorporate cuts, additions, and alterations
which were made during rehearsals; in many cases these will
have been considerable.

Naturally a director will be apt to take with a new or youthful playwright a rather more dominant line than would be seemly if the author were an established heavyweight. This can cut both ways. The novice's work may be butchered; but it may, on the other hand, benefit extremely from experienced and judicious guidance.

And now, what does the director do?

He bears to the preparation of a play much the same relation as an orchestral conductor to the rehearsal of a symphony. But the symphony is performed by the conductor with each member of the orchestra playing under his leadership. He does not play the leading part. He does more. He interprets, shapes, guides, inspires the entire performance.

The theatrical director's work ends before the first performance. It is his duty to prepare the work; but when the time has come to show it to the public, the performance goes forward without him. Theoretically, each actor in rehearsal is no more than an instrument in a concerted performance. But in practice the actor has infinitely more technical latitude and a far more creative task than the orchestral player.

This is because the script of a play reveals so much less of its author's intention than does the score of a symphony. This may seem paradoxical, because every literate person can read the text of a play whereas to be able to read a full symphonic score is an accomplishment.

But, once you have mastered the business of reading it, the musical score will indicate in precise terms the pace, pitch, and rhythm of the sounds which are to be heard; how a melody is organized, and a phrase shaped; the logic of counterpoint and harmonic progression. From these instructions an interpreter can deduce, not with precision, but with only moderate margin of error, the color of the different sounds required, the balance of instrumental tone, the relation of one musical statement to others and to a whole work; all sorts of technical and interpretative deductions which enable a con-

ductor, even if he is merely competent and industrious, to re-
create a great deal of a composer's intention.

But now consider the text of a play.

Take a single speech from *Hamlet:* "To be or not to be."
The text gives a precise indication of its syntax, and in
broadest and simplest terms, its rhythm. The pace, pitch,
stress, melody of the speech must be invented by the actor.
Much of its meaning, and hence many indications as to how
to speak it, can be deduced by study of the rest of the work.
But this study makes far more severe demands upon the intelligence, feelings, intuition and education of the actor than
are ever made upon an orchestral musician.

It must, of course, be admitted that the technique required
of a violinist, for instance, demands long training and endless
practice; whereas a well-graced actor, with a voice which is
naturally well-produced, can play Hamlet with comparatively
little technical drudgery. But the intellectual and intuitive
demands made upon the actor, because of the incomplete
indications to be derived from a play's text—these are what
make his work creative and interesting. It is to reinforce, but
not to supplant, his own intelligence and intuition that he
principally needs a director.

It can readily be seen that a great complicated masterpiece
like *Hamlet* needs a director more than a neat little comedy
of modern manners in a conventional, naturalistic style. The
latter hardly needs any artistic direction. Someone must
choose the actors, plan the set, make practical arrangements
of various kinds. In most plays of this kind the choreography,
if such it can be called, is very simple. Actors enter through
one door to indicate that they have come from the street;
from another if they have come from kitchen or bedroom;
meals occur round a table; love scenes on the sofa; hostesses
plump cushions; guests light cigarettes, exchange elegant
badinage and forward the plot in a series of almost preor-
dained postures; so rigid are the conventions of this kind of
piece. And yet the moment someone with a spark of originality, a quirk of invention, gets to work on the actors, sets

them in unconventional positions, cracks the old gags in a
new way, how much more lively is the result!

For *Hamlet*, or any of the masterpieces, or for any play
which is not in an obviously familiar style and whose interpretation is not clearly charted and signposted, much more
is required of a director.

First, he must decide what he thinks the play means—to
him. The meaning of any work of art is subjective. It is not
what the author thinks it means. If the objective meaning
of a work of art were known, there would be no point in its
existence. It exists merely to suggest many ways in which an
undefined truth may be approached. Every interpretation is
subjective. Some will be nearer to objective truth than others,
but not on that account necessarily more interesting or of
wider appeal than others.

To face the fact that your own interpretation of a work
of art is consciously and flagrantly subjective always seems
to be regarded as an arrogant attitude. But I think the truer
view is that an interpretative artist can only make his own
comment upon the work which he endeavors to interpret, and
that to do so humbly is the only possible attitude to the
"creator" (or, more truly, the expressor) of the "original"
idea.

Throughout my own career I have been criticized for impertinently attempting to express my own subjective, and
admittedly limited, comment upon the masterpieces which
I have been privileged to direct.

I consider such criticism misplaced. I know perfectly well
that my comment upon *Oedipus Rex, Hamlet* or *All's Well
That Ends Well* is not the final, any more than it is the first,
interpretation of these works. My collaborators and I have
merely added one more comment to the vast corpus of
criticism, admiration, revulsion, reverence, love and so on,
with which a masterpiece of human expression is rightly
surrounded.

Performance in the theatre seems to me the right way to
make such comment upon works which were written in

dramatic form, which exist as the raw material for performance. Shakespeare, for instance, wrote his plays, often in a hurry, for a specific group of players. So little was he interested in the plays as literature that there is no record of their being printed, or published, during his lifetime. And when, shortly after his death, his two friends Heminge and Condell endeavored to get together the texts of his plays for publication, they could only find prompt scripts full of errors, omissions and, we may be sure, "improvements," added in rehearsal or performance.

Scholars have performed service of inestimable value in the elucidation of textual difficulties and in the discussion of many problems, primarily in the literary and intellectual fields. But there are limits to the usefulness of purely intellectual and literary criticism of works which are intended to be realized in theatrical terms.

One of the minor tragedies of the historical development of European culture has been the divorce between the theatrical performance and the literary study of drama. Through a series of historical circumstances, the stage, at a period which began during the latter part of Shakespeare's life, became discredited as a serious vehicle of spiritual expression, became relegated to the category of entertainment and as such was regarded by serious people as a frivolous and, for the most part, licentious and pernicious form of exhibitionism.

For about three hundred years educated people, partly under the influence of Puritanism, partly irritated by the shortcomings of almost every interpretation of a masterpiece upon the stage, have been inclined to divide into two isolated categories *Drama*, a minor but not entirely negligible tributary of the main stream of literature, and *Theatre*, a medium of entertainment largely concerned with the commercial exhibition of handsome men and women.

This all ties in with the theory, which survives from a period when the fight against material poverty was man's chief preoccupation, that life was divided into two mutually exclusive compartments entitled Work and Play. Work was serious and important because it aimed to better the economic condition of both the individual and the community. Play was only important insofar as with no play Jack became a dull boy.

In an age of increased material prosperity, when machines lighten our physical labor and mental calculation, when more people are working for shorter hours, but at dreadfully dull, monotonous tasks, we find that congenial work is, as it has always been, more congenial than merely frivolous play; that what we do with our increasing leisure time is at least as important as our vocational time.

For three centuries the myopic examination of texts, their pedantic classification as tragedy, comedy, pastoral-comedy, tragical-comical and the like; laborious exposition of minor points of punctuation, of whether Hamlet says "oh that this too too *solid*" or "too *sullied* flesh" and so on—all this has been considered work, and as such worthy of respect and good wages. Whereas the performance of plays has been lowly regarded and theatrical practitioners have only been well paid when they offered successful commercial entertainment.

Now a change is occurring. The serious theatre is seen to be something more than mere frivolity. Now a distinction is apparent between the mass media and the living theatre; and, in the living theatre, between "show biz" and what has a serious and intelligent aim.

Drama is still academically charted as a backwater in the main stream of English literature. In schools and universities the fact that Shakespeare, Ben Jonson, Congreve and Sheridan were men of the theatre is still overshadowed by their status as men of letters. And their works, as well as those of other dramatists, are still studied as literature. This is, of course, a more convenient and infinitely less expensive way of studying them. But it now begins to be widely realized that, as a method of extracting their meaning, it has grave limitations. University faculties who once maintained the ridiculous paradox that Shakespeare was better appreciated in the study than on the stage are beset now by grave doubts about the ultimate importance of studious, philosophic ponderings, such as those of Bradley, utterly divorced from the exciting two hours' traffic of the stage.

Now the general attitude of educated people is to look with a certain indulgent superiority on those branches of the theatre which can be classified as show biz; to admire the great entertainers—Chaplin, for instance, Grock, Harry Lauder or Danny Kaye, and to find in their antics a "significance" which the perpetrators would be the first to disclaim; to accord too much reverence to great artists who were also great exhibitionists, such as Bernhardt, John Barrymore, even Max Reinhardt; and to expect of something known as the serious theatre a great deal of the light and leading which our grandfathers expected of bishops and statesmen.

So that now the serious theatre is in grave danger of being divorced from any pleasurable or amusing connotation. It is becoming something which we must take, like pills, because it is "good" for us.

I dread the word "educational" when it is applied to the theatre and the great masterpieces of the stage. I see reluctant school children herded into performances of *As You Like It*, *Twelfth Night* or *The Merchant of Venice*, because these are supposed to be simultaneously masterpieces and "nice" plays, containing little to corrupt youthful innocence (a total misconception of the plays, of corruption and of youthful innocence) and thereby being taught to loathe and shun forever three potential sources of great wisdom and great joy.

The serious theatre at this moment stands in danger of being hanged in the noose of its own new-found respectability; of succumbing to the temptation of playing up its educational value and eschewing its duty to entertain. It is possible to get money from Authorities—educational, civic, and philanthropic—if we subscribe to the popular misconception that education and entertainment are mutually exclusive; if we

go cap in hand and beg to be allowed to educate and uplift
our fellow citizens.

I suppose beggars must always go cap in hand. But it seems
to be dishonest to go in cap and gown, rather than in the
traditional cap and bells.

There are two criteria by which the educational potentiali-
ties of a theatrical enterprise are judged. First, is it likely to
produce material which is on the syllabus? Funds can be
given or withheld by dullards who ask whether a play will be
performed because it is a prescribed text, which young people
are forced to cram, in order to be examined in a subject called
"literature."

The second criterion is more general and far more sensible.
It is concerned with the question whether drama, in general,
or a particular dramatic enterprise is, or is not, in a wide
sense "educational."

To the official, the fund-bestowing, mind I have found
the following is fairly typical rating: Shakespeare, yes. Greek
tragedy and the great classics of the French and German
theatre, less definitely, but still yes. Restoration comedy, very
definitely no. Sheridan and Goldsmith are near the borderline. Ibsen, Shaw, Chekhov, Bridie and O'Neill are even
nearer the borderline. A "modern" play or a new play, no.
A modern, foreign play, quite definitely No.

Even Shakespeare is not entirely reliable. Most of his plays
are concerned with quite uneducational ideas, like adultery
and murder; even the "nice" plays are full of uneducational
words like "whoremaster" or "belly."

Ideas as to what constitutes education are inextricably
intertwined with ideas about morality. Consequently theatrical people who hope to get money out of educational authorities have no alternative but to pretend that their job is to
do good to their fellow men, rather than to amuse them.

I am an unashamed advocate of what dry-as-dust peda-
gogues derisively term the "play way," for education and all
other activities. I contend that you really only apprehend
what you *want* to apprehend and that the best form of educa-

tion is to find means of inducing a student to want to teach himself.

By bitter experience we have all learned that, if people say a thing is good for you, it is merely a ruse to induce you to undergo a thoroughly unpleasant experience. And so conditioned are we that, conversely and perversely, we are disinclined to accept a thing as good for us unless it is also thoroughly unpleasant. No one thinks well of a medicine which tastes nice; to be good for you it must taste filthy and if possible smell filthy, and look filthy too; disinfectants must *sting*; a good book must be a penance to read—one of the reasons why the Bible is printed as it is.

But isn't it the case that we really only learn from experiences which touch us emotionally—either with pleasure or pain? And that the more intense the emotion the more powerfully the experience is etched on the plate of memory? That is why most of us have long forgotten the greater part of the knowledge which was stuffed into us at school. Important, interesting things are clean forgotten because they were never emotionally etched upon the mind; whereas we remember absurd scraps—the population of Cork in 1910, the specific gravity of cotton—because for some usually irrelevant reason such scraps are associated with an emotional experience.

For this reason the theatre should assert its claim to be educational, not because it is a short cut to examination answers nor because it is morally uplifting, but because it widens the imaginative horizon by presenting ideas in the most memorable way. The ideas evoked by the theatre are, if the actors are doing their work adequately, primarily emotional. They drive consciously at the sources of pleasure and pain; and by that means produce impressions, not only far more vivid but also far more lasting, than experiences which are more purely intellectual.

Therefore those who are concerned with education do well to be wary of the influence of the arts, and particularly the arts of the theatre. That must be admitted. The mistake, however, they commonly make is to apply the customary Puritan formula: *what is good for you must be unpleasant* and its converse, *what is pleasant cannot be good for you.* What is pleasant *can* be, and usually is, good for you. Nature sees to that. What is bad for you is boredom, being made to undergo experiences which have for you no meaning, which do not ring your bell.

There is today a tendency for the theatre to be divided into two categories: first, show business, which is fun, sexy and frivolous, educational only in the same sense as drunkenness or rape; second, the serious theatre, which is educational in the same sense as quadratic equations, and is a thundering, pompous, unmitigated, but anemic, bore.

The first is so popular a diversion that it is able to operate profitably under what is flatteringly termed private enterprise. The serious theatre can operate only if it is given constant injections of public money.

No one expects universities, public libraries, museums, art collections, opera, symphony orchestras to pay their way. I do not know how honestly they plead their cause. I suspect that they all have to pretend to be more concerned with uplift and less with pleasure than in fact they are. I would like the theatre to be an honest beggar, not to pretend to be other than it is.

Why should the Muses be supported on other terms than science and religion? Hospitals, research laboratories and churches command support for what they are. They do not have to plead that they are educational.

Artists are ministers. Artists bring healing and knowledge. The theatre is a temple. I would like us to ask authority for alms as ministers of a temple where levity and mirth are not excluded, but where it is recognized that levity and mirth are all part of one emotional axis at whose opposite pole lie gravity and tears; that if Jehovah is to be glorified, so also is Baal to be mocked; that fun can be serious; that seriousness need not be pompous.

There is a further danger for the serious theatre. Not only
are we tempted to corrupt our purposes by pretending to be
more educational than we are, we may now aim at a pretentious and spurious "immortality."

Hitherto the charm of theatrical art has been that it was
writ on water. Of the greatest performances no trace survives
but in the memories of spectators. Caruso, Melba, de Reszke
poured forth their glorious cascades and half an hour later
what was left? Fading bouquets; tashed properties carried
back to store; the costumes of Mephisto, Faust, Marguerite,
limp and discolored under the armpits; and—a Legend. Some
thousands of men and women were transported, carried away,
as they never had been before and never would be again. They
recounted their rapture to their friends, their children, their
grandchildren. Something—not all, but something—of the
rapture survives; with the years it grows greater, not less, more
mysterious and exciting. The reality of the performance grows
into legend.

Of course, most performances are forgotten in a matter of
hours, of weeks; a few last for years; a very few last for generations. "My father's grandfather saw Kean's Iago. He could
describe...." That is the sort of fame which seems to me
appropriate for actors, less lasting by a few centuries than a
cathedral, but "immortality" is strictly relative; what matters
a few centuries?

Of performance, only what is glorious survives. Inglorious
performance is deservedly and mercifully forgotten. But the
printed word knows no such nice distinction. The dull thought
survives alongside the inspired one. The shelves of libraries
groan under the weight of literary comment upon the great
dramatic masterpieces, some of it interesting, even exciting;
most of it consists of boring, dated, deadly dull pronounce-
ments.

It fills me with dread to think that the theatre of our day
may survive in tangible form, recorded upon film or tape or
wire. That posterity may remember not the legend of Helen
Hayes but will see her image, with period hairdo, long out-

moded shape and gait, ranting and carrying on in the theatrical conventions of our own bygone epoch; that posterity may
in Laurence Olivier hear nothing but the laughably quaint
accents of a long defunct British upper class; or in Marlon
Brando the humphs and grunts and inarticulate croaks which
experts in the period may identify as "Method" acting.

For my part I would rather write on water; be remembered
by a few and for a while with warmth and joy, or else be
totally forgotten, than survive in crude mechanical reproduction to be analyzed, laughed at, misunderstood, or—worst of
all—falsely reverenced by a posterity which, through no fault
of its own or of ours, can never bridge the unbridgeable, because indefinable, gap between one historical context and
another.

To return to the function of a director, how is his intention
to be achieved, once he has decided how a play is to be
interpreted?

Many of the important decisions are taken before the actors
begin to rehearse.

Their interpretation will be enormously conditioned by
the casting. If A, B and C are to play Othello, Iago and
Cassio while X and Y are Desdemona and Emilia, before a
single rehearsal has been called, it is fairly clear what the
general attempt of a director will be in this particular
production.

Conferences with those who are to design and make the
scenery and dresses will determine how a play shall look. A
good director will not dictate to his collaborators in these
departments, but they will look to him for general lines of
guidance. For instance, in a classical play he must indicate the
period, the scenic convention required; some general direction
about color, about the "key" of this scene and that. Even the
simplest modern comedy in the most obviously realistic single
interior set demands that he state where the doors, windows,
fireplace and furniture be placed; whether the curtains are
to be cottagey or grand. A wise director will know how much,

or how little, direction or suggestion to give. Some designers like to work, as it were, on ruled lines; to others a wink or a nudge is as good as three columns of closely typed instruction. It is vital that the designer's creative talents be encouraged, not frustrated; equally vital that other, and possibly more important, aspects of a production are not butchered to make a designer's holiday. With dominant designers this sometimes happens, particularly in our era, when what is seen tends to attract more interest than what is heard.

But while the general shape and feeling of the production will have been settled before the actors assemble for the first rehearsal, nevertheless it is from now on that the most vital and interesting work of interpretation is done.

How can a director communicate his ideas to the cast?

It is usually better to attempt this by implication rather than explication. There is a method of direction, more prevalent in America, Germany and Russia than in Britain, which believes in giving long talks, and in encouraging long discussions among the cast about the meaning of a play and the process of its interpretation.

This may lead to great results in plays which depend upon teamwork and upon achieving a precise and subtle counterpoint between one voice, one movement and another—such plays as those of Chekhov. But, if the process is to succeed, it must essentially be slow and thorough. The voices of the shy and unimportant persons should be heard as well as the more assertive. At the Moscow Art Theatre, where a permanent company, each member of which is like a member of a family, studies one production over a period of many months, the method of discussion probably works excellently. In London or New York, a hastily assembled group of strangers works for three or four weeks. In such conditions the discussion method is likely to be unfruitful.

This is not entirely to disregard the value of discussion. Far from it. But I regard it as an adjunct to, rather than a substitute for, other work. And, where time is severely limited, the discussions ought to be conducted out of working hours.

In all conditions, the lecture method seems to me a bore, an expression of the director's egotism rather than a practical plan of action. Of course the director must from time to time express theoretic ideas about the work in hand. But such expression should be brief and rare. Naturally, there can be no hard and fast rules. No one in his five wits would rehearse *Three Men on a Horse* in the Spirit of the Moscow Art Theatre preparing *Uncle Vanya*, or by similar methods.

In the preparation of *Hamlet*, for instance, it is essential for the director and leading actor to be in the closest accord. But such accord should have been reached before the rehearsals begin. It is not necessary for the actors who play Barnardo or the Second Gravedigger, or who shout offstage that Laertes shall be King, to know all the considerations which govern the production. It is boring for them to sit around while director and leading actor thrash out theoretical ideas about the Oedipus complex, the meaning of this line, the importance of that move. And in the time available for rehearsing any play with which I have ever been connected, it is out of *all* question that the smaller fry should air their views at rehearsal. They are naturally entitled to views and to express such views to the director when they are relevant to their own parts, but not otherwise, and not publicly.

Of course the contribution of the smaller parts is an important ingredient of the dish. But it is largely determined by the casting. For instance, in *Hamlet* it is possible to use the gravediggers as comic relief. It is also possible, and in my opinion more interesting, to have them make a simple but serious comment on the transitory nature of human existence—"passing through nature to eternity." It is possible to make this comment and still be amusing. The casting of the gravediggers largely determines the comment which their scene makes, the style in which it is made, and the weight it carries.

What concerns them can be explained to any actor-gravediggers of ordinary capacity in a few seconds. Their cooperative suggestions can be made during the rehearsal of their scene. They do not have to be present at all the discussion of the far more complex scenes between Hamlet and Ophelia, Hamlet and his mother, the Ghost, Claudius and even Polonius.

If attendance of the whole company is compulsory at rehearsals of scenes which do not concern them, the production, rather than being more closely integrated, is far more likely to be disrupted by the boredom and disaffection of the smaller-part players.

In theory, a director should not instruct his actors in the detailed playing of their parts. General aspects of a scene or a speech must be directed. It must be explained why this passage must go fast in order to contrast with a slow passage preceding or following; how this scene must be underemphasized in order that more emphasis may fall elsewhere. The focus of attention must be directed. The audience has to be shown where, at a given instant, it must look; to what, at a given instant, it must listen. Naturally there are many technical devices to do this. All of them depend upon the directed cooperation of the actors.

But, in addition to this, every actor depends upon a director for criticism or advice. Even the greatest and most proficient performer will pay attention to the advice of a director he trusts. It would be highly absurd if a director were to try to teach an actor far better qualified than himself how to play a scene or to speak a speech—if I, for instance, were to offer to teach Laurence Olivier. But Laurence Olivier will look to me for technical criticism and suggestion: "Try this a bit faster. Don't pause there." And the actor will depend upon the director to implement in practice theoretical points upon which, in discussion, they will have previously agreed; that such a scene shall be played for comedy; that such a scene shall be dark and shadowy; that emphasis shall be placed here, or there; that the climax of a scene be made in this way or that.

But frequently, with the less gifted or intelligent or experienced actors, the director must coach the performer, show him where to breathe in a speech, which word to stress, when to move, when to keep still.

It is always a sign of failure when a director makes an actor copy him. The failure may be the actor's: there are some so dull that they can only imitate. Far more often it is a failure of communication on the director's part.

He should be able to indicate a move, an inflection or other piece of expression; and the actor should be able to see the idea and express it in his own terms, not by a literal copy. Such indications can be verbal. But nearly all directors find it far quicker and more vivid to sketch the idea in acted terms; and I believe that, provided the actor is confident that such a sketch is not offered as a model which he must slavishly copy, he will find it immensely more helpful than a verbal disquisition. The *how* and the *why*, incidentally, seem rarely to be verbally definable or logically separable.

While a good director may often offer helpful criticism and valuable coaching or supply interesting, even thrilling, interpretative ideas, perhaps his most useful contribution to the work of rehearsal is not "artistic" at all, but consists of being a good chairman.

It is in this capacity that he arranges the agenda of each day's work, sets the pace and determines the amount of time devoted to this or that. Above all, it is principally from the director that a rehearsal takes its tone, derives its atmosphere.

Even in factory work this matter of tone or atmosphere is important. A good foreman, just and vigilant, who makes no favorites among his subordinates, who commands their trust and respect, creates an atmosphere in which work gets done pleasantly and easily. The preparation of a play is like factory work in that the product is the result of cooperative effort. It differs from factory work in that frequently the workers have to reveal themselves in an uninhibited way which, in the wrong atmosphere, could easily be embarrassing, even disgraceful. Directors must try to create an atmosphere in which efficiency is maintained to create a finished product by an ineluctable dateline, and in which, at the same time, all sorts of strange, intimate, and often uncouth images can be created, all sorts of emotional experiments conducted, without embarrassment or self-consciousness.

This is not perhaps so hard to do as it sounds. Efficiency is supported by the excellent discipline which normally prevails in a theatrical company; first, because actors are usually doing what they want very much to do; and, second, because there are always more actors than jobs. They know that if they are a nuisance they will find it very hard to get work. Then, too, a suitable atmosphere is not too hard to create because most actors are exhibitionists, not only unafraid, but delighted, to tear off the veils which convention drapes around many aspects of our human nature, and to which persons of another temperament cling with the desperate modesty of virginity unlawfully assailed.

It is the strange paradox of acting that the more a person disguises himself in another character, the more, to a discerning eye, does he reveal his own. Actors know this about one another. It makes them tolerant of much that, especially in sexual matters, society at large regards with a very puritan eye; and, in consequence, society is apt to think of actors as "odd" and even "loose." Perhaps I have lived too much in their company to be very detached, but it is not my experience that actors are odder or looser than any other group of people, plumbers, say, or clergymen. They are, perhaps, a little more inclined to admit to kinds of looseness which plumbers endeavor to deny, to flaunt oddities which clergymen not always successfully conceal.

Actors are also artists in the sense that they approach a subject with analytical detachment, trying to apprehend the nature of the material which they must interpret, just as a painter analyzes the proportion, texture and coloring of a model and with no more emotional involvement than the surgeon feels for the inert lump on the table under the lights.

The director, then, is partly an artist presiding over a group of other artists, excitable, unruly, childlike and intermittently "inspired." He is also the foreman of a factory, the abbot of a monastery, and the superintendent of an analytic laboratory. It will do no harm if, in addition to other weapons, he arms himself with the patience of a good nurse, together with the voice and vocabulary of an old-time sergeant-major.

The all-important thing for a director is not to let rehearsals be a bore. The chief practical means to this end is to keep people busy, not to keep them waiting around with nothing to do. This is largely a matter of sensible planning—the factory department. It is also a matter of seeing that work proceeds at a good brisk pace, not at that of the slowest wits. Better to rush the dullards off their feet than to bore and frustrate the brighter spirits.

Again I do not wish to oversimplify. There is far more to directing than just not being a bore. But I have so often seen men and women who have so much to offer in the way of intelligent and sensitive appreciation of a text, who have so much knowledge and wisdom to pass on to actors, but who simply cannot make a rehearsal "go with a swing," and therefore simply cannot infuse the proceedings with the vitality and good will which can bring anything into being.

So far I have only discussed the director's communication with the actors on a conscious level and predominantly in technical terms. If there is indeed an *art* of direction—and I believe there is—if it is not just a matter of being a good chairman, with a bit of vitality and warmth, and some knowledge of various theatrical crafts, then much more important is the director's relation with the players, not on the conscious and practical level, but on a plane where communication is not articulate in words and signs, where influence is exerted not by precept but by evocation.

I think I can best make this point by instance.

I was told the following story by Julius Gellner, a gifted director and theatre man in Germany, who in middle life was obliged to seek refuge in Britain. As a young actor, no more than nineteen or twenty, he was working in a German provincial company. He was personable and talented and it was suggested to Max Reinhardt, then at the zenith of his power and glory in Berlin, that this young man was worth considering.

Reinhardt summoned him to Berlin for an interview, all expenses paid, first class. Naturally the boy was thrilled at the possibility of professional advancement and young enough to be no less thrilled by the glories of first-class travel, the sleeping car with all its gadgets, and a stupendous breakfast on the train. It was his first time in Berlin. The weather was glorious: crisp, brilliant October sunshine.

The Deutsches Theater was then the mecca of every German actor. He remembered walking from the station, drawn there almost as one in a trance. He remembered the grandeur of the entrance hall—thick carpets, glossy paint, crystal chandeliers. He presented his letter of appointment to a personage —a lady he thinks, but with the years her identity has become hazy—and was wafted through a door; up a flight of wide steps thickly carpeted in crimson; along a passage; up another flight of narrower steps, thinly carpeted in brown; along another passage, and another, down some steps which were not carpeted at all.

He entered a big room. He recalls long windows running all down one side, and the autumn sunshine streaming in and patterning the floor. At the far end some members of Reinhardt's company—gods and goddesses—were rehearsing a play. With awe he recognized some of their celebrated faces. Then he noticed that, right beside him, sitting on a table, there was a little figure, swinging its legs, backwards and... it could not be... it *was!* The Professor! But so small, so ordinary! And then, with the sweet idiocy of youth, he felt himself stirred with profound humility and affection just because this giant was so small, this genius so ordinary.

The professor, with a friendly nod, motioned to him to wait. The rehearsal proceeded.

Julius was intensely interested. He knew the play. They were acting well. But what he awaited with breathless expectancy was the stream of pure knowledge, the fountain of inspiration which would spout from the Master, the golden garment of praise which should envelop a good and faithful servant and—this he awaited most eagerly of all—the flame of invective in which wrongdoing must shrivel to white ash.

The rehearsal went on. At last the scene came to an end. Now, now, the oracle *must* speak. It did.

"*Quite* nice," it said. "Go back to the maid's entrance; and you, dear, carry the tray in the *other* hand."

He watched all morning. Mostly the master just swung his legs in silence. Utterance, when it came, was not profound. Yet, Julius says, it was the most stimulating and the most fruitful rehearsal he has ever attended. I believe him. We must allow for the excitement of a young man in his particular circumstances. But no doubt the stimulation and excitement must have been there to have made such a strong impression and such a lasting memory.

My own experience and that, I believe, of any other old pro, confirms that it is not by talk, by planning, by taking thought, that a great director achieves results. Reinhardt, on this occasion, did not direct the interpretation; he evoked it. He was an audience to whom the players were directing their efforts—an audience of one, but one whose attention they were determined to hold, whose appreciation they deeply needed.

From instance to analogy: the same process of evocation takes place when a great conductor is in charge of an orchestra. I remember an old orchestral player saying of a conductor— I cannot remember whether it was Toscanini or Beecham —"It isn't that he makes you play as well as you can. He makes you play better than you knew you could."

This process of evocation is not conscious. The conductor, or director, does not deliberately try to pull the performance out of the players. He seeks only to interpret the work. Without conscious intention on either part, without either being aware, a relation establishes itself between them. It is intermittent, it rarely lasts for more than a few minutes, indeed

a few seconds, at a time. It is unpredictable. It certainly does
not come by being sought. All artists know how vain is the
search for inspiration, how defeating to its own ends.

When a name is forgotten the worst way to remember it
is by conscious effort; you must think of something else;
then, not always, but as likely as not some association will
be established, and the name will just fly into your head.
So in the fields of creative imagination and of artistic communication, sometimes, not always, and never as the result
of conscious effort, a fruitful association will be established
between idea and reality, a fruitful artistic relation come
into being between person and person, so that *jointly* they
express an idea, which no one of them singly has originated.

No one knows for certain when this state of inspiration
begins or ends; often, as with the two disciples at Emmaus,
no one knows that the God has been present till after he
has disappeared. Moreover, I do not think anyone can be
sure of distinguishing true inspiration from that which is
false or assumed. The eye rolling in a fine frenzy is not always that of the poet. But we must not on that account leap
to the conclusion that eyes rolling in fine frenzy are always
bogus. Because, upon one celebrated occasion, God spoke,
not in the whirlwind, but in a still, small voice, is not a wise
reason to ignore the whirlwind.

Everyone, not just the artist, knows the experience of being
taken in charge, carried along by a force which apparently
has nothing to do with the "usual self"; whose power is infinitely greater than anything of which the "usual self" is
normally capable. Nearly all great decisions are taken under
such influence. Few people really know why, or even when,
they decided to do the things which really exert the most profound influence on their lives, by means of which they express
themselves most fully. Why, or when, did I decide to marry;
to run away to sea; to join the Catholic Church; to adopt
Fluffy, Snowball and Tibbs?

It is impossible to be precise about what we vaguely and
metaphorically term inspiration. It is, for me at any rate,

impossible to deny its existence. It is when inspiration takes over that the competent and experienced craftsman becomes an artist. A theatrical director must be a craftsman first and foremost; must devote all his energy to learning the intricacies of the trade. If, now and again, craftsmanship is ennobled by inspiration, let him not be puffed up. Inspiration bloweth where it listeth. It is not a wage earned by the industrious apprentice working overtime; it is a gift; its possessors are not usually happy and it quite often happens that, were you or I at the head of things, we should find ourselves quite unable to award them more than five out of ten for conduct. Like any other of God's gifts it is hard to know whether those upon whom it is bestowed are being rewarded or punished.

I am often asked, by young people who want to be theatrical directors, how to begin. It is not an easy question to answer. If you want to be a general in the army you begin as a recruit. But in the theatre there is no promotional ladder.

It is often suggested that aspiring directors should begin by working on the stage-management staff. I think the only advantage of this is that it may be a little easier to get a job as an assistant stage manager than as an actor, especially if you are not particularly handsome. It is important to get into a theatre, to watch what is going on and to do any small job for which someone will pay you a wage. But, in fact, I do not think that an assistant stage manager is in any better position to learn the crafts of direction than an actor, a scene shifter or anyone else who happens to work backstage.

If you want to learn to tie knots in a string it is presumably better to work in a rope factory than a scent factory—but only because you are likely to find rope more accessible. The only way to learn to tie knots is to get a piece of string in your hands and tie it into knots. So, the only way to learn how to direct a play is to get a play, to get a group of actors who are simple enough to allow you to direct them, and direct.

It is unlikely that at first the actors will be anything but amateurs, and probably very raw amateurs. It is unlikely that at first there will be any money to spend upon scenery, lighting or dresses. None of that matters. No one should judge his own early efforts by success. Amateur theatricals are apt to seem more successful than they have a right to be. At this stage, as at any stage, of a theatrical career it is very hard not to be unreasonably exalted by success, unreasonably cast down by failure. Ultimately, like any other artist, you must discover that success and failure are largely fortuitous.

What matters is this: can you make a rehearsal into a lively experience for those who take part? Can you feel the material growing and taking shape and beginning to live as you and your collaborators work? Do you get a passionate satisfaction out of this work? If these three questions get from you a ringing and spontaneous affirmative, then press on. If not, better stick to that nice steady job in the bank, or go chase wild bulls and bears on Wall Street or elephants in Africa.

II

West End

&

Broadway

I HAD NOW been working in the theatre for more than ten years, but, so far, never in the West End of London. Rightly or wrongly, this seemed to be a part of my theatrical education which could no longer be neglected. I did not want to be completely involved in the commercial or fashionable theatre, but without at least some success in this sphere no one is regarded as fully professional.

The West End was already, as it still is, dominated by the remarkable personality of Hugh Beaumont. Although his name never appears upon a playbill, and hardly ever in a newspaper, he has been associated with most of the successful and many of the significant productions of the past twenty-five years. He has had a profound influence on managerial policy, and even upon public taste. More than any other single individual, he can make or break the career of almost any worker in the British professional theatre.

In 1934 he asked me to call at his office. At that time I had heard his name but knew very little about him. I just knew that he worked for a firm called Howard and Wyndham which owned good theatres in a number of the large provincial cities.

What I met was a very slight, fair young man with a glib line of fashionable expressions and a pair of very shrewd, watchful gray eyes. He was making me an offer to direct a new play which he intended to produce, with Diana Wynyard in the leading part. Miss Wynyard had just returned from a successful trip to Hollywood and was all set to be a big star. Mr. Beaumont's talk about the project was amusing, human, unpretentious and extremely commercial. I liked him very much.

The script was amusing, human, unpretentious and extremely commercial. I liked it very much. It was called *Sweet Aloes* and the author was Joyce Carey, an actress who joined the cast of her own play.

I met Miss Wynyard. She was even more beautiful than her photographs, with a sensible, straightforward manner, delightfully at odds with all the glamorous publicity which surrounded her.

The play was a novelette about a nice girl who got into trouble with a nobleman. In content it was about the caliber of a story in a woman's magazine, but its stagecraft was skillful and experienced. Always, just when it seemed about to be uncomfortably mawkish, the author would save the day with a really good joke.

The management never intruded, but it was always helpfully available. Orders came in the form of pleasant little requests; if something had to be forbidden, the interdict would come in some such form as "Might it perhaps be better to. . . ." The iron fist was wrapped in fifteen pastel-shade velvet gloves, but no one who has known Binkie Beaumont can for a moment fail to realize that there is an iron fist. Oddly enough, I have never heard of his being caught, so to say, with his gloves down.

This production was in his early days of management. I do not know much about his beginnings; few people do. He had been a box-office clerk. He became friendly with H. M. Tennent, a man considerably older than himself, of great

charm and theatrical experience. The two of them were working for Howard and Wyndham; finding it difficult to book
what they considered suitable attractions for their firm's theatres—these were the days of transition when the old touring companies were becoming obsolete because of the
all-pervading movies—they decided to produce suitable attractions themselves.

This production was one of their early efforts and also one
of their last under the aegis of Howard and Wyndham.
Shortly after this they went into business on their own account, as H. M. Tennent Ltd., today by far the biggest and
most important production firm in London.

At this stage Binkie Beaumont was still comparatively
green. But he was far too bright to pretend to knowledge or
experience which he did not have. His confidence for a man
of his age was astounding.

Only a few months before I met him he had been concerned
with the management of a play by Clemence Dane. The
director was quite well known and experienced; the cast was
led by Gertrude Lawrence, supported by three or four senior
actors of the highest professional eminence. They opened
in Bournemouth and the performance passed off without
mishap. The leading players were invited to supper by Mr.
Beaumont, champagne was quaffed and all was merry as a
marriage bell.

Over coffee Mr. Beaumont, who was aged twenty-three
—any of the others were the right age to be his parents—
very quietly began to pull the performance apart. The direction had seemed to him a little conventional (that is Binkie's
way of saying outrageously dull); Miss Lawrence had seemed,
here and there, just the least bit hesitant (that meant "you'd
better learn your words, dear, and learn them fast"), and so
on down the line. The criticisms were of deadly accuracy
and shrewdness, offered in a manner which not even the
vainest or most sensitive actor could consider rude or even
uppity.

It is not given to many managers after a not-too-disastrous

first night to take five bulls by the horns, to say nothing of
so glamorous and sacred a cow as Miss Lawrence, give them
a good scolding and send them off to bed. Bear in mind that
this particular manager was barely past his majority, utterly
unknown and merely a paid hand of the firm which was
presenting the play.

Binkie was still so inexperienced that for our play no designer was engaged. Now the firm has become an important
and fastidious patron of stage design. But at this time the
plans of the scenes, their color and character were sketched
by me on the backs of envelopes and carried out by con-
tractors. I chose the furniture and supervised the little woman
round the corner who stitched on slip covers. It was like
being back at Cambridge.

The dresses, however, were made by Molyneux. Unfor-
tunately, no one saw any sketches. We merely saw the finished
and infinitely glamorous articles at the dress rehearsal. No
doubt Captain Molyneux had read the play, but his idea of
what was suitable—even possible—for middle-class ladies
living quietly in the country differed from mine. Character-
istically, Binkie backed his director; he admitted his own
mistake, made an amiable, fair, and I expect advantageous,
settlement with Molyneux, and sent the character actresses
off to Oxford Street to buy suitable dresses off the hanger.

Sweet Aloes did a long tryout tour. We visited half the
big cities of Britain. These were the early days of tours preliminary to a London opening. I do not know if this practice
was already current in the U.S.A. It was new in Britain and
was introduced, I believe, by Binkie and Harry Tennent as
part of their policy for keeping the theatre going in the
provincial cities. All the time Binkie kept urging us on to
more and more work—"Don't you think last night they were
restless at the end of Scene Two? I had my eye on a fat
woman in row K. . . ." He would sit in a box, or stand at some
vantage point at the side and concentrate on three or four
individual members of the audience—contrasted types. It
was a sort of private Gallup poll. I used to wonder that the

guinea pigs never seemed to be aware of those gray eyes
following every shade of their reaction; noting where, and
guessing why, they laughed, or fidgeted or wept—it was a
weepy play—or ate candy. Many's the line or piece of business which we altered because at that moment the fat woman
had eaten a candy.

Eventually London, Wyndham's Theatre; poor notices for
the play; all the critics commented, justly enough, on the
novelettish quality of its story and failed to notice the craftsman's cunning with which the rather flimsy bones had been
articulated. All agreed, however, that Diana Wynyard was
very beautiful and womanly and acted a great deal better
than anyone has a right to expect of beautiful, womanly
women.

The play ran for well over a year, which in those days was
great going.

After the opening Binkie gave an enormous party. The host
has since confessed to me his agony of nervous apprehension
in case this large mob of guests should find themselves at
the requiem for a flop. It taught him a lesson, he says, never,
never to give large omnium-gatherum parties after an opening.
Now, after a Tennent first night, the cast and a few trusties
get their supper—a far more sensible arrangement. Success
can be cosily celebrated, failure inconspicuously mourned.

This business of first night parties is just a small instance
of the realistic commonsense approach which brought Binkie
Beaumont to the top, has kept him there and will keep him
there as long as he cares to go on working. He is methodical,
reasonable, good-tempered—qualities usually associated with
a certain stodginess; their possessors usually function in low
gear. Not so Binkie Beaumont: his mind moves like lightning; he is observant and uncannily intuitive. If his long reign
as the monarch of his particular realm can be seriously criticized it is because, for all his courage and buoyant ingenuity,
he has broken so very little new ground. He has been content
to farm, with splendid efficiency, soil which has proved its
fertility and to leave the pioneering to others.

Not long after the production of *Sweet Aloes*, Binkie Beaumont asked me to produce a play called *Hervey House*, written by Jane Cowl in collaboration with Reg Lawrence. Hervey House was a fictitious ducal mansion in London; the story was romantic, set in the Edwardian era. There were the duke, very handsome; the duchess, equally handsome and very pure and good; the duke's mistress, very handsome and, to make up for not being very pure, very charming; the duke's secretary; "character" aunts and uncles; a devoted lady's maid; a good old butler and dear knows how many footmen, tweenies, grooms, gamekeepers and pantry boys. The scene changed at least fifteen times, from attic to basement of the great house. It had no particular resemblance to real life, but it was written with great verve and conveyed a rather charming admiration for the good old days and the good old English upper orders in a way which no English writer could have managed except tongue in cheek.

We thought it would be an appropriate offering for King George V's Jubilee, done on the grand scale with a whopping star cast and lavish production. Nicholas Hannen was engaged to play the duke, with Fay Compton as his duchess and Gertrude Lawrence in the comparatively small, but grateful, role of the mistress.

We agreed that various alterations were desirable and I was to go to America to persuade the authors to make them.

Joyce Carey had left the cast of *Sweet Aloes* and was now acting in New York with Katherine Cornell in *The Barretts of Wimpole Street*. She knew Jane Cowl quite well and volunteered to arrange our meeting. Miss Cowl was about to go on tour but there was just time for us to meet before she left New York.

We met in the lobby of some hotel, very old oaky and chintzy—can it have been the Algonquin? Miss Cowl, although she had only come down from her room to the lobby of the hotel, wore a tremendous fur stole and a huge, floppy, black gauze hat. I have the further impression of a great many crimson roses; but perhaps I presented them.

Mr. Lawrence was pale, fair and friendly, and let his partner do the talking. Miss Cowl was gracious and flattering;
she declared that my Irish brogue was charming and asked
if I did much hunting. I am afraid she was disappointed not
to find that I too was glamorous. I wished that I could have
been wearing Life Guard's uniform, or had a beard and the
ribbon of the Legion of Honour.

Miss Cowl was raising her Martini in a little exquisite
gesture of salute. A small orchestra struck up Waltzes from
Vienna from behind some rubber plants. I raised my glass
and, trying to "look worlds" over beaded bubbles winking
at the brim, I essayed a little toast, the sort of light nothing
that Prince Vronsky might have said to Anna Karenina. The
light nothing turned to a shrill cough; beaded bubbles winked
embarrassingly all down the front of my neat blue suit—
policeman's uniform cloth, grotesquely heavy and hot for
a New York hotel.

I decided that Prince Vronsky was not my part and that
I had better endeavor to impress Miss Cowl with my honest,
decent common sense.

"About *Hervey House*," I said in a firm, Rugger-blue tone.

But Miss Cowl continued beading at the brim. "His accent!" she said. "Is your home in a bog?"

As a matter of fact it is. So still in a firm tone I answered
"Yes."

"Divine!" She gave a little thrilling, trilling laugh and
proceeded to describe my home, but not very accurately because her impressions of Ireland derived strictly from *Arrah-na-
Pogue* and *The Colleen Bawn*.

"Now about *Hervey House* . . ."

"More d'inkies; me's firsty," said Miss Cowl, and asked
for my impression of the London season.

I though she meant the theatre season and began what
was meant to be a bluff, common-sensible critique.

"No, silly! The Season! The Parties. Ascot. Goodwood.
Cowes. D'you know Pussy?"

"We *have* a cat. A nice tabby called Lizzie."

But Pussy turned out to be a Duke; and Joe was a Viscount and Toots was the Dowager Countess of Chrome.

The minutes were flying past and so were the waiters, all bringing Martinis.

Miss Cowl was now launched on a Pilgrim's Progress through Debrett. We hopped from Wilton to Knowle, from Chatsworth to Mentmore.

"Tubby," she said—Tubby was Master of the Rolls—"Tubby and I were in the Orangery at Champneys Maltravers . . ."

"Listen!" I heard a terrible, loud, rough voice behind me. "Listen!" it said again.

I whirled round and caught only my own reflection in a glass, alarmingly red in the face.

"I've not crossed the Atlantic to talk about Tubby and you in the Orangery."

There was a silence like death. Not a sound in that chintz and oaken hall. The band had stopped.

"No!" said the voice even more aggressively. A pause.

"No?" said Miss Cowl in a voice like rose water falling in a fountain of pearl. "Then what?"

"I've come here to talk about *Howvey Herse.*"

Like the man in the song, she was off to Philadelphia in the morning, but a further meeting was arranged. Joyce Carey and I must have supper with her after the play on Thursday.

In a way this was rather nice. For three days I had nothing to do but look around New York at the expense of my management. I cabled to Binkie explaining the situation, and regretting the extra expense.

Joyce Carey was a wonderful guide to New York. It was divine weather, bright and cold. We did nice touristy things: up the Rockefeller Center, then very new; Radio City Music Hall—Shirley Temple in *Curlytop* and millions of Rockettes performing the dullest antics; we took the ferry to Staten Island; we "did" the Metropolitan Museum of Art and the Frick; we went to a matinee of *Tristan* at the Met; *The Petrified Forest*, in which Humphrey Bogart had just made his first big success; and *Anything Goes* with young Ethel Merman and young William Gaxton. The vim and pep and sheer gusto of a good American musical were a revelation; so were the impudence and wit of the book. In this field the New York theatre seemed already ten years ahead of London.

Compared to the smartness and glitter of hotels and restaurants and department stores, the theatres were incredibly dowdy and fusty. It was odd the way the audience read the evening paper in the intervals, as if traveling in a suburban train. The absence of foyer or bar was odd; I fancied that some of the theatres smelled of drains and that none of them had been painted or upholstered since the Civil War.

Thursday found us in Philadelphia, where, in the Walnut Street Theatre, a small audience seemed inattentive during the acts but mightily interested in the evening paper at intermission. The piece was a very conventional drawing-room comedy, and Jane Cowl was giving an almost academic display of drawing-room comedy technique; cushions were plumped, cotton tiger-lilies were sniffed, telling exits were made through french windows slap into painted oleanders; there were thrilling, trilling laughs and experienced dabs with a lace-edged hanky. It was perfunctory, but also incredibly skillful; you could see that, with a good play, good direction and her heart in the job, this was an actress of remarkable caliber.

At supper Jane was cheerful and businesslike; this was man-to-man evening, but I could see that she had no intention of making the alterations. She conceded one or two very minor points with a great show of giving in; on all the more important ones she was pleasantly, blandly adamant. Mr. Lawrence, as before, was pale and mute.

By-passing the alterations, Miss Cowl started to discuss the style and scale of the production. I explained that His Majesty's Theatre was very large and that Mr. Beaumont's intention was to make a lavish and spectacular production. Miss Cowl said that a large theatre would kill the play, which was intimate. I queried the economic possibility of presenting in a small theatre a play with such a huge cast. She said they could double up, and with a pencil made an efficient plan for this on the tablecloth. I countered with the large number of sets. More plans were drawn, showing how it could all be staged with three good bits of furniture and some plywood screens. The tablecloth began to look like the plan of a maze.

At two o'clock the party broke up, leaving Miss Cowl undisputed mistress of the field.

Next morning I sent another long cable to Binkie. Hardly had it been dispatched when Mr. Lawrence appeared. He agreed with some of the suggestions and would like to discuss them in further detail. After two hours we were in agreement and had produced what we thought was a workable outline to present to Jane.

That evening came Binkie's reply to my cable: unless the alterations were made to my satisfaction he would not put on the play. I was to use my discretion about telling this to Miss Cowl.

In the dead vast and middle of the night I was wakened by the telephone: Miss Cowl on the line from Philadelphia. Miss Cowl was in one hell of a rage. She accused me of suborning her partner, of going behind her back, of coercing him into ruining *her* play; she kept saying "I thought Irishmen were sportsmen. This is not cricket." With the daemonic energy of the star actress she went on and on and on. Her thrilling voice ran up and down the scale. For minutes on end I put the telephone down and walked about the room and grieved for her when she would be faced by the telephone bill.

Towards the end she spoke more in sorrow than in anger; once I thought I caught the hint of a sob. Before my eyes, and I hated myself for it, rose the picture—not of a lonely and aging widow, as indeed she was, fighting for the life of her brain-child, as indeed she was—but of the experienced actress giving experienced and stylized flaps of a tiny lace-edged hanky. Her last words were that I might come, if I liked, and talk it over again, next week—in Chicago.

In Chicago we had a quiet, reasonable showdown. I told her that it was the alterations or else, and she accepted the situation with the philosophy and realism which underlies the froufrou of all professional performers. I sometimes wonder whether actors and actresses ought not to manage our public affairs instead of politicians. It would seem so much more sensible to entrust things to people who are steady and realistic underneath the meringue of a fluffy and flossy exterior than to people who are fluffy and flossy behind a steady and realistic stone façade.

In the end the play was a failure, and for just the very reason which Jane had foretold. It *was* a small, intimate piece, which in my production was blown up to a size in which its charm was lost. The actors did well; the sets by Molly Mac-Arthur were handsome, but so complicated that, on the opening night of the tryout in Manchester, one of the actors got lost and flew about in a frenzy through room after room, pre-set on a turntable. The actors on stage, making up lines and pretending to look for their lost colleague in the garden, were startled to see him crawl through the fireplace.

The production cost a fortune and must have involved Binkie in tiresome and embarrassing trouble with his directors. It is characteristic that he never uttered one word of blame or reproach, although it had been on my advice that the production was as it was. In failure—even spectacular failure—he is as calm, and as ubiquitously helpful as in success.

Miss Cowl is dead; I have regretted often that I never made an opportunity to admit that she was right, and give her at least the tiny satisfaction of hearing my apology and knowing that I was genuinely sorry that misjudgment of mine had spoiled her play.

A few months later I was back in New York, again as an employee of Beaumont, but this time in association with the Theatre Guild. The play was *Call It A Day* by Dodie Smith.

It was my first experience of working on Broadway, but this was hardly typical because the cast were almost all drawn from the ranks of the British contingent in New York, led by Gladys Cooper and her husband, Philip Merivale.

I had never met Gladys Cooper, though I had often seen her act, and admired the way she had turned herself from a beautiful, pale-pink English rose into a well-equipped actress. She has never made the slightest pretense to being a dedicated artist, but is rather one of those people who have a living to earn and decided upon a career where her great physical beauty could be a legitimate capital asset. She graduated from the chorus of musical comedy and soon achieved a very good position. For ten years in England she operated as an actor-manager, running at her own theatre a series of solid business successes. There were no great plays, not even ambitious ones, just a series of capably written, acted and managed hits.

It was interesting too to meet the heads of the Theatre Guild, whose names were already legendary in Britain as well as in America. This was 1935 and many of the Guild's founders were still active. Philip Moeller, rolled up in a muffler, seemed to be conducting rather ninetyish university reading parties, or seminars; you half expected that Richard Le Gallienne, Edna St. Vincent Millay or John Jay Chapman might be going to read a paper. I was grateful for the kind and friendly way Moeller treated me, not as a senior and eminent director dealing with a junior and, worse, a know-all Limey, but simply as one enthusiast talking shop with another. Lawrence Langner was in and out, delightfully merry and genial, still a busy lawyer playing with the theatre as a grown-up plays with an electric train. Theresa Helburn was briskly friendly; but at that time I always had the impression that she was interested in something important and secret, which had either just happened somewhere else or was just going to happen the moment I left her room. We and our project seemed to be pieces of rather secondary merchandise in the back part of a busy warehouse.

I saw most of Lee Simonson, who was designing the sets, and found him wonderfully glamorous and stimulating. He did nothing by halves. Everything was extreme. From extravagant gaiety he swung to the lamentations of Jeremiah. His work was the same.

Our play was about an upper-middle-class family, whose home had to be comfortable, in good, conventional and essentially "English" taste. Lee would produce sketches of marble halls, hung with tapestry, chandeliers, Gainsboroughs and Romneys by the dozen, carpeted with Aubusson overlaid by polar-bear rugs. When I hinted that the sketch suggested something rather too grand, he would pout, then shrug, then smile with endearing and warming humor, and next day there would be a sketch for the same set which suggested the slums of London during the plague.

Towards the end of rehearsals he caught a cold: even the cold was larger and louder than life. He coughed like Marguerite in the last chapters of *La Dame aux Camélias*; wound a turquoise woolen muffler right round his face, and looked out with the infinite sadness of an ailing marmoset; the end seemed hourly due and I had planned the little speech which I would make to his widow. Suddenly he felt better. The scarf was unwound, color returned to the fading, wasted cheeks and we had a delightful evening, laughing over old photographs and downing the remains of the cough mixture laced with brandy.

Miss Cooper's approach to the rehearsals was briskly professional. Early in the morning she used to go out sliding on the ice in Central Park with her youngest daughter. She would arrive at the theatre, punctual and casual, and give the impression that, while moderately interested in her work and entirely willing to do her best, her real interests were elsewhere.

One thing was disconcerting: she never seemed to learn the words. Gradually everyone put away the book and everyone seemed to have his part well under control—except Gladys. She rehearsed in big horn-rimmed glasses, carried the book everywhere and never lifted her nose out of it. In the part she never stopped pouring tea, or putting on children's overcoats or working with account books or making parcels, so the omnipresent book was more than a bit of a bore. Madam performed prodigies of one-handed dexterity, but nobody can really tie up a parcel with one hand.

She saw I was getting worried: "It's all right, dear. I always do this. It'll be all right and I won't be a nuisance to the others."

Even at the dress rehearsal she carried the book and did not seem to know the words at all.

We played in the Morosco Theatre, which is very small and has no orchestra pit and no footlights. A man in the front row of the orchestra impudently placed his derby hat right on the stage. Gladys, making her first entrance, when most players are half-paralyzed with nerves, saw the hat, advanced upon it spouting her part a mile a minute and, dead accurate, gave the hat a tremendous kick and sent it flying over the heads of the audience into the nethermost darkness of the pit. There was a laugh, a round of applause, and Madam proceeded with the business of the play as cool as a cucumber.

In the preparation of this production I learned how hard it is in New York to get a scene to look even remotely like an English home. In America there seems to be no halfway house between brand-new, glossily smart furnishings and expensive antiques. What this play needed was a general effect of good taste and good breeding, without being in the least bit elegant or wealthy; a mixture of styles harmonized and humanized by the shabbiness of long wear and tear. Lee Simonson was in sincere agreement and tried hard to find suitable stuff, but a crisis arose over a bed.

The first scene represented a bedroom. We agreed to compromise on the set, which was in shades of chestnut and deep blue, unquestionably in good taste, but somberly, totally unlike St. John's Wood. Never mind; the alternatives had been a sort of operating theatre in dead white or a jungle of pink rose-trellises with emerald chintz frills. But the bed provided by Mr. Simonson was a gigantic double bed in mahogany with a heraldic coat of arms at its head. It was designated "Toodor." Six people could have slept on it without being at all crowded, but access was only possible by standing on a chair.

Miss Cooper made what, if it had not been so dignified, you might have called a fuss. Mr. Simonson was what *he* called a little upset—the symptoms were like the burning of a ruined city. Finally he shouted that he would have some alternative beds sent in; Miss Cooper could damn well choose.

We were rehearsing in what was then called the Guild Theater, which had a great many doors. Every few minutes, after much thumping and pounding, one or another of the doors would open to admit a group of men, grunting and sweating under the weight of gigantic and extraordinary double bedsteads. Gradually the entire orchestra was full of them: four-posters, brass bedsteads from Victorian lodging houses, Empire beds, Chippendale beds, Sheraton beds, Biedermeier beds, topped off by the arrival, in the late afternoon, of a gang of six Negroes, who triumphantly deposited a bed supported at each corner by an outsize, oxydized metal swan. The rehearsal broke up in agreeable disorder. Simonson and Miss Cooper went off to Macy's arm and arm and bought entirely innocuous twin beds extremely cheap.

The next Anglo-American crisis arose because our friends at the Theatre Guild kept reminding us of the extraordinary rapidity of what they called the "tempo" of American goings-on.

"You must find that we move at a bewildering speed," Miss Helburn would say, as we hurtled in a taxi down Sixth Avenue at fifty or sixty miles an hour.

"Bewildering," I would reply, as we scrambled back onto the seats, whence we had been thrown when the taxi screeched to a halt at the lights.

"Simply bewildering," I would add, as minute ticked after minute, before we again plunged forward, this time striking our heads against the rear window.

It was implied that plays were acted rather slowly in London. Nobody said anything at all rude or hurtful; simply

that our nonchalant, infinitely leisurely style was rather
gracious.

I determined that this time at least the silly old European
tortoise must not lag too far behind the American hare. Every
line was spoken at top speed, every cue was taken at least three
syllables before the end of the previous speech. Everyone
moved at a run. It was like a newsreel in the movies in 1910.

Langner and Moeller and Miss Helburn attended the dress
rehearsal. "Delightful," they said, "delightful. But *much* too
fast. You must slow it all down. Remember we in America
don't take things in such a dreadful *rush* as you people over
there."

After *Call It A Day* I stayed on to direct *Sweet Aloes*,
which, on the strength of its success in London, had been
bought for New York. It was another, and rather painful,
lesson in the deceptive differences which underlie the similar-
ity suggested by a common British and American language.
The jokes, which had amused the London public, were not
for export. They depended upon an awareness of all sorts
of small and entirely local customs, turns of phrase and dis-
tinctions of class. In New York they fell painfully flat. Without the jokes the play seemed heavily mawkish, and folded
after three sad weeks.

We left America with regret. It had been a wonderfully
stimulating experience and we had made many friends.
Within a year of our departure, the persecution of the German Jews began: the writing was on the wall. The gap between our present departure and our future return was destined to be ten years; quite a span in the short lifetime of a
human creature. At the end of this particular ten years the
entire world, ourselves and our friends included, would be
so changed that now, looking back after another decade, I
can hardly believe that I am trying to chronicle events and
ideas in my own life rather than that of some long-dead, or
even fictitious, character whose name and appearance I
happen, by an odd coincidence, to bear.

12

Old Vic &
Laurence Olivier

WHEN IN 1936 an offer came to return to the Old Vic I was very glad to accept. The interim had taught me to appreciate the difference between a theatrical institution with a policy and the haphazard conditions of the commercial theatre, where no manager, not even Beaumont, seemed to have much more of a plan than to produce "a success," or to look farther ahead than the current season, or at very most, the next but one.

I had now worked long enough and in a sufficient variety of conditions to have a fairly realistic opinion of success. I had learned that it can only be reliably measured in terms of ticket sales, a solely quantitative standard; that any judgment about artistic success must be merely subjective, a matter of taste; learned further that what I considered the best plays and the best productions very rarely succeeded; and that the greatest successes rarely seemed to me interesting or of lasting value. I saw too that the exigencies of the commercial theatre make it difficult, if not impossible, to aim at anything other than the advancement of one's career by being associated with the greatest possible number of the greatest possible successes.

Success of this kind brings rewards in the shape of money and celebrity; but high income tax takes a great deal of gloss off a high salary; and in the theatre, while it is fairly easy to achieve a sudden and resounding success—much easier than, for instance, in engineering or any of the so-called learned professions—it is also much easier to come a no less sudden and resounding crash, from which the recovery may take years, from which there may indeed be no recovery.

Most of the people at the top of the theatrical tree live in continuous and justified anxiety lest they be knocked off their eminent perch. The desirable thing is to be steadily employed in a kind of theatrical work which, though not necessarily the best paid or the best publicized, you believe to be stimulating and useful.

Such employment an institution with a policy can offer. Moreover, it offers to its employees an attachment to something more interesting, and of more lasting importance, than their own careers.

My little excursions into the commercial theatre had further convinced me that only now and again in that world would productions be offered which would really satisfy my artistic aspirations or stretch my technical and imaginative range. Merely to earn a living, let alone to maintain a place somewhere near the upper branches of the competitive tree, it would be necessary to spend nearly all my working life in the preparation of small comedies in the realistic manner, most of them mere "vehicles," lightweight buggies designed to display a high-stepping star. This prospect had only limited appeal.

Moreover, I felt eager for another grapple with Shakespeare. Now that more than a year had passed since my first season at the Vic I began to have a bit more perspective on it, to be able to assess the quality of our productions, to see not only how things had been, but why they had been so.

Mentally reviewing that past season made me long to put into practice some of the lessons I had learned. While I cer-

tainly felt some sense of artistic responsibility, I shall not
pretend that my decision to go back to the Vic, at very much
lower pay than I could now expect to earn in the commercial
theatre, was entirely governed by artistic integrity. I also believed that it was a wise move for worldly reasons. Only by
a series of respectable classical productions could I establish
the sort of reputation which I would like to have, and be
considered for the sort of work I wanted to do.

This, I suggest, is an aspect of their worldly, as opposed to
artistic, careers to which young people in the theatre, especially in America, attach too little weight.

The classics are the only measuring rod by which the stature
of an actor or a director can be measured. It is not possible
to compare Mr. A's performance in one ephemeral comedy
with that of Mr. B in another. Such comparisons are made;
but with rare exceptions it is the personalities, rather than
the art and skill, of the artists which are the point of comparison. Criticism degenerates into gossip. But it *is* possible, and
it is a matter of great interest and of serious critical value, to
compare the Hamlets, let us say, of Barrymore, Gielgud,
Olivier, Maurice Evans, Christopher Plummer, and the host
of others who from time to time attempt the part and risk
the comparison.

Occasionally a performer will be so outstanding in a certain role as to make it his own for at least a generation. In
London, Edith Evans has done so as Millamant, Sybil Thorndike as Medea. I have already mentioned such a performance
by Laurette Taylor in *The Glass Menagerie*. Other instances
come to mind: Tallulah Bankhead in *The Little Foxes*, Ruth
Gordon in *The Matchmaker*, Helen Hayes in *Victoria Regina*.
But in each case the actress was supported by a play of sufficient weight to be at least a runner-up for classic stature.

Oddly enough, I cannot think of a male performance quite
in this category. No doubt there are such. But on the whole
the men tend to be remembered by their work in the classics.
Can it be because the classical plays—classics in the English

language at any rate—offer comparatively small opportunity to the women, that the outstanding female performances occur in the other field?

Yet no seriously ambitious young actress can really afford to forego the chance to play Ophelia, Rosalind, Desdemona or Viola while she is still young enough to do so. Every seriously ambitious young actor should have played at least three of the important *young* classic roles at the right age—Hamlet, say, Romeo and Benedick; or Mosca in *Volpone,* Young Hard-castle in *She Stoops to Conquer,* and Valentine in *Love for Love.* To neglect this opportunity is to neglect two things: first, the comparison with one's own contemporaries and with the young actors of previous generations. Such comparison is essential in the establishment both of contemporary status (apart from mere success, in terms of a big salary, fan mail, one's picture in the newspapers) and also of posthumous re-membrance, the legend, by which alone great acting survives the contemporary moment. Second, no artist can afford to neglect the technical and imaginative development which only great parts in great plays can bestow.

To an actor a classic repertory is as essential to his develop-ment as it is to a musician. No one would dream of taking seriously a pianist who had not at one time familiarized him-self, imaginatively and technically, with Bach's preludes and fugues, Beethoven's sonatas and at least three or four of the great concertos. Yet actors presume to consider themselves serious artists without ever having made any real attempt to come to grips with any single one of the great classic roles which lie within their range.

At the present time this is a more difficult problem for young people in the American theatre than it is in any other civilized country, because, with the simple exception of the American Shakespeare Festival at Stratford, Connecticut, there are no classical productions prominently offered in American terms. On the rare occasions when a classical play appears on Broadway, it is given either by an imported en-semble (Old Vic or Comédie Française or the like) or by an

American cast carefully bolstered up, and for very sufficient reason, by experienced European artists.

Obviously, this is not because American actors lack talent. It is because they lack a suitable kind of experience. But if they felt that their lack of this particular kind of experience were a serious detriment to their imaginative and technical development, they would take more energetic action to remedy the existing situation.

My own motives in rejoining the Old Vic were a mixture of artistic ambition and integrity with an element of worldly calculation. But I think the dominant reason was to attach myself to something more significant than my own career; to feel part of something more permanent, and rooted in more serious intentions, than the short-term, superficial professional alliances of the commercial theatre.

I wanted, in short, to be part of an institution. *Institution* is a dreary word, suggestive of lunatic asylums, homes for indigent widows; of long, draughty, antiseptic corridors, of huge turnip fields in flat country being hoed by supervised inmates. And yet I can find no other which covers the same ground—Organization, Foundation, Establishment—all synonyms ring the same knell. And I cannot help reflecting that if a word, especially a name, carries depressingly ominous overtones it must be for a reason. Institutions do tend to be dreary; they do tend to house the indigent, the insane, those who for some reason or another have failed to fight life's battle on their own.

Can it be that to want to be part of an institution bespeaks a weakness, that one is turning oneself, so to say, into an indigent widow, a supervised inmate? Does the strong spirit, moving breast-forward up the mountain, proceed alone? Surely, if wise, he will not shun the support and company of other pilgrims; if kind, he will want to offer his support and company to them.

Or is the desire infantile? Do we fly into institutions as to a rather grim, gaunt mother's breast?

When I returned to the bosom of the Vic was I abrogating

the manly independence with which I had resisted Wellington with its Iron Dukery; or was I learning at last a lesson in humility and brotherhood, or could it just be that one institution was congenial and the other was not?

This time I was received at the Vic with open arms. Miss Baylis allowed me to see that, though she did not feel warmly towards me, she recognized me as potentially useful and that time might draw us together. She also gave a good deal more attention to the suggestions and requests which, in this new and more summery climate, I ventured to make. Of these the most important were the engagement of a stage manager of my choosing, George Chamberlain, and the decision to establish the Shakespeare Company in sole possession of the Old Vic, with the Opera and Ballet companies at Sadler's Wells.

Since the opening of the Wells in 1930 all three companies had operated, turn and turn about, in both theatres. This was an unsatisfactory arrangement in many ways: the transport of scenery and dresses was extremely expensive and, frequently, especially in bad weather, caused great damage. On one stormy March morning the entire scenery of *La Traviata* blew off a truck as it crossed Blackfriars Bridge and was lost forever in the muddy, turbulent waters of the Thames. Another trouble was in the box office: angry old gentlemen from Putney, trying to book for *La Bohème* at the Vic, would find it had moved to Sadler's Wells; while at the self-same moment the Wells' box office was fending off an even angrier old lady from Wimbledon who wished to see *King Lear,* which had just been transferred to the Vic.

The Wells, with a larger stage, a larger capacity and more dressing rooms, was clearly more suited for opera and ballet, which were cramped at the Vic. The more intimate conditions of the Vic were better for Shakespearean plays, which were lost in the wide-open spaces of the Wells.

The practical reorganization was easy. The reason it had been so long postponed was constitutional. The charters of

both theatres, under which they were subject to H. M. Charity
Commissioners, specified that Shakespeare, opera and ballet
should be played in both houses. Alteration of the charters
was a long, tedious legal business which the board of governors had long contemplated, but been deterred from achieving partly by sentiment and partly from inertia. With the
energy of a new broom I was able to sweep Miss Baylis and
the governors into action.

George Chamberlain and I had worked together in a
production for Beaumont of a play which had starred Marie
Tempest. It was called *Short Story* and was the 'prentice effort
of Robert Morley, then a desperately shy and almost conspicuously unsuccessful actor.

Miss Tempest, the greatest light comedienne of a generation, was by now seventy and a tremendous tartar. She was
a fascinating, brilliantly clever and talented little woman,
but she had a considerable sense of her own importance and
expected others to have the same. The prompter is at rehearsal the whipping boy of actors like Marie Tempest. If
they fail to give a prompt not merely at the moment when it
is wanted (and at seventy she wanted plenty of prompting
in the early stages of rehearsal), but the moment before, then
there is hell to pay with compound interest.

George Chamberlain, prompting Marie Tempest, was the
absolute model for the craft. He would anticipate a dry-up
with the intuition of a Tiresias and offer the prompt with
the tact of a great hostess. But once he spoke too soon.
Madame whirled round on him with blazing eyes:

"Did you speak?"

"Yes. I gave you the line."

"Are you acting the part or am I?"

"You are trying to, and you always dry up on that line."
For the assistant stage manager thus to address Dame Marie
Tempest was like a corporal giving a back-answer to a field
marshal, like a rowboat ramming the *Queen Mary*.

There was a long and terrible moment; but neither common sense was lacking in Marie Tempest, nor humor.

"*Quite* right," she said, and smiled the smile which no one was ever able to resist.

I knew then that George Chamberlain was a man with whom I would like to be associated.

When I went to the Vic, I persuaded him, with the greatest difficulty, to come to stage-manage the company. Now more than twenty years later he is still at the Vic. After a considerable period as stage director, then as general manager of the Old Vic and Sadler's Wells, he is now clerk to the governors of the Old Vic and a governor of the Sadler's Wells Trust.

In some other respects my advice to Miss Baylis was less fortunate. I had the idea that, instead of recruiting a full Shakespearean company of twenty or thirty actors, we should offer a seasonal engagement to a nucleus of no more than six or seven. This had the advantage of saving money. The whole of a large company is never employed to full advantage. Some are either free during part of the season and paid to do nothing, or else miscast, or else playing parts which could be adequately cast for half the salary.

The drawback was that neither backstage nor between the company and the audience was there quite the solid, cosy family-feeling which is so important an asset of a permanent company. Nor, taking a longer view, were we training in smaller parts the actors who would eventually succeed to larger ones.

There was a considerable saving of money, but on balance, the loss in intangible advantages was greater than the monetary gain.

The season opened quietly with *Love's Labour's Lost*, which introduced Michael Redgrave to the London stage. Our second production was *The Country Wife* by Wycherley. The Vic had done Congreve's *Love for Love* a year or two earlier and, although there had been some unfavorable comment and a letter or two in the press complaining of the lapse in the Old Vic's usually uplifting moral tone, no great harm had been done. But *The Country Wife* is a great deal more indecorous than *Love for Love* and, while funnier, a good deal less witty.

We had a particular inducement to put it on. Gilbert Miller had seen Ruth Gordon as Mrs. Pinchwife in a summer stock production at Westport, Connecticut. He was so entranced with the performance that he planned to present it on Broadway with decor by Oliver Messel. Messel persuaded him to let the Old Vic do it first and then transfer Miss Gordon and the scenery to New York.

We found ourselves therefore tempted to put on this licentious work by the offer of the use, without charge, of sumptuous decor by Oliver Messel and a performance of which the fame had already crossed the ocean. I am glad to say that neither Miss Baylis nor I wrestled very long or hard with Satan.

Around Miss Gordon we were able to collect a cast of extraordinary brilliance. It included Michael Redgrave, Alec Clunes, Ernest Thesiger, James Dale, Eileen Peel, Freda Jackson, Iris Hoey, Kate Cutler and, as a glittering centerpiece, Edith Evans.

It was a glorious success, clouded only by a first-prize rumpus among the governors. As with *Love for Love* in the Laughton season, objection was raised to the production by the Old Vic of a play which some of the governors considered indecent. A London charitable foundation of great wealth, antiquity and influence, which had for fifty years been one of the few sound pillars in the extremely shaky edifice of Old Vic finance, threatened to withhold its annual grant.

A special meeting of the governors was convened. Fur flew. Noblewomen called other noblewomen "damned old fools." Proconsuls, accustomed to the absolute obedience of Honduras or Bechuanaland, squealed like pigs at a fair. Miss Baylis very wisely kept mum and left her chairman to restore order.

Her chairman was Lord Lytton, and never can anyone have more perfectly looked the part of a belted earl. He was a small man, but beautifully made, with the most patrician manners imaginable. Towards the end of his life he became a little deaf. He would incline his elegant white head towards you and say, very, very quietly, "Would you please speak more clearly." As a result everybody at the meetings spoke loudly, even raucously, because they were self-conscious; the chairman's replies were in the lowest of silvery tones; occasionally at random, but always perfectly phrased, perfectly lucid, and delivered with Delphic assurance. His authority was total.

On this occasion he let the objectors make their case, then reminded them very gently that whatever their personal opinion of the play might be, Wycherley was a master of the English tongue acknowledged by nine successive generations; that the morals of a play cannot be judged irrespective of context; that some of the morality in the play was admittedly at odds with our own; but so was much of the morality in Shakespeare's plays; so, for that matter, was much of the morality in the Old Testament. He gave a concise summary of the dangerous futility of censorship, reminded his board that they had not been appointed as censors, and wound up with a simple peroration which I shall quote verbatim. You must imagine him sitting at the head of the storm-tossed table looking the embodiment of *ancien régime.* "For my part," he said, in tones more silverly urbane and lower than ever, "I abominate censorship as much as I enjoy the vigorous performance of a masterpiece, even a masterpiece of smut."

That was the end of that. The battle continued in the correspondence columns of *The Times.* But goody-goody letters expressing horror at the depravity of the Old Vic's current offering were naturally a shot in the arm of the box office. And even these were finally silenced by a brief, witty thunderclap from Bernard Shaw.

We played to capacity every night of a run, which was limited by the date when Ruth Gordon and the scenery had to go to New York.

I do not think the New York cast had either quite the same star appeal or the same gusto as the Old Vic team. Miss

Gordon's performance was suitably admired but the evening as a whole had less impact.

Meantime at the Vic we presented *As You Like It* with Edith Evans as Rosalind, Marie Ney as Celia and Michael Redgrave as Orlando in a charming production by Esmé Church, with decor by Molly MacArthur in the style of Watteau.

Edith Evans was nearer fifty than forty and I think that, for the first five or six minutes of her performance, audiences may have had reservations about the wisdom of this marvelous, but quite evidently mature, actress playing the part of a young girl wildly in love and masquerading as a boy. For my part I had no reservations whatever; from beginning to end the performance swept one along on the wings of a radiant and tender imagination. It was a comment upon womanhood and upon love, more interesting and moving, not less, because it had the ripeness and wisdom of experience. It was a feast of spoken music—a revelation to me of how Shakespearean verse, when wonderfully spoken, gilds the meaning of words and opens the windows of the imagination in the way which the theatre uniquely can, but seldom does. This was a great performance.

But let not lesser artists suppose that they too in middle age can assume the rhapsodic passions and freshness of youth. Nothing has done greater harm to Shakespeare than the presentation of his young parts by ladies and gentlemen twenty or thirty years older than they are pretending to be.

It is easy to see why this sort of casting occurs. Managers feel that they dare not offer a Shakespeare play without the insurance of a star or two in the leading parts. Stars, except in the cinema, where appearance counts for so much more than skill, are rarely less than forty years of age. Actors are rarely able to acquire either the technique or the authority for important parts until they are too old to be suitable for any of the younger characters. Also, it is a temptation to the mature star to have a shot at parts which he ought to have played years ago but for some reason never did. His name means

money at the box office, so a presentation can always be arranged; his friends will flatter him into the belief that at
forty-five he can still play Romeo, Benedick or Hamlet. And
so, in a sense he can. He will bring to bear, as Edith Evans
did on Rosalind, a developed technique and a mellowness of
emotional experience beyond the range of youth. Now and
again, as with Evans' Rosalind, the result will be justified;
but only rarely.

In general I would rather have the freshness and energy
of youngsters in the young parts and put up with the inevitable shortcomings of immaturity. Otherwise there is a grave
danger that a tradition will develop, or at all events a rooted
public preconception, that the world of Shakespeare is peopled
entirely by booming big guns, surrounded by parents, uncles,
servitors, statesmen and warriors all in the very last stages of
doddering senescence.

After *As You Like It* we did *The Witch of Edmonton* by
Dekker, directed by Michel Saint-Denis. In striking contrast
to a glittering Lady Fidget in *The Country Wife* and radiant
Rosalind, Edith Evans appeared as a crone in rags. The production was interesting but neither critics nor audience found
it acceptable.

Then the production of *As You Like It* was transferred by
Bronson Albery across the river to his New Theatre, and the
Vic recruited an almost entirely new company for *Hamlet*.

Laurence Olivier now joined us. Since as a boy in school
theatricals he had played Katharina in *The Taming of the
Shrew*, he had only made one appearance in Shakespeare.
In a production by Gielgud of *Romeo and Juliet* he and
Gielgud had alternated in the parts of Romeo and Mercutio.
The critics had praised the young Olivier's vitality but faulted
him for verse-speaking. With this criticism I did not agree.

Not yet quite thirty, he had already had considerable success both in New York and London and was on the threshold
of fame. Offstage he was not notably handsome or striking,
but with make-up he could achieve a flashing Italianate,
rather saturnine, but fascinating appearance. The voice al-

ready had a marvelous ringing baritone brilliance at the top; he spoke with a beautiful and aristocratic accent, with keen intelligence and a strong sense of rhythm. He moved with catlike agility. He had, if anything, too strong an instinct for the sort of theatrical effect which is striking and memorable. From the first moment of the first rehearsal it was evident that here was no ordinary actor, not everyone's cup of tea—no very strong personality can be that; not necessarily well cast for Hamlet, but inevitably destined for the very top of the tree.

Hamlet was followed by *Twelfth Night*—a baddish, immature production of mine, with Olivier outrageously amusing as Sir Toby and a very young Alec Guinness less outrageous and more amusing as Sir Andrew.

It was now the spring of 1937 and the Coronation of King George VI was imminent. We thought that a ringingly patriotic *Henry V* would be appropriate and that Olivier would be well suited to the part. It was, and he was. Motley did a simple but extremely ingenious decor of flags; the supporting company, over a hundred strong, was excellent; the finale was, as a royal betrothal should be, fully choral and a dozen sopranos from the Opera used to hurtle down in cars from Sadler's Wells just in time to appear, in their *Tannhäuser* frocks, and lend great body to a final high B flat.

The production was, I think, my best to date; and, when a few years later I saw that one or two little notions and wheezes had been incorporated by Olivier into his film, I was sincerely flattered and proud.

A successful season ended with a nice loud bang and an invitation for the company to take our production of *Hamlet* to Elsinore to inaugurate an annual festival performance in the Castle of Kronborg.

Elsinore was no picnic. The performances were arranged by the Danish Tourist Board and were to take place in the courtyard of Kronborg, a seventeenth-century castle on the sound which divides Denmark from Sweden. This was the first venture of the kind and the Tourist Board, understandably enough, was hardly conversant with the peculiar problems of theatrical management.

We had sent over plans of the stage set and a list of requirements for rehearsals, dressing rooms and so on. We were assured that all would be in perfect order and that, for good measure, we should have the full cooperation as "extras" of a hundred of the Corps of Officer Cadets who were quartered in the castle.

We arrived a week before the performance. The cadets were perfect—a hundred blond and intelligent young men ready to do or die in the service of art. A stage set had been built to the design of a Danish artist, who was considerably huffed when we insisted that the use of his set would involve rearranging the entire production, and that the whole thing must be rebuilt in precise conformity with our plans. More serious was the fact that the authorities in control of the castle had never been informed that we needed to rehearse.

The castle was open to visitors all day and the authorities were not prepared to close it. Accordingly we rehearsed all night. Even this arrangement was rather upsetting to the authorities, who were convinced that theatre was in some way synonymous with fire; reluctantly they permitted us to rehearse from midnight until six in the morning, but insisted on our employing a large posse of elderly firemen in steel helmets with axes in their belts. Since the courtyard is built of stone, with walls at least a foot thick, and since the weather was exceedingly wet, the precaution seemed excessive, but the firemen did us no harm and seemed, dear old things, to enjoy the play.

We were quartered in a pleasant summer hotel, all verandahs and Venetian blinds. It was May. The lilacs and laburnums were glorious. By day we slept, not quite enough, played tennis and boated on the sound. Each day was sunnier than the last, and each evening wetter; towards midnight we would sally forth in raincoats to the castle and to work.

I had never before done a production out-of-doors, and

was amazed to find how much less quickly we all got tired in the fresh air. The stuffy, frowsty atmosphere of most theatres and rehearsal rooms makes work much more physically exacting; after six or seven hours everyone is tired, has a headache, needs a break. In these rehearsals, although it was pretty cold in the small hours and we were often soaked through and through, we would find ourselves full of energy at the end of the long night; the great problem was not how to keep awake, but how in the freshness of a May morning to commit what seemed the sacrilege of going to bed and trying to sleep.

Miss Baylis was in her element. She was naïvely enthusiastic about Abroad, loved the hotel, was childishly greedy about the interesting foreign food, solicitous and motherly to us, her company, her children, determined that we too should enjoy the trip, and no less determined that we should be "good" and give the foreigners a nice impression of the Old Vic.

Like a good commander she shared the hardships of her troops. Night after night she sat through the rehearsals, dispensing from a window sandwiches and lemonade. We used to break for twenty minutes at about three in the morning: the company and the cadets and the orchestra—military musicians resplendent in skin-tight, sky-blue uniforms with silver lace. One night the rain was more persistent and more violent than ever before. Miss Baylis was not at her usual window, but in a sort of porter's lodge, and word got round that she had laid in a keg of rum. Came the break and with it an ugly rush towards the porter's lodge. At the head of the hunt was the colonel who commanded the band.

"Not you," screamed Miss Baylis in the raucous tones which Englishwomen reserve for foreigners who, naturally, are stone deaf, "Not you," and we heard a resounding whack on a sky-blue behind, "You're just band. This stuff's for *my* people."

The opening was to be an important occasion—the Tourist Board had left no stone unturned. Royalty was to be present; a special train was chartered to convey the royal party and the diplomatic corps from Copenhagen. The press was there in force. And that night it rained as never before.

The performance was at eight; at seven-thirty the rain was coming down in bellropes. Miss Baylis, Larry Olivier and I held a council of war. It was out of all question to abandon the performance, indeed the special train had already steamed out of Copenhagen. To play in the open air was going to be nothing but an endurance test for all hands. We would give the performance in the ballroom of the hotel. There was no stage; but we would play in the middle of the hall with the audience seated all around as in a circus. The phrase hadn't yet been invented, but this would be theatre in the round.

Larry conducted a lightning rehearsal with the company, improvising exits and entrances, and rearranging business; George Chamberlain and I, assisted by the critics of *Dagbladet*, the *London Daily Telegraph* and *Paris-Soir*, arranged eight hundred seventy basket chairs in circles round the ballroom. Miss Baylis put on her academic robes and kept things going with royalty and ambassadors till we were ready.

The audience thought it a gallant effort and were with us from the start; actors always thrive on emergency and the company did marvels. But *Hamlet* is a very long play. After two hours of improvisation the actors became exhausted and a little flustered. The finale was a shambles, but not quite in the way the author intended. Still it had been quite a good evening; royalty looked pleased, ambassadors clapped white-gloved hands and the press next morning acclaimed a "sporting gesture" and a *Hamlet* of more than ordinary vitality.

The performance would have worked better if we had been permitted to use all the entrances to the hotel ballroom. But one—the most effective one, a double door at the head of a short flight of steps—was strictly forbidden. The head porter, six foot six, in frock coat and brass buttons, was obdurate. "This door cannot, it must not, it will not open." Ours not to reason why; besides, there was no time for argument. The reason emerged next morning. I asked the man, who seemed a reasonable and friendly person, why he had been so firm.

"I will show you," he said, and tiptoed down a verandah towards the double door. In the architrave was the nest of a pair of blue-tits; the little hen, nervous but gallant, fluttered about our heads. "If this door had been used, she would have deserted her eggs; you wouldn't have wanted that."

The excursions and alarums of this Danish trip had, for me, two important consequences. They drew Miss Baylis and me together. At Elsinore we saw more of one another, and in far more revealing circumstances, than had ever been possible in London. She thought that I had shown some qualities of leadership in the various emergencies; more important, she decided that I was not just a worldly and calculating man who was using the Old Vic as a professional springboard. She now considered that I was trustworthy; that I had some understanding of what she had tried to do during her many years at the Old Vic, and some respect for what she had, in fact, achieved.

She realized that my conception of the Old Vic's function, my aspiration for it, were not precisely the same as her own —we discussed this frankly; but she was far too shrewd not to realize that, with the years, changes not merely in tactics but in strategy were inevitable. Already—this was 1937—the whole social and economic context had changed vastly, not only from the time of the Old Vic's incorporation as a charity in 1880, but from the time she herself had taken over its management. Already it was becoming apparent that the uneasy interlude between two world wars was drawing to its end; that still vaster changes were soon likely to occur. She felt herself an aging woman, and I think from this time she consciously began to regard me as one of the possible Elishas upon whom her mantle should fall.

The Danish trip had a second, and for me, important effect. The impromptu and rather haphazard performance in the hotel ballroom strengthened me in a conviction, which had been growing with each production at the Vic, that for Shakespeare the proscenium stage is unsatisfactory. I should never have suggested staging this rather important occasion as we did if I had not already had a strong hunch that it would work. At its best moments that performance in the ballroom related the audience to a Shakespeare play in a different, and, I thought, more logical, satisfactory and effective way than can ever be achieved in a theatre of what is still regarded as orthodox design.

During the next two years the prestige of the Old Vic remained at a high level. It is always a good indication of a theatre's prestige if the leading actors of the day are willing to play under its banner.

In the course of the next two years the Vic included in its casts Diana Wynyard and Robert Morley (Eliza and Higgins in *Pygmalion*), Marie Ney (marvelous in *Ghosts*— one of the finest performances I remember), Emlyn Williams, Sybil Thorndike, Judith Anderson, Alec Guinness, John Mills, Anthony Quayle, Jack Hawkins, Andrew Cruickshank, André Morell, O. B. Clarence, Freda Jackson, Pamela Brown . . . the list is not exhaustive.

The most successful production was *A Midsummer Night's Dream*, with the full Mendelssohn score and beautiful decor in early Victorian style by Oliver Messel. Ralph Richardson, as Bottom, led a team of "mechanicals" which included Alexander Knox. Helpmann was Oberon, Vivien Leigh Titania; we had a splendid quartette of lovers; Ninette de Valois lent fairies from the Ballet and directed the dances. We even had fairies flying on wires. The production played to capacity business.

The Queen brought the two young Princesses to a matinee and the heiress to the throne nearly lost her life by falling from the box; so interested was she to see how the fairies flew that she hung out by the heels. On the same afternoon, Helpmann and Miss Leigh were brought round at the interval to the Royal Box, to be presented. In the process of making their bow and curtsey the elaborate wire headdresses of the Fairy King and Queen became inextricably twisted together. The pair remained head down, literally with locked horns, until wrenched apart by the Queen and the two delighted children.

Othello, soon after, promised to be exciting. Olivier returned to play Iago to Ralph Richardson's Othello—a prelude to their great postwar partnership. But the production was a disappointment. Olivier and I were full of theories about the psychological relation of Iago and Othello. We spent two long evenings with Dr. Ernest Jones, Freud's biographer— for us, evenings of the greatest interest and excitement. But Richardson would not go along with us. The more "psychological" Iago became, the more embarrassed and inhibited became poor old Othello.

I think a good row might have cleared the air. But everyone behaved too well. Each of us thought that by the next day the clouds of misunderstanding would lift and all be well. Friendships remained unimpaired but the production was a ghastly, boring hash.

My own best productions, I think, were Ibsen's *An Enemy of the People* and a modern-dress *Hamlet* with Alec Guinness.

In the Ibsen play Roger Livesey as Stockmann, Edward Chapman as his brother, the Mayor, Ursula Jeans and a splendid group of character actors propelled the play clearly, humorously and forcibly. A most laudatory criticism in *The London Times* was headed "Ibsen's tremendous Metaphor from Sewage." Other notices were no less favorable and made the evening sound equally dreary. The business in an otherwise prosperous season was the lowest within living memory at the Old Vic.

As Hamlet, Guinness, then in his early twenties and quite unknown, gave a fascinating performance. His youth, combined with rare intelligence, humor and pathos, realized a great deal of the part. He had not yet quite the authority to support, as Hamlet must, a whole evening, or to give the tragedy its full stature. The performance demanded that the public reach out and take what was offered. To this demand the public is rarely equal. It is necessary to make an audience open its mouth, shut its eyes and swallow the physic. The ability to do this distinguishes the accomplished old bird from the fledgling. The medicine which Guinness offered was already wonderfully compounded, but he had not, at that time, quite the authority to force it down the patient's throat.

As production succeeded production in the two and a half years between Elsinore and the outbreak of war, I became more and more certain that Shakespeare cannot adequately be presented on a proscenium stage. The only Shakespearean productions of my own during this period which gave me even moderate satisfaction were the Guinness *Hamlet*, in which modern dress threw (or so I thought) a new light on many aspects of the story and its characters, and *A Midsummer Night's Dream*, in which both Messel's decor and my direction were a deliberate pastiche of early Victorian style.

I found myself more and more attached to the Old Vic as an institution—its aims, its tradition, the comradeship engendered in its service. At the same time, suspicion that a theatre of this shape was not suitable for the presentation of Shakespeare was, by each fresh attempt, gradually hardened into certainty.

13

The Picture Frame

SINCE ABOUT the middle of the seventeenth century all European theatres have been built with a proscenium arch. The proscenium is the space between the curtain or drop-scene and the orchestra. The proscenium arch is, as it were, the frame which encloses the stage picture; indeed in many theatres it is decorated, like a picture frame, with gilt moulding. Just inside the proscenium arch hangs a curtain behind which scenery and stage effects can be prepared, unseen and, in theory, unheard by the audience. Then the curtain rises . . . Lo and behold!

The proscenium arch divides the front of the house from the back. Within is the stage and behind that again the actors' quarters. Without is the auditorium, with seats arranged usually in a horseshoe and in several tiers rising one above the other, so that all the spectators face the stage. All, that is, save the occupants of the stage boxes. These are placed close to and at either side of the proscenium arch and command a close but a poor view of the stage, and then only if their occupants crane and peer out sideways over their shoulders. This, however, is not important, because those who occupy stage boxes are rarely so concerned to see the stage, as to see, and be seen by, the other persons in the audience.

Theatres have not always been built on this plan. For instance, in the Elizabethan theatre the audience sat almost completely round the stage, which jutted out into the auditorium. There is evidence that sometimes the plan of the theatre was round, sometimes octagonal and sometimes square.

Evidence is doubtful as to the exact architectural arrangement at the "back" of the Elizabethan stage behind the acting area. Certainly in some, if not most, theatres there were dressing rooms, probably on more than one level. The upper level of dressing rooms would give onto a balcony in view of the audience. This balcony provided an alternative acting area where scenes could be played, either with other actors on the balcony, or with those on the main stage below.

There is a theory that the space beneath the balcony, on main stage level, could be curtained or screened from view, and that here, unseen by the audience, thrones or beds or other furniture could be set while action proceeded outside.

This sort of theatre went out of favor and theatres with proscenium arches came in, for two main reasons—one practical, one theoretic.

The practical reason was the vogue, which spread from Italy all over Europe, for musical works, or opera. So great was this vogue, that for nearly a hundred years it completely dominated theatrical business and enormously influenced, then and still, theatrical art and consequently theatrical architecture.

It can be readily understood that in opera it is desirable that the singers should be able to see their conductor. He stands in the orchestra, facing the stage; they stand and, so far as is possible, move in a way which enables them to "get the beat." It follows that, in order to see and hear the singers to the best advantage, the audience should be arranged facing the stage, watching the faces of the singers, or actors, or dancers, and the back of the conductor.

When theatres began to be rebuilt in conformity with the conventions of Italian opera, not only did the audience and actors now face one another; a great gulf was fixed between them. In this gulf sat the orchestra, grouped round its conductor.

This was only partly a matter of practical convenience. It also marked the social chasm, which separated the predominantly courtly and aristocratic audience in the stalls and boxes from the socially inferior persons who were paid to entertain them. The separation was reinforced by yet another practical and symbolic barrier of fire—the footlights. From the seventeenth through the nineteenth century these were a perpetual source of danger. Fires, followed by panic, were not uncommon, and gradually all over Europe there came into force a whole budget of precautionary regulations, including the provision of yet another barrier, the iron curtain, now a world-famous political symbol of separation or *apartheid*.

Just as the proscenium stage was an extremely practical solution of the problem of presenting operatic singers, so are footlights a practical solution of the problem of lighting actors by artificial light. The theatres of Greece and Rome, of medieval Europe and Elizabethan England were none of them roofed over. Performances were given in the light of day. If a performance has to be lit artificially, no better way has yet been found than to have at least part, if not the greater part, of the light originate from a source in front of and below the actors.

Gradually, however, the new arrangements began to have results which their practical originators can hardly have foreseen. With the whole stage picture isolated from the audience, brilliantly and obviously artificially lit; and set against a painted and again obviously artificial background; with the grouping and utterance of the performer stylized to the requirements of opera, an immense emphasis was thrown on to artifice.

In comparison, the intimate, daylit relation of the Elizabethan actor to his audience and, at any rate in the public theatres, the far more democratic character of that audience, made the Elizabethan theatre seem to the next few generations a crude, rough-and-ready, even barbarous institution. We know how superior Pepys and, after him, Dryden felt about Shakespeare. They acknowledged that there was some merit in his woodnotes wild but felt that time had marched on, leaving him and the sort of theatre for which he wrote pathetically and forever outmoded.

Artifice was all-important. Scenic effects and surprises played an important part in the entertainment. That these effects might be prepared unperceived and then revealed as a surprise, the drop-curtain came into vogue.

Meantime another tendency was at work. Acting, writing and production all aimed to be more realistic, to be a closer and more literal imitation of life.

I do not think any theatrical historian would challenge the fact, instanced by the plays themselves, by the writings of actors and observers, and by theatrical paintings and engravings, that from about 1660 until the movies really began to grip the public imagination in the first decade of this century, the paradoxical situation prevailed of the theatre trying, with more and more artifice, to be more and more natural.

I suppose the zenith was reached with the famous production of A *Midsummer Night's Dream* at His Majesty's Theatre in London, with real rabbits frisking around the Beerbohm Trees. This was the *reductio ad absurdum* of naturalism. Also by this time the Bioscope was already beginning to achieve supremacy in the field of realistic imitation. The death knell of theatrical realism was sounding.

But an idea so firmly rooted in tradition as theatrical realism does not die quickly. Fifty years have passed since Tree's real rabbits, and naturalism is still the current mode. Nine new plays out of ten in any given season in London or New York are written and produced naturalistically: that is to say, they try to make the fictitious persons of the play, and their environment, seem as real as possible by means of literal imitation. It can readily be seen that this aim cannot thor-

oughly or consistently be achieved. It is hard to get very near to realism in exterior scenes—gardens, streets, forests, and so on. These scenes are, at best, a rather uneasy mixture of solid elements (tree trunks, imitation rocks, houses, pavilions, flights of steps) with representational painting. But you can, within a proscenium arch, achieve a plausible imitation of a domestic interior. Any evening in New York or London you can see expensively mounted drawing-room comedies with real, solid doors which lock or bolt; with ceilings, often with solid cornices; with moulded wainscots and walls which do not, by shaking or by revealing joints, betray the fact that they are not solid; carpet, furniture, pictures, ornaments, are all as real as money can buy.

The room, however, has one or two rather markedly *unreal* features: one side of it has no wall; through a blank space some thirty feet wide and maybe twenty feet high, several hundred people are looking in, from their seats in that other very large, dark room where they are seated in rows. Also the sunshine in this unreal-real stage scene comes not from the real sun but from a number of powerful lamps.

Similarly, realistic acting can only be realistic within limits: even secrets must be spoken loud enough to be heard by all those people out there in the dark; every significant action must be broad enough for them all to see. Even a quick glance must "register."

Even the script of a realistic play is only comparatively realistic, insofar as it must, in the short course of one evening, convey not necessarily a complete story or a conclusive argument, but at least a coherent impression. In so doing it must eliminate most of the dull and irrelevant remarks of which all real human converse largely consists.

In brief, even the most realistic productions of the most realistic plays—Chekhov interpreted by Stanislavsky or Odets by disciples of the Method—are not realistic at all; they are an elaborate exercise in style, in the selection and emphasis of some elements of real life, the elimination of others, and the precisely realistic representation of only a very few.

What is the aim of such realism? Is it to create an illusion of reality, to make an audience mistake the fiction of the theatre for reality? In many cases, I think this *is* the aim. It is one to which I do not subscribe, and the question is going to be discussed more fully in Chapter 21. In the present context, the aim, or underlying theory, of theatrical realism is not the point so much as the mere fact of its existence; its persistence, moreover, as the still-dominant manner of contemporary practice.

For my own part, I lost interest in naturalism when I began to believe that the cinema was a better medium for naturalistic expression than the theatre. I suppose the reaction was exactly analogous to that of painters in the late nineteenth and early twentieth centuries when they found that the camera could in many respects achieve a more literal, precise and objective "likeness" than they could themselves. From the moment of that realization painters began to be more concerned with interpreting rather than imitating nature. Henceforth they were more and more inclined to a subjective approach, to abstract expression.

The cinema can achieve a far more complete and consistent realism than can the theatre. Backgrounds are photographs of the "real thing." Similarly the actors in a screen play are photographs of real people and therefore "in key" with their background in a way which is never possible in a theatre. Also, the scenic backgrounds of a film can be much more ambitious and various than those of the theatre; the action can take place now on Mount Everest, now in a coal mine, at sea, in a cafe in Vienna, a street in Chicago; and the changes, so cumbrous in the theatre, can be effected more easily than turning the page of a book. The acting can also be far more natural.

Whether such "natural" acting can ever be as interesting and thrilling as "theatrical" acting is another question altogether. In the theatre the actor must "project," and though this is apt to make his expressions more interesting and exciting, it is fundamentally unnatural.

In the cinema the focus too can change; we can perch with Cecil B. DeMille upon a high place and look down upon hundreds, maybe thousands, of extras milling in long shot around Moses or Samson; and then, with no ado whatever, we can peer at an object in close-up—a single face in the crowd, a piece of business which the director wishes to emphasize—a note, say, passed secretly by one spy to another.

All this flexibility of the cinema, contrasted with the comparatively clumsy and limited devices of the stage, disenchanted me forever with theatrical realism. But not with the theatre. On the contrary, I began to see wherein for me the real magic of the theatre lay. It was, I discovered, charming, interesting and exciting not the nearer it approached "reality," but the farther it retreated into its own sort of artifice.

What had gone wrong was that the proscenium stage was being misused. Created for that most artificial of all art forms, Italian opera, its use had been gradually perverted.

Most of us have rather naïve and childlike taste. The element of the proscenium theatre which, almost from the day of its inception, proved most popular was its peep-show quality. Audiences loved, in a naïve and childlike way, the "surprises" which awaited them when the curtain rose; the doll's house interiors—"just like real." It soon became apparent that to gratify this taste was for a manager good business. More and more money and effort went into more and more elaborate spectacles. Performances were staged with real water, real fire, live horses, live girls in "exotic" surroundings and flimsy dresses. And, where the object of entertainment was not primarily spectacular, the background was expected to conform to current notions of realism; and such notions tended to become steadily more and more elaborate.

In the early nineteenth century the theatre, following poetry, the novel, painting and music, was dominated by wildly romantic and picturesque ideas presented in a wildly romantic and picturesque manner. Then—in the eighteen-sixties—Tom Robertson wrote and the Bancrofts produced

Caste; and there was born the "cup-and-saucer school" of naturalism.

Ibsen was the most distinguished and important master of this school. Its influence has pervaded the whole European and Western theatre; it has been intellectualized by Shaw, poeticized by Chekhov, democratized by Clurman and the Group Theatre and thence Methodized. It is still the dominant influence in playwriting and production all over western Europe. In America it is virtually the only influence and serves effectually to insulate the American theatre from the contamination of some of the older foreign influences—from such dramatists as Aeschylus, Racine, Ben Jonson and Congreve. Dramatists like these, unenlightened by the sun of naturalism, uncheered by the chink of cup and saucer, unflavored by the quintessence of Ibsenism, are rightly regarded as a dangerous and disruptive foe to the established naturalistic order. Prudently enough, Broadway relegates them to outer darkness.

My feeling about the proscenium theatre is not that it is an out-of-date mechanism which should be scrapped at the first opportunity. It is realism which I find out of date. Such realism has, it is true, largely been engendered on the proscenium stage; but as I have tried to show, this has been a corruption of the proscenium's highly practical purpose as a means of presenting Italian opera. It is ironic that a method so splendidly adapted to display the artifice of the theatre should have become today the fortress wherein are beleaguered the reactionary forces of realism.

The proscenium stage is certainly not out of date. It probably never will go out of date. But it cannot any longer be regarded as the only kind of stage upon which a professional production can be satisfactorily presented. For certain kinds of play—almost all those written since about 1640—it is suitable, because it is the sort of stage which their authors had in mind when they were writing. But quite a number of plays, and indeed quite a number of interesting and important plays, were written before 1640; and it by no means follows that, either in theory or in practice, the proscenium-arch theatre is the best mechanism for their production.

Let us take a particular instance, a familiar comedy of Shakespeare, *Twelfth Night*. In the first six or seven minutes the scene changes five times: Orsino's house or near it, the seacoast of Illyria, Olivia's house, then back to Orsino's house and back again to Olivia's house. It is theoretically possible by the use of elaborate machinery—and I doubt not but that in Germany it has been tried—to create the necessary three "realistic" sets and to shift them about at incredible speed. But, however fast the changes (if only three seconds), the mere fact of change is an interruption of the audience's concentration; and paradoxically, the faster, the more magical the change, the greater is the interruption—its very magic causes comment irrelevant to the matter of the play.

In fact, the usual solution of the problem is by compromise: either a composite, permanent set does duty for all localities, suggesting all of them vaguely and none of them literally, aiming rather to interpret the mood, atmosphere, or feeling of the play. Or else there are one or two elaborate full-stage pictures—outside Olivia's house is the obvious choice in *Twelfth Night*, since the greater part of the play's action can be plausibly arranged to take place there; the other scenes are played on the front of the stage before a series of dropcurtains painted to represent various other localities—Orsino's house, seacoast, street, cellar, and so on. While these front scenes are going on, the next full-stage set can be prepared and the actors out on the front must holler good and loud to drown the thuds and rumbles and blasphemy which accompany scene changes.

This latter was the method in vogue in the nineteenth century. In principle, this is how Irving's great productions were staged at the Lyceum in London. The main scenes, perhaps two or three or four, were very elaborate and magnificent. Irving lighted them by gaslight with great skill, and they evidently made a tremendous impression upon audiences which most certainly were not simple unsophisticated hay-seeds. The front scenes were necessarily skimpy and sketchy; but the text was hacked and rearranged (Bernard Shaw says "butchered") with great ingenuity to squeeze the plays into the scenic formula which Irving's presentation demanded.

Then came William Poel and after him Granville-Barker, who between them revolutionized British, and thence American, ideas of Shakespearean production. The text must be inviolate. If realistic scenery cannot—and it cannot—be suit-ably adapted to the constant changes of environment and atmosphere indicated in the text, then realistic scenery must go.

Poel's productions were given on a bare stage; Barker, less austere, used very simple "stylized" indications. Like most other directors who during the last thirty or forty years have seriously grappled with Shakespeare, I agreed with Poel and Barker that the first consideration must be the text, that Irving and his contemporaries were wrong to subordinate this to scenic convenience, and that Shakespeare must not be tied to a literal realism.

Yet, that Shakespeare is to some considerable degree a realist cannot be denied. I assume that in dramatic art it is always essential that some recognizable correspondence be established between the imitation and the thing imitated; between the character which the actor is playing and the situation of that character and a recognizably similar character and situation in real life. If an audience is to be interested in his assumption of Hamlet, Lady Teazle or Harpagon, then the actor must embody to a considerable extent the audience's notion of a prince of Denmark, a squire's young wife or a miser. To do this it is not necessary to present a stereotype. A good actor will not dream of doing so. The merit of his acting will lie in the fact that his characterization is recogniz-ably valid without resort to stereotype. But this cannot be achieved without resort to realistic imitation of observed phenomena.

In writing, as in acting, the same principle holds. We recognize the greatness of Shakespeare not only because of the music of his verse, the sweep of his philosophy, his artifice in theatrical construction; he is also great in the minute observation and precise record of individual character and mannerism. Justice Shallow is a great creation and, though created of a different species in a different manner, bears no less surely than Othello the stamp of genius. But Shallow is a piece of realistic art and must be realistically interpreted.

However, Shakespeare is only intermittently concerned with realism. In the main, he is not writing realistic dialogue or dealing with realistic characters or situations. Most of his characters have great reality but this effect is not, as a rule, achieved by a literal imitation of life. Intermittently he uses a realistic method to establish a correspondence between his figments and recognizable fact; but not as an end, only as a means. He uses a realistic method to contrast life-sized personages—Justice Shallow, for instance, Pompey, Froth and Elbow in *Measure for Measure* or the gravediggers in *Hamlet* —with heroic characters, larger than life-size. But for the most part Shakespeare, in the highly artificial form of blank verse, is creating characters who are larger than life.

Further, his dramatic construction, conditioned by the sort of building in which his plays were first performed, does not demand—does not permit—realistic scenery. When it is important to indicate where the characters in the play are supposed to be, such indication is given in the text. Consider the duet between Lorenzo and Jessica which opens the finale of *The Merchant of Venice*; this is not only a great piece of music, it sets the scene: "How sweet the *moonlight* sleeps upon this *bank* . . . look how the floor of Heaven is thick inlaid with patines of bright gold." The whole passage paints the scene, lights it and furnishes it—with genius. If these lines are to be spoken, does it seem a good idea to reinforce them with blue limelight, a back cloth stuck with sequins and a structure of chicken-wire covered with grass matting? Instances of such indications of weather, time and atmosphere can be multiplied. Surely the point need not be hammered.

Therefore, Shakespeare should not be produced as though
he were a realistic dramatist. The intermittent realism of
this or that scene or character must be faithfully interpreted.
But actual indications of time, place, atmosphere and so on,
must be avoided; as must a reduction of great tragic conceptions to life-size; or no less damaging, a reduction of romances—*The Winter's Tale*, for instance, or *As You Like It*—
to make them plausible. One of the charms of a tall tale is
its very tallness.

The Old Vic, where I now found myself grappling with a
program almost entirely dedicated to Shakespeare, is an early
Victorian opera house. Its stage, framed by a proscenium
arch, is entirely adequate for the usual pictorial demands,
but bears no resemblance whatever to the sort of stage for
which Shakespeare wrote. Players and audience are related
in an entirely different way.

Successive producers had tried all kinds of devices. In the
nineteen-twenties Robert Atkins had built the stage out in
a wide arc over the orchestra, so that in front of the curtain
there was a reasonable acting area, proscenium or forestage.
In the thirties I attempted a permanent and abstract set (the
Wells Coates set, see chapter 9). In general it was a failure,
but certain features of it—for instance, access to the forestage
from the orchestra pit by means of curved stairs—remained
as almost a part of the permanent structure of the theatre.

In 1947, under the influence of Michel Saint-Denis, the
whole forestage was remodeled by a French architect, at great
cost. The result looks handsome and dignified but bears no
stylistic relation to the architecture of the auditorium; and,
more serious, it makes a number of seats unsalable because
from them actors on the forestage cannot be seen. It also
fails to solve the main problem because behind this dignified forestage there remains a proscenium arch; and inside
that arch—here's the rub—is a perfectly conventional stage,
framed by the arch which the whole audience faces, inside
which they have been conditioned to expect "a picture." So

long as that picture frame remains, some kind of a picture has to be put inside it.

Granville-Barker and his immediate successors tried to make a very simple and abstract picture which, with easily and quickly made adjustments, would do duty for all scenes. Nothing can be simpler and more abstract than curtains; but either with long straight folds or elaborately draped curving folds, they make a very emphatic and often very unacceptable pictorial statement.

Also it is illogical and annoying if a stage which has been designed as a peep show, which has all the mechanism—ropes, pulleys, lighting apparatus—for creating visual interest, is then denied its whole function. Also, assuming that a satisfactory compromise can be reached in regard to scenery, a picture which is also not a picture, the problem still remains of how to relate the actors to their audience in the manner which the author presupposed when he was writing.

As far back as 1936 I had felt convinced that there could be no radical improvement in Shakespearean production until we could achieve two things: first, to set the actors against a background with no concessions whatever to pictorial realism, the sort of background which the Elizabethan stage provided and which the picture-frame stage, designed precisely to create a picture, and traditionally associated with "illusion," cannot achieve; second, to arrange the actors in choreographic patterns, in the sort of relation both to one another and to the audience which the Elizabethan stage demanded and the picture-frame stage forbids; the manner, in fact, envisaged by Shakespeare when he wrote his plays.

Let me elaborate each of these two points. First, background: if we are to avoid scene changes, and avoid the impertinence of parodying Shakespeare's verbal indications in canvas and paint, there should be no pictorial backgrounds. The only way I can see to avoid them is to have, behind the actors, a structure with the facilities—balcony, windows, stairs—which the particular play requires, which is obviously functional rather than decorative and unmistakably part of the permanent structure of the theatre, not a temporary, *ad hoc* contrivance put up to create the illusion that the audience is in Padua, Illyria or wherever the text may indicate.

Second: choreography. On the picture-frame stage two of the main considerations that govern grouping are to keep the actors facing the audience and to prevent their masking one another, that is to say, standing between other actors and the audience. These considerations often make the movement and grouping of actors more difficult, and less expressive, than it would be if they were disregarded. This is now generally agreed, and in any naturalistic production of the last twenty years you could observe actors playing with their backs to the audience, and even occasionally masking one another. Nevertheless, the architectural form of the theatre does make these considerations important: they can only be disregarded occasionally and with caution.

The Elizabethan type of stage, jutting out into the midst of an audience which surrounds three sides of the quadrilateral (or virtually quadrilateral) platform, makes it physically impossible for actors to face the entire house; and they can never completely avoid masking their partners in a scene unless they are placed on different levels.

If you reflect that Shakespeare must have *known* that the speakers of his soliloquies could not face every member of the audience all the time, you are virtually forced to this conclusion: the soliloquies must have been spoken by the actor either on the move, or rotating on his own axis, so that at different moments everyone in the house could see his eyes and the expression of his face.

When this idea first occurred to me, I tried speaking "To be or not to be"—a soliloquy which, in my opinion, demands repose and not movement—rotating slowly on my own axis. With a little practice I felt that I could have made my expression clear to everybody, if they had been in a circle around me, and still not seem to be fidgeting. The movements had, of course, to be carefully planned and executed very slowly and smoothly. I then tried to speak the speech sitting in a chair; and again I found that I could turn and direct my glance round a full circle without any fussy or fidgety movement. Technically, the trick seemed to be to move the eyes first, then let the head follow, then let the shoulders slowly follow the head, and so on down to the feet.

Now consider those many scenes in Shakespeare where quite a number of actors are engaged. He must have known that they would mask one another; yet he must still have considered that the scenes could be effective.

Two conclusions can be drawn: first—the disadvantages of masking can certainly be compensated in some degree by greater fluidity of grouping and by the greater naturalness which follows if a group of actors can form circular patterns, arranged around whoever, or whatever, is supposed to be the focus of their attention.

Second—if, at a given moment one figure, out of several or even many, must command the audience's attention— Henry V, for instance, before the breach at Harfleur—he must be raised above them, so that the audience gets an uninterrupted view of him over the heads of his colleagues. Henry V must either be on the balcony, on some raised platform on the main stage, or be lifted and held on the shoulders of the other actors.

And now, finally, consider the physical relation of actors to audience, or rather to auditorium. The conventional theatre with horseshoe auditorium facing the stage is, as we have seen, logical for opera, but it is wasteful of space. If the audience sits round a larger segment of a circle (or round three sides of a rectangle—the principle is similar), more people can be accommodated near the stage. The Globe Theatre of Shakespeare's day held three thousand people. To accommodate an audience of three thousand, a picture-frame theatre would have to be very large indeed, so large that it would not be possible to act with any degree of intimacy.

Now we must switch for a moment to the economics of theatrical production. Shakespeare's plays require large casts, many costly costumes and accoutrements. The production therefore has both high production and running costs. To make ends meet it must play in a house of large capacity. Large capacity in a theatre of conventional design means that those in the remote seats are a long way from the stage. To make the play interesting, even intelligible, to these people the actors must speak loudly and slowly, and their glances and byplay must always be exaggerated to operatic proportions.

It is because Shakespeare has almost always been played in huge theatres that a booming, bellowing, bombastic style of acting has become associated with his plays, that it is commonly regarded as "the Shakespeare tradition," and that the plays seem on the stage to be grandiose affairs. The subtlety, intimacy, and elaborate detail which is apparent in the study entirely disappears in the theatre.

The fact is that there is no Shakespearean tradition.

One of the great assets of the Comédie Française is that there exists an unbroken tradition of how the French classics were, in their day, acted. It has been handed on from actor to actor, from Molière down the generations to the present day. In England there exists no such tradition, because twenty-four years after Shakespeare's death the Puritans succeeded in shutting all the public theatres. For twenty years the theatre went underground. When, with the restoration of the monarchy, it was again lawful to give theatrical performances, the Elizabethan and Jacobean tradition had completely disappeared. The new theatre was an opera house; its architecture, repertory, style of acting and the quality of its audience were all entirely different.

What we of the twentieth century have inherited is not a Shakespearean tradition, it is merely a legacy of nineteenth-century theatrical conventions.

The nineteenth century adored rhetoric. Shakespeare was chiefly admired for the opportunities which his works afforded for "spouting." In the early and middle years of the century

—indeed, it was customary until the dominance of Irving in the seventies—when an actor came to one of the great Shakespearean purple patches, he would step down to the audience and belt it straight into the house; then, after suitable applause, he would rejoin his colleagues and the action would proceed. This was called "making a point." Of course the custom has been completely discredited; but it has left its scar on contemporary Shakespearean performance, because nowadays we are so scared of this kind of vulgarity that actors, when they come to a purple patch, feel bound to treat it gingerly, with good taste, to bury it under a tumulus of "Methodist" introversion, and pass quickly on to the next Freudian symbol.

What, above all, the acting of Shakespeare demands is good speaking. It is impossible for an actor to do his best with the lines if he is forced to adapt himself to the demands of a huge auditorium. It is not generally appreciated what prodigies of virtuosity are displayed by our best contemporary rhetoricians—Gielgud, Maurice Evans, Olivier, for instance— when they make their lines seem natural, when they give to their speeches variety of pace, pitch and color inside the rigid limits imposed by the large opera houses in which Shakespeare has perforce to be played.

The ideal house for Shakespeare must be designed so that every spectator is near enough to the stage to enable the actor to use the full range of his voice from a shout to a whisper; to speak, when necessary, as fast as ever he can, and to mime the action with the subtlety and delicacy which it deserves.

At the same time, the building must hold a large number of spectators; partly for economic reasons, but also because only a large audience can generate the large-scale response which great classics demand. A thousand seats, I suggest, would be the minimum. There is only one way in which a thousand people can be packed into really intimate contact with the stage: by putting the stage in their midst.

For the last fifty years the movie houses have aimed at a huge, and mainly unsophisticated, public. One of the main

attractions offered has been luxury and grandeur in rather
unsophisticated terms: phony Temples of Karnak; organs
in silver and opalescent chrome rising, in three-four time,
from the bowels of the earth; troops of hussars to usher
Madame not to her seat, but to her fauteuil, of multidimen-
sional plush.

For the last fifty years theatres have not aimed to make
themselves more practical pieces of mechanism. That would
have involved the troublesome task of thinking what the
theatre, as opposed to other forms of art, entertainment and
commerce, is trying to do. Instead it has been easier, if idiotic,
to imitate what has been commercially successful, to emu-
late the grandeur of the movie palaces, to try, with limited
budgets, to turn theatres into poor man's phony Temples
of Karnak, to offer Madame a fauteuil, but in fewer dimensions of less expensive plush.

Audiences can rather easily be made *too* comfortable. I
do not expect this opinion to be widely shared, especially
on the American continent, where there is a tendency to
confuse physical comfort with civilization. But it is my conviction that audiences ought not to be coddled. They must
be warm; no one can concentrate if his feet are cold; in
summer they must be cool; no one can concentrate if the
sweat is running down his spectacles. But the idea of ever
larger and plushier seats is deadly. They induce not concentration but somnolence; and the larger the seats the fewer of
them can be got into any given space. Also the mere fact of
everyone being jammed together helps to create in an audience
a feeling of unanimity. One of the reliable measures of how
well a play is going is the degree of unanimity the audience
achieves. Ideally, it should be one single, massive, composite
beast, not a number of isolated individuals. Further, people
value more dearly what is dearly bought. Pleasure is the
keener for being purchased at the cost of moderate physical
discomfort.

One more point before we leave the question of Elizabethan
versus picture-frame theatre. If the audience is, as it used in

the Elizabethan theatre, to sit round at least three sides of a rectangular stage (or a large segment of a circle), then a large part of the audience sees the players against a background, not of scenery, as when you look through a proscenium arch, but of other spectators. It is like the spectators at a boxing ring: behind the boxes they see faces, rising tier on tier, of other spectators.

Is this destructive of illusion? I suppose so. But is it therefore destructive of enjoyment? I think not. Rather the reverse.

I suggest that enjoyment is enhanced if you are constantly reminded that it is being shared, that you are one of a crowd similarly concentrated. Furthermore, I do not think that an audience's enjoyment of a play is dependent on illusion.

This point will be discussed more fully in Chapters 21 and 22. But it is relevant here as being one of the important differences, practical and theoretic, between the open stage of the Elizabethan theatre and the Italian opera stage, now almost universally accepted as "right," with its stage isolated from the auditorium behind the triple barrier of orchestra pit, footlights and curtain.

In the foregoing I may possibly have given the impression that the Old Vic is particularly ill adapted to the production of Shakespeare. This has not been my intention; nor is it the case.

The Old Vic, since its recent rehabilitation, is neither a picture-frame stage nor an open stage. It is an uneasy compromise. The stage at the Shakespeare Memorial Theatre at Stratford-upon-Avon is a similar, but even more uneasy and unworkable, compromise.

The Old Vic permits a more intimate contact with the house and more flexible grouping. The lines of sight at Stratford demand that, if every member of the audience is to be treated to a fair view of the play, then the grouping must be like the Gilbert and Sullivan operas: principal personages in the center, well downstage, and all the rest in a semicircle behind.

At both Stratford-upon-Avon and the Old Vic, director

after director, faced with what I consider the insuperable problems posed by the architecture, falls back upon elaboration of spectacle. To give the public something for its money, a Pageant is mounted to the accompaniment of a Shakespearean text.

Rightly, and often, the dramatic critics point this out. But, as is so often the case with critics who are not practitioners, they perceive a symptom and believe the symptom to be the cause, not the result, of a malady which they have not diagnosed.

The only theatres in New York where I have staged Elizabethan classics have been the Broadway and the Winter Garden. In both cases the vast acreage of the auditorium made it completely impossible for the actor to establish any intimate or subtle relation with the audience. The performances had to be broad and noisy. There was no alternative.

14

War Years

BY THE TIME I returned to the Old Vic in 1936 it was established as a national institution of artistic importance. It was no longer a charitable enterprise in the slums of London. It was the Old Vic which was invited to represent the British theatre and to inaugurate the series of *Hamlet* performances at Elsinore. Now, if we asked the leading actors of the day to head the company, they would be inclined to accept; now every London newspaper sent its leading critic to opening nights. Now, in fine, we occupied a recognized position on the theatrical map, not just of London but of the world.

Meanwhile at Sadler's Wells, the Opera, and more particularly the Ballet, had created for themselves a similar position. As the creator and the head of these three companies, Miss Baylis was, from now until the time of her death less than two years later, not just the embodiment of an extraordinary legend peculiar to herself, but the most important theatrical manager in Britain, probably in the world. She died rather suddenly in November 1938.

A few months afterwards I was appointed by the governors as her successor and given the title of Administrator of the

215

Old Vic and Sadler's Wells. Within weeks the war with
Germany was declared and a new epoch had begun.

So far as my own professional life was concerned, these
years were a diversion of energy from what I consider the
main stream of my life. I felt like a river which for a section
of its course is diverted from its channel, in order that the
force of its current may turn a mill wheel. The mill wheel in
this case was to keep the Old Vic and Sadler's Wells in existence. I was told by the Ministry of National Service that this
was considered a useful and necessary job and, during those
years, we were given a good deal of official assistance—the de-
ferment of National Service, for instance, in the case of certain
indispensable singers and dancers without whom the companies could not have continued to function.

I was completely inexperienced as a manager and as a man
of business. This inexperience, I now see, affected me far
too keenly and allowed a feeling of inferiority to oppress a
customarily resilient nature and to make me overcautious,
penny-wise and painfully indecisive. This was foolish. At a
time when established institutions were toppling right, left
and center, when new precedents were being created, new
experiments and expedients being tried as never before, my
inexperience, if I had capitalized it boldly, could have been
an asset, not a disadvantage. But at the time I could not understand what I now see clearly: that in war, death and destruction, though terrible and horrible, are not entirely disastrous;
many of the things which are destroyed are better away.
There is a great destruction of precious things, but there is
also a great and necessary clearance of rubbish. Under the
stress of war there is an intense liberation of feeling and
thought which only such a violent stimulus seems able to
achieve. At the time I could see and feel only the deadly, depressing closing-in of calamity: winter had come and, like
a savage or an animal, I could not, although I tried, feel
sure that spring would ever come again.

The Ballet was able to take care of itself. Carried on a
flood tide of public demand, it was not hard for the Ballet to

survive and make money, or too hard for it to achieve the
almost legendary reputation with which it finished the war.
This is not, I hope, to imply the least detraction of Ninette
de Valois' extraordinary qualities of leadership. I have great
professional respect for her and great personal admiration.
At this period we had our differences and I still do not know
who was right. De Valois was impatient with what she rightly
regarded as my timidity and overcaution, resentful that I
wished to make the comparatively easy success of the Ballet
finance and further the aims of its sister company, the Opera.
At the time, rather than precipitate a first-class rumpus, I
gave way. I do not know whether this was right or wrong.
De Valois had created the Ballet; she considered that her
work was being frustrated and possibly even ruined. She suggested, and I agreed, that the Ballet should be managed by
Bronson Albery, for whose integrity we both had the greatest
respect. From 1941 the Ballet, for all practical purposes,
ceased to be part of the organization which Miss Baylis had
built up.

In short term this certainly gave de Valois what she had
a perfect right to demand: scope, financial and artistic, to
exploit the current vogue for ballet, to build up the efficiency
of her company, to make it world-famous and to establish a
British National, or as it has become, a Royal Ballet at
Covent Garden.

These were aims with which I could not, and cannot,
entirely sympathize. Covent Garden I have always regarded as
an artistic graveyard; its cubic capacity is enormous but it
holds a comparatively small audience; it is "grand"—and
the grandeur certainly pays a dividend on the three or four
occasions in a year when royalty is present in full regalia—
but on most nights of the week when the audience is just the
usual middle-class crowd, of which all ordinary modern audiences are composed, the building's grandeur is just an inappropriate and wildly costly memorial to bygone glories.
Covent Garden has the quality of swallowing up all but the
most powerful and penetrating performers and performances.

It is essentially a "star" house. Great personalities can dominate it and be seen to advantage but the minor talent, the
subtle effect, the delicate work go for nothing at all.

De Valois has been aware of this and has deliberately
broadened the style of her Ballet to suit the house. In the
process, much of the old repertoire which suggested at one
time that some significant content might be developed—
Ashton's *Dante Sonata*, for instance, or Helpmann's fascinating commentary on *Hamlet*—became, in the new and vast
surroundings, quite ineffective.

Without content, ballet has no right to the pretension
that it is an art on an equality with opera or drama. In my
opinion ballet has got above its station and should have
been content to remain no more than an adjunct to the
opera.

In essence, this was the rock upon which de Valois and
I split. I consider that events have justified my view; ballet,
despite the réclame, the financial success and the Royal
Charter, has not grown up. It remains a mere sweetmeat on
the theatrical menu. But by the defection of the Ballet the
development of the Sadler's Wells Opera was gravely handi-
capped. The work of the two companies should have been,
but never really was, complementary. Similarly at Covent
Garden the Royal Ballet and the Opera Company merely
occupy the same premises; the one does not enhance the
quality of the other.

The policy of the Sadler's Wells Opera was to give opera
in English and to develop a native operatic repertoire and
company. Somehow opera has never taken very kindly to
British soil. It has never become an indigenous plant, but
has remained a delicate, waxy, hothouse exotic. The kind of
opera which is most admired in London is the same as that
most admired in New York: the nineteenth-century classics
produced on the enormous scale for which, in an opulent age,
they were planned; sung if possible in a language which most
of the audience does not speak but pretends to understand,

by the most celebrated stars of the day; and sold at a price
which prohibits wide popularity and gives the performance
great snob-appeal.

Sadler's Wells, dedicated to a policy of cheap seats and
opera in the vernacular, could offer neither great stars, mam-
moth productions, nor snob-appeal.

Most works of the classic Italian and German repertoire
seem to defy the art of the translator. The English versions
slide uneasily from pomposity to a vulgar colloquialism. English singers, unless they assume foreign names or return
laurel-crowned from abroad, rarely excite the imagination
of their compatriots. Somehow it is possible for a tubby little
Italian tenor called Giovanni Stotti, singing, often screaming,
the works of his native land in his native language and with
native fire, to conquer the British public. The conquest
would never have occurred had a similar tubby little personage been called John Stott and sung the gobbledygook of
the Verdi and Puccini translations in a Lancashire accent.

The Sadler's Wells Opera Company had many excellent
singers, many distinguished productions had been given, particularly of works of Mozart, under the influence of and in the
fluent and literate translations of Professor Edward Dent.
The orchestra, small for the grander grand operas, was better
than merely competent. The chorus was first-class. There were,
in my opinion, the elements of a splendid ensemble; but even
the excellencies of the company were worthy rather than
exciting; a little dowdy, a little stodgy; they were something
which no theatrical performance can afford to be—snob-
repellant.

The Ballet, on the other hand, was, to the highest degree,
snob-fodder. It had glamour. But I felt that by itself the
Ballet, for all this glamour, was a little vapid; that what
Sadler's Wells could, and should, do was to wed the elegance
and charm of its Ballet to the serious solidity of its Opera.
Out of this union there might have emerged that lyric theatre
which, except for the brief and possibly transitory glory of

the Savoy operettas of Gilbert and Sullivan, Britain has never achieved, but for which British literature, music and humor seem to offer such a favorable tradition.

Who can tell? Evidently this was not the moment and I was not the priest to solemnize this marriage. The two companies went their separate ways.

At the end of the war the Ballet emerged as a national institution with a brilliant company, a school, world fame, the honor of its Royal Charter, but still no significant repertoire. The Opera emerged solvent—an achievement which only those who have had the financial responsibility for an opera company can appreciate—with one great artistic triumph to its credit, the first production of Benjamin Britten's *Peter Grimes*.

Joan Cross, the greatest British singer of her time, and Laurance Collingwood, as director and musical director, were primarily responsible for the company's survival. I think it was a mistake, at the end of the war, that public money was used to found at Covent Garden another opera company, thus dividing in two the available funds, talent and support, which were barely sufficient for one. I do not know who was responsible. Neither I nor Miss Cross was consulted; we were presented with a quietly accomplished fact. At the time I was too much exhausted either to object or to grasp its implications for the future of opera in Britain.

By far the most important consequence of the war for our profession was the acceptance by Parliament of the principle that the state has some responsibility to see that the serious theatre survives. As so often happens in politics, in medicine and in all human affairs, the patient was rightly treated for the wrong disease.

In 1941, just after Dunkirk, when Britain stood alone and in the gravest danger, the government decided that the arts must be protected, as far as possible, against the coming holocaust. It was remembered that in the 1914 war public taste had revolted against anything serious or difficult. Artistically ambitious efforts had died horrible and unlamented deaths. It was also expected that our principal cities would be, as they were, severely bombed; and that their inhabitants would be, as they were not, confined to underground shelters.

If serious arts are to survive, it was argued, they must be financially "encouraged" and enabled to disperse their services wherever at a given moment they might be most useful. The initiative was taken by The Pilgrim Trust, an Anglo-American foundation administered by Dr. Tom Jones, a remarkable Welshman. The Trust persuaded the government to put up pound for pound to create a fund which would be administered by a *Council for the Encouragement of Music and the Arts*—CEMA for short. The first beneficiary of this fund was the Old Vic. The offer was made through Sir Lewis Casson. He and his wife, Dame Sybil Thorndike, had been asked by CEMA to tour the mining areas of South Wales. They were willing to head a company if the Old Vic would undertake the organization and management.

This was the beginning of a long series of tours of mining and industrial areas all over the country and a close association with CEMA.

It soon became apparent that the premises underlying the foundation of CEMA were only partially correct. Instead of the frivolity of the 1914 war, public taste was serious. Libraries all over the country reported a rise in the demand for serious and classical books. Sadler's Wells Opera met with enthusiasm in cities not hitherto renowned for musical cultivation. Welsh miners acclaimed Sybil Thorndike; and *King John* played to capacity in places like Lancaster, Ulverston and Burnley.

The Ballet was a sellout always and everywhere. I recall an anxious conference with de Valois the first time, very soon after war was declared, that the ballet company was invited to tour the garrison theatres. Nervously we decided that it was our patriotic duty to accept and to expose the company to the jeers and whoops and wolf-whistling of uncouth creatures called troops. Little did we know. *Les Sylphides*, with a young gentleman whirling around in white tights among white muslin coryphées to waltzes and mazurkas of Chopin, proved exactly the stuff to give the troops. Indeed, what everybody wanted almost as much as food or drink during those years was to see youthful and beautiful creatures beautifully moving through ordered evolutions to a predestined and satisfactory close. It was the antidote to the drabness and dullness and monotony of a life which seemed to be moving in disorder to a predestined and highly unsatisfactory close.

Soon after the air raids began on London, Sadler's Wells was commandeered by the Borough of Finsbury as a rest center. When houses in the neighborhood were rendered uninhabitable, the people who had lived in them were sent to Sadler's Wells, where they were fed and housed until more suitable accommodation could be found.

When the theatre was taken over, the borough authorities requested us, the staff, to manage the rest center on their behalf. We at once moved into residence in the dressing rooms and "stood by" to receive forty-eight "guests."

Air raids were then a nightly occurrence. The very night after we became a rest center our district received a more than usually severe attack. Instead of the forty-eight guests for whom we were prepared, a hundred forty persons arrived, many of them considerably shocked, with nothing of their possessions left but the clothes they had on. The eldest of our guests was eighty-two, the youngest had been born two weeks previously.

We then had the Opera, the Ballet and two drama companies all on the road. Communication between London and the provinces was seriously disrupted by the raids. We could only keep in touch by telephoning in the small hours of the night when the lines were less busy than at more normal times. After seven weeks I decided that we must transfer our headquarters from London.

Burnley, a large cotton-weaving city in East Lancashire, seemed a good center. It was unique in this: the manager of the theatre there, Mr. Jess Linscott, was eager to have our companies come to Burnley and was willing to make his theatre available.

In all the other large towns we were, at this time, having the greatest difficulty in booking dates. With the London theatre virtually, but temporarily, out of action, all the managements were competing for the principal theatres in the provinces. Against the big stars and a crop of commercial comedies, our companies, at that time reduced for financial reasons—we were virtually broke—to skeleton proportions, did not stand a chance. The secondary theatres preferred the burlesque shows to which their audiences were accustomed and felt no inclination to take a chance on opera, ballet or Shakespeare, which they regarded as box-office poison.

At this point, Linscott, to his great credit, was willing to offer what we needed: a theatre in the provinces, to which our companies could come in turn, which should be a temporary headquarters where new work could be prepared and whence the administration could be conducted.

For almost two years our home was the Victoria Theatre, Burnley, which saw and gave enthusiastic support to opera, ballet and classical plays. Our period in Burnley gave us the necessary respite to reorganize and, as we began to earn money, expand our forces. During these two years we learned to grapple with the problems of wartime production—the shortages of material of every kind and especially of manpower—and gradually to take advantage of the great public demand for what our companies had to offer.

At the beginning of that period we were crippled by debt. We could scarcely find the money for salaries if one of our companies did a bad week's business. At the end of eighteen months we looked forward to paying the interest on our debts and had substantially reduced the principal. We were able to look ahead with confidence and to plan expansions and improvements on a scale still modest, but no longer hand-to-mouth.

It is a sad little footnote to the story that the old Victoria Theatre is now defunct; Burnley makes do with the movies and the telly. The plaque placed on the theatre's wall to commemorate our tenancy now rests in the Town Museum.

As the war dragged on, the work of CEMA expanded and in 1942 a reconstitution took place. Lord Keynes, the economist, was also an enthusiastic Maecenas. His immense prestige as a financial wizard emboldened the government to accept a more responsible role as patron of the arts. The Pilgrim Trust bowed out and support for the arts was now forthcoming, on an increased scale, from the Treasury, administered on behalf of the Board of Education by the Arts Council of Great Britain, with Keynes in the chair.

By this time (1942–1943) I had formed a close alliance with my old friend, Bronson Albery. He agreed to become joint-administrator of the Old Vic and Sadler's Wells and from 1942 until the reopening first of Sadler's Wells in 1945 and then of the Old Vic in 1950, our companies used his New Theatre as their London home. Each company played there in turn, touring between their London seasons.

Meantime, our efforts in the provinces, sincerely attempting to fulfill what I had been encouraged to believe was still the official policy of decentralization and mobility, began to seem to Lord Keynes rather dowdy and dull. Clever Mr. Beaumont, always sensitive to public taste and alert to seize any managerial advantage, was pursuing in London the policy which had once been peculiar to the Old Vic, and offering an interesting series of classical productions, better mounted and more starrily cast than ours. He had an advantage. We were operating on a very low budget, guaranteed against loss by the Arts Council up to a very limited amount. Beaumont was able to use the profits of his commerical company (H. M. Tennent Ltd.), earned out of popular comedies with small casts and wide appeal, to finance the operations of a non-profit company (Tennent Plays) which presented "prestige" productions of excellent quality.

Suddenly we found that we, the Old Vic and Sadler's Wells, were no longer the beloved only twin children of the

Arts Council's theatrical family. A new, and very much more glamorous, baby had appeared.

Lord Keynes, great man though he was, was a "sucker" for glamour. Lewis Casson was now the Drama Director of the Arts Council and as such, subject to Keynes as his chairman. The two men did not get on very well. Keynes, a complete amateur, kept overriding the advice of his more experienced subordinate and leaned more and more heavily in the direction of Tennent Plays.

For a year or two the Old Vic trod a distinctly thorny path. In this game of theatrical politics we seemed to have been completely outmatched; our prestige waned; it became harder and harder to get the actors we wanted because they all preferred to work for Beaumont. The one feather in our cap was the reopening in November 1942, under Old Vic management, of the Liverpool Repertory Theatre, which had closed after the severe bombing of Liverpool in the winter before. We operated it for four years successfully and very profitably. For a period, under the direction of Peter Glenville it was, I think, the liveliest theatre in the country.

Gradually, however, the alliance between Tennent's and the Arts Council became rather strained. At this period the entertainments tax was remitted to productions operating in connection with the Arts Council. There was a growing feeling, whether justified or no I cannot say, that Tennent's were merely using the Arts Council as a means of escape from entertainment tax. This feeling became more and more articulate, and when Tennent Plays were granted remission from tax on a highly profitable production of A *Streetcar Named Desire* there was a scandal. The rights and wrongs of the matter are irrelevant here. Charles Landstone, one of Lewis Casson's successors as Drama Director of the Arts Council, has chronicled the whole controversy in his book *Off-Stage*. The eventual upshot did not occur till 1950 when the Arts Council—I quote Landstone—"solemnly cast out Tennent Plays with bell, book and candle."

Meantime, as far back as 1944 the Old Vic was beginning

to reap a certain advantage from the controversy. We were
now the good, if plodding, child—high marks for Liverpool—
working away and giving no trouble.

In 1944, after many conversations, first between myself and
Ralph Richardson, then between myself, Richardson and
Olivier, it was agreed that, if the Old Vic could procure their
release from the services, they would join the Old Vic. The
governors broached this plan to the Arts Council. Backing,
generous for those days, was promised for a season in which
we hoped that the Old Vic would make a resounding comeback.

Lord Lytton, Chairman of the Old Vic governors, wrote
to the First Lord of the Admiralty requesting the release of
the two actors on the ground of their outstanding reputation
and indispensability to the rehabilitation of the Old Vic,
which he hoped would be regarded as a matter of national
importance. The request was granted. We prepared three
plays—*Peer Gynt, Arms and the Man, Richard III*. A strong
company supported the two stars, including Sybil Thorndike,
the Old Vic's staunchest champion, and a youngster from
the Birmingham Repertory called Margaret Leighton.

We were to play in the New Theatre, but while we rehearsed the Opera Company was in occupation there with
so much scenery that we had to rehearse elsewhere. We were
lent rooms in the National Gallery whence the rightful occupants, the masterpieces, had been evacuated to secret caves
to protect them from bombs. The Doodlebug raids were in
progress and if, as frequently occurred, one seemed to be
headed straight for the National Gallery, the rehearsal would
stop while we all lay down on the floor. It was shaming how
relieved we all felt when a bang, and the ensuing shattering
of timbers and glass, would proclaim that someone else had
"had" it.

The season opened with triumphant success. Soon after,
but perhaps a little more important, the war ended. The
emergency was over. I was completely exhausted and decided
that the best thing I could do for the Old Vic was to leave.

The Ballet was on its own and brilliantly successful.

The Opera was rent with schism and I was not eye to eye with the governors about how to deal with either present problems or future policy.

The Shakespeare Company was now being operated by a triumvirate—Olivier, Richardson and John Burrell. I had agreed to the arrangement and already had misgivings about it. Burrell, considerably younger and less experienced than the other two, could not be expected to have the authority and weight to stand up against their towering reputation and powerful personalities.

It should have been apparent—and I was much to blame for not seeing it—that what did happen, would happen. The period of glory was brilliant but brief. In spite of enormous houses, no money was saved. In less than two years it began to be apparent that the two stars must decide either to be actors, making films and radio appearances, going to America, Australia and so on, or else to be managers of the Old Vic. They tried, and failed, to have the cake and eat it. The Old Vic fell once again into serious financial and organizational difficulties from which it did not emerge for seven years.

My years of management thus came to a not particularly glorious end. All three companies were solvent, for which I take a little credit, though most of it goes to George Chamberlain, once stage director, at this time general manager. But the triple empire of Lilian Baylis was falling apart. Perhaps this was inevitable and perhaps it was not a bad thing. Yet I think united the three companies could have been stronger, more useful to one another and to the public than the three can ever be apart. The fact that it was during my regime that their courses began to diverge I count the most serious failure of my professional life.

15

New York

WE LEFT FOR AMERICA in 1945. The year before, we had revived at the Liverpool Playhouse Repertory *He Who Gets Slapped* by Andreyev, in a new version by my wife. It had been admirably acted by Peter Glenville, Audrey Fildes, Noel Wilman, Arnold Marlé and Eileen Herlie. Alfred Lunt and Lynn Fontanne had seen a performance and liked the version and the direction well enough to suggest to the Theatre Guild that they should ask us to revive the play for the Guild in New York.

The blaze of lights, the abundance of food and drink and warmth and material comfort were simply staggering. Everyone was enormously kind and hospitable. In a vague way, they realized that Britain for the past five years had been rather uncomfortable. The typical attitude was that of a pleasant and fully intelligent lady to whom I was introduced: "From London? Oh, you poor dear, the bombing must have been ghastly, just ghastly, but *do you know* I've just got in from Cleveland and I had to stand, to *stand* in the train—*for forty minutes!*"

I see now that it was idiotic to expect any better understanding, to be irritated in restaurants when plates arrived

228

loaded with what we had become accustomed to regard as a week's meat ration for three people, idiotic to be shocked at waste, to be angry when people made fusses because they couldn't get cream or had to queue for a taxi. Gradually we saw that *we* were the self-centred ones to expect anything else; and in the years that followed I noticed that my own imagination did not stir very vigorously on behalf of fellow creatures in Korea, for instance. "Ghastly," I thought, "just ghastly but *do you know* . . ."

There seemed to be a superabundance of actors as of everything else in New York. The Theatre Guild had a charming and intelligent casting director and, for six or seven hours daily for several weeks, actors came and went and were looked over in the process of casting *He Who Gets Slapped.*

I had not before encountered this slave-market technique, and was horrified at the way the actors accepted it. Some of them really seemed to want to open their mouths so that we could see if their teeth were sound. The only reason I wanted them to open their mouths was to hear what sort of noise they made and what sort of ideas they had. But no one seemed to think any of that important. The emphasis was heavily on physical appearance. Such troops of beautiful young women, dripping with furs, with jewelry, with allure! Young men too, likewise magnificent, sunburned, athletic, and only a little too consciously virile!

The odd thing was that none of these young beauties seemed to have any professional grounding. Some of them had been to drama school; some had majored in something called drama at a university which turned out to be five hundred miles from any professional theatre; a few had walked-on "off Broadway," or even played a bit part in a Broadway show. None of them had played a series of parts in a variety of kinds of play. It was borne in on me that there simply was no opportunity for them to get such experience. I thought, and think, that it was not beyond the wit of man for these young people to create such opportunities for themselves; not merely to wait around, untrained, for chance in-

troductions to useful people; not just to rely upon personality
—the great euphemism for sex appeal, male, female or middle-
sex.

Another odd thing: there seemed to be hardly any elderly,
or even middle-aged, actors and actresses who had never
achieved the top of the ladder, but who nonetheless had behind them a lifetime of professional practice and human
experience. Every director in every European capital knows
masses of actors like this, reliable, skillful, many of them
highly intelligent and educated.

In New York that winter I hardly met any such; and even
in subsequent years with a larger local experience and a better
idea of where and how to look I have found them extremely
scarce.

I think there are two reasons: first, a great proportion of
such actors have migrated to the coast. There, in movies
and even more in television, they get more varied and more
highly paid work and can live more cheaply and in a better
climate. The other reason seems endemic to the current
American way of life. The accent is so heavily on youth. Both
men and women keep up as long as they possibly can an
illusion of being boyish and girlish. Then suddenly the illusion vanishes; overnight they are tired, old, old men and
women. Moreover, in a tremendously buoyant and expanding economy it is comparatively easy to "succeed," in the
sense of making money. There is a conventional pressure
towards such success, a conventional disapproval of failure,
because it makes people poor, and worse, odd, such as I do
not think has ever existed in the world before. A considerable
measure of success can rather easily be won comparatively
young. If by forty you have not achieved the conventional
emblems of success, a car, a house, clothes, manners, club,
vacation, all of the currently fashionable style, then you
must either be conspicuously rich, in which case it is smart
to be odd, or else you must be a failure.

An actor who by forty has not got somewhere usually either
leaves the stage or takes to the bottle or retires to some

analogous nirvana. I have known around New York a number of pathetic and unreliable victims of middle-aged shipwreck, but extraordinarily few senior people who work contentedly and skillfully in the theatre without ever expecting to be rich or celebrated. Economic and social pressure makes such an attitude possible only to people of resolute conviction, even dedicated certainty.

He Who Gets Slapped is a rather ninetyish Russian play about the circus. Romantic melodrama is delicately, sophisticatedly, even decadently, packaged in poetic symbolism. In Liverpool the cast had been able to convey both poignancy and humor; something strange and interesting and true emerged. The casting in New York was less felicitous. The whole effect was like Chopin scored for military band. Stella Adler gave a fascinating performance but the audience had not the least idea what she was trying to do. I think it was the humor of the whole thing which missed fire. In a broadly dramatic way there were several effective performances, but without the counterbalance of the play's melancholy and sophisticated humor, they only added up to a rather old-fashioned and obvious drama, with a gothic capital *D*. It seemed to me that neither the audiences nor most of the cast had any feeling for a humor which does not expect the response of laughter.

Years later I found exactly the same thing with *The Matchmaker*. It was immensely popular in America. The public warmed to its vigor, to the broad fun and homely good sense. But the pathos and even underlying melancholy of its humor evoked no response. Not that *The Matchmaker* is at all like *He Who Gets Slapped*. It is a farce, derived by Thornton Wilder from a number of sources, rather as Shakespeare derived and transmuted the material of his farces and romances. The plot comes from a Viennese adaptation of an old English comedy; situations are borrowed from here and from there; one whole passage of dialogue has been lifted bodily from Molière. In the hands of a merely industrious pedant this

learned pilfering would have achieved nothing. Wilder is
learned but no pedant. I have never met anyone with so en-
cyclopedic a knowledge of so wide a range of topics. Yet he
carries this learning lightly and imparts it—the important
with the trivial, the commonplace with the exceedingly bizarre
—in a style and with a gusto which is all his own.

The manner is confidential and quite giggly; incredibly
rapid utterance, accompanied by a series of stabbing gestures
and jerky curlicues executed with the forefinger, as though
he were tatting an invisible and refractory wire net. He has
been everywhere, has known—and knows—everyone, and is
fond of a sort of name-dropping which might seem snobbish
if its purpose were not obviously the further embellishment
of an already ornate conversational style. "Texas Guinan
and I were in a goat-carriage on Michigan Avenue . . . Ber-
trand Russell dipped *his* in brandy . . . Ernst Lubitsch leaned
across my plate and whispered to His Holiness. . . ."

If you sat opposite to him in a plane or train, and you
probably have, since he is a ceaseless traveler, perhaps you
took him, with that clipped gray moustache, to be a slightly
eccentric major on leave or an excitable country doctor or,
noticing those strong, incredibly restless hands, an artificer,
a maker of precision instruments or, maybe, a piano tuner.
You would expect him to be anything but a *savant*, a notable
wit and the author of three or four works which, of all written
in our time, are probably at the head of the queue for classical
status—not because they are learned and funny and technically accomplished, not even because they are filled with
wisdom and feeling, but because (to me at any rate) they
express the profound intuition with which, over and above
the literal meaning, between the lines of story or play, one
human soul speaks to another.

I once traveled with him in a local train in Canada. For
two hours on a baking summer morning he gave me an
absorbing critique and intimate biography of Henry James.
Thornton left the train and I went on. An old man came
along the coach and plumped down in the empty place.

"Say," he said. "Been watchin' the two of yer. Couldn't hear a word, mind ya; but that was a jolly old joker. Bet he could tell ya a few good yarns."

He could, and has.

The Matchmaker had made its first appearance as The Merchant of Yonkers—a wittier, more allusive and altogether better title, in my opinion, but tarred with the brush of failure. This first production opened with a splendid cast headed by Jane Cowl and directed by the greatest master of the craft, Max Reinhardt. But the date was 1940; the public was in no mood for antic farce, Miss Cowl was no farçeuse and Reinhardt was grappling with a foreign tongue and all the psychological tumult of exile. The Merchant of Yonkers did not thrive.

Ruth Gordon and I had become fast friends when she came to the Old Vic to act The Country Wife in 1936, and had long hoped for another opportunity to work together. During the winter of 1951–1952, rehearsing Carmen at the Metropolitan Opera, I was her guest. During those long quiet firelit winter evenings in New York, from seven way on till seven-fifteen, we would turn over plans and projects. It was Garson Kanin, Ruth's husband, who suggested that The Merchant of Yonkers might revive. We all knew the play well and loved it. The most serious drawback seemed to be that it bore the stigma of failure—something which, I have tried to suggest, is in present-day America far more damning than a conviction for rape or arson. The Kanins suggested that though the play is American as clam broth, it might still possibly be acceptable in London; that if we tried and succeeded in London it might then return to New York, cleansed of the guilt of failure, redeemed, restored to a state of grace.

Hugh Beaumont agreed to present it—a good omen. Tanya Moiseiwitsch designed the decor and it was arranged that we should open as one of the dramatic offerings at the Edinburgh Festival of 1954. The play went like clockwork; Miss Gordon shared the honors with Eileen Herlie; the barometer of the box office registered set fair. Halfway through the two weeks' run in Edinburgh, on a Sunday evening, an act of the play was presented on television. They took it "live" from the theatre with an invited audience in front. Wisely, I think, we made no pretense that what was seen was supposed to be "really" happening; it was obviously and admittedly a performance from a theatre—uproarious farcical ongoings on the stage were intercut with shots of the laughing audience, and a gay half-hour was achieved. This proved, contrary to some forecasts, a splendid fillip to the business of a long provincial tour which followed.

Beaumont, as usual, was courteously, gently relentless in keeping us on our toes. Thornton was compelled to rewrite and the cast to rerehearse. The first act gave us a lot of trouble; as so often with farce, the exposition took rather long and the laughs were slow in the first twenty minutes.

After a good run at the Haymarket Theatre in London, the first time I had worked in the house with which my great-grandfather Tyrone Power had been so closely associated, the play was transferred to New York under the management of the Theatre Guild, and, more actively, David Merrick. We had a week's rehearsal in New York in de luxe conditions: scenery, props and an almost complete staff. Then we opened in Philadelphia.

The theatre was enormous, far too large for the play, and the company, after nearly a year in the intimate conditions of the Haymarket, was not quite adjusted to its scale. But the really disconcerting thing was to find what a completely different play the American audience made it seem. They were quicker on the uptake, they were more quickly on to the play's intrigue, far quicker to take jokes about money and sex, but almost totally blind and deaf to what I thought had been the play's great charm, its humor, the fact that the best jokes were not just laughs but had a serious undercurrent; that the best situations were not funny, but pathetic, even poignant. Pathos and poignancy had gone for good. It was not just the first night in Philadelphia which missed this bus;

in the face of audience reaction throughout a four-week tryout the whole performance became sharper, harder, tougher
with—in my opinion—considerable loss of charm.

In Philadelphia, business was good but the laughs were
few and far between. Mr. Merrick was alarmed and declared
with some heat that this was not the play he had bought in
London. Thornton Wilder was infected with some of the
same fever. He saw a matinee performance in which every
line was spoken, every bit of business performed, as exactly
and meticulously as it had been for more than a year by an
experienced and well-disposed company. He and Merrick fell
upon me as if I were a fraudulent dog-breeder who had sold
them a mongrel with a forged pedigree. Undignified scenes
in hotel rooms kept coming to the boil and were only averted
by the extreme tact and good sense of Garson Kanin who,
an old friend both of Thornton and myself, could act as a
sort of umpire and impose order and restraint on us two
foolish, excited, elderly gentlemen.

Things were better in Boston. But we still were not out of
the wood. It was arranged that before the official opening
in New York there should be a week of benefit performances.
At each of these the house had been sold *en bloc* to a charity,
which then sold the seats to its supporters at an exorbitant
profit. On one evening I heard that up to fifty dollars had
been given for orchestra seats.

Never have I known such audiences. They came late; they
talked loudly all through the performance, often commenting
on the actor's personal appearance in tones perfectly audible
to the stage. The last twenty minutes of the dialogue used
to be rendered totally inaudible by the hubbub in the audience: "How's about it, Mildred?" a gentleman would yell to
his wife sitting four seats away on the other side of their
guests: "Shall we stick it out or shall we go now while we
can get a cab?" If Mildred elected to go, they would stand
right up and pull on their overcoats, talking a mile a minute
and good and loud so as not to be interrupted by all that
gabble on the stage. I suppose the attitude was that Frank

and Mildred and four guests amounted at fifty bucks apiece, to three hundred, and that to be asked to pay, in addition, a little attention, and even a little respect, to the actors—well *that* was just *ridiculous*.

The cast, warned by all their fellow professionals that these preview benefits were sheer bloody murder, stood it manfully. When on opening night there actually seemed to be human beings out front they were too relieved to be nervous. The notices could not have been better if we had written them ourselves, albeit on the lines of zany antics, roaring laughfest; it was not the fault of critics, author, players, or even director, that the subtle shades of humor had been obliterated. As always, the public extracted from the performance only those elements which it wanted to find there. What was not acceptable, or was not perceived, just disappeared, ceased to exist.

Soon after *The Matchmaker* I was hired by the Phoenix Theatre to direct a production of *Six Characters in Search of an Author* by Pirandello. I wanted to work with the Phoenix because I admired its directors, T. Edward Hambleton and Norris Houghton. To the best of my knowledge they were the only managers in America who seemed to want, or to see the need for, a long-term policy more interesting and more serious than just making money and having a great success.

Six Characters has always been one of my favorite plays. We had opened our Cambridge season with it years ago; I revived that production in London a year or two later, and had directed the play a third time in Liverpool during the war. I do not think the play's philosophy is very profound, but Pirandello manages to say something about the nature of reality in splendidly vivid theatrical terms. Instead of talking *about* various degrees of reality, he embodies them in highly colored characters who simultaneously lecture the audience and one another, and demonstrate the lecture in action. The published translation into English, authorized by the author's representatives, is, in my opinion, neither very

accurate nor written in good English; nor are either the lines
or situations as theatrically exciting and amusing as in the
original. I had prepared a version which the Phoenix directors
were willing to produce, but they had also gone some distance
in negotiating the production of yet another version by an
actor called Michael Wager. The matter was pleasantly
settled by an agreement that Wager and I should amalgamate
our two versions; I should direct and Wager would act the
part of the Son.

Again the casting was not entirely satisfactory, principally
because of my limited knowledge of available actors, but
partly because of what seemed to me a failure of *rapproche-
ment* between myself and first the cast, then the critics, in the
matter of humor.

I certainly do not mean to imply that I was right and that
the actors and critics were wrong. That would be the height
of arrogance. Nor was it a question of right and wrong; merely
of two different ways of approaching a play. Nor do I wish
to imply that the critics were unfair or unfavorable; they
were neither. Nor that there was dissension between myself
and the actors; our relation couldn't have been more cordial.
It was a subtler and more interesting difference than mere
disagreement.

Most of the younger members of the cast, including
Michael Wager, were ardent disciples of The Method. They
approached the play as a psychological document and with
the doctrinaire preconception, which I consider the Method's
chief error, that all serious plays can be brought to life if
the acting is "real." They looked for something called truth.
They tried to find in their parts some relation to their own
experience; but to the expression of themselves few of them
brought sufficient stage experience or adequate vocal technique.

I regarded the play as a light-hearted and essentially theatrical *tour de force*, a juggling trick with metaphysics in
place of billiard balls or playing cards. It bore only a remote
relation to real life; was hardly concerned at all with truth,
whatever that may be; and must be acted, not with deep

feeling and painful gropes into the subconscious, but with a display of histrionic virtuosity, brilliant rather than profound.

They were disturbed by what they considered my levity, the superficiality of the approach and by my insistence that things must be done because they were effective rather than because they were necessarily true. I was disturbed by what I thought their heaviness; their disinclination to see that what is serious can also be funny, and vice versa; and the lack of technical equipment which prevented them from giving possibly a superficial but still theatrically effectual expression to emotions or ideas which they themselves did not "feel."

The upshot wasn't too bad. It was not as pyrotechnic as I would have liked, nor as true as they would have liked. The critics, so far as I could gather, and I daresay the public also, would have preferred a more solemn approach. It is the current mode: serious things must be very serious, whereas a joke's a joke. To treat serious topics with levity, or to make a joke which has serious or even pathetic implication, is in bad taste. I am not sure whether it really is a current American, as opposed to European, mode. I seem to have been much more conscious of it in America. But perhaps this was only accidental.

Right after *Six Characters* I embarked upon one of those strange adventures which make the New York theatre so different from London and so interestingly falsify any slick generalizations based upon a rapid skim of show biz.

Roger Stevens and Robert Whitehead decided that, in partnership with the governors of the Shakespeare Festival at Stratford, Ontario, they would present a revival of Marlowe's *Tamburlaine the Great*. I was to direct and Anthony Quayle, who had just ended four brilliant years as director of the English Stratford, was to play the enormous leading part.

Three years before, I had directed the play at the Old Vic.

Sir Donald Wolfit then played Tamburlaine; he and I jointly made an "acting version," cutting the enormously long original to manageable proportions. We omitted about half the campaigns, and more than half the subsidiary personages; and arranged the play into two parts. The first traced Tamburlaine's rise from obscurity to be Emperor of the world; the second showed his degeneration and eventual death, with the implied dissolution of the ephemeral Empire. We must have done quite an efficient job for the play had a wonderfully successful opening and a good press.

The American production rehearsed and opened in Toronto; the scenery, dresses and props, designed by Leslie Hurry, were made in the Festival workshops at Stratford, Ontario; and a fine job they were, elaborate but barbaric, a visual complement to the splendor of Marlowe's verse. Anthony Quayle, a muscular, handsome heavyweight and a superb technician, led the Stratford Canadians who attacked the piece with tremendous verve. I think it was my best production. The great technical difficulties of the "score," for the play is as near to opera as you can get without crossing over the quite indefinite line from speech to singing, were met boldly and, I think, resourcefully.

We did two weeks of tremendous business in Toronto. But we knew that we floated on the stream of good will engendered by the success of the Stratford Festival. We came to New York well aware of the difficulty of interesting a public to whom neither the name of the author, nor those of any of the actors, meant anything at all.

We played in the Winter Garden, a huge wide-splayed house. On the first night, to mark an occasion of Anglo–Canadian–American cooperation, it was half-heartedly decorated with rather grubby bunting, and the presence of the *corps diplomatique* had been requested in order that in the theatre's many boxes there should be an array of glamorous international personalities. Ruritania, for instance, was represented by the aunt, from Newark, of the second commercial attaché.

Ten minutes before the curtain rose, any experienced person could deduce from the many empty seats and the many obvious "deadheads" with bad colds that the performance would have a hard time getting across. It did, and the next day's press put the nails, so to speak, in the coughing. I have never read notices which, while praising the performance and the performers really handsomely, yet contrived to convey so clearly to a reader that the evening was a great, thundering, cavernous bore.

Naturally, we did no business at all; and, reasonably, the management withdrew the production mighty fast. Yet I have never been associated with so helpful a flop. I think it did more good to my reputation and Quayle's and that of the Stratford Festival than if it had been a success. Enough of the right people came to see it, and liked what they saw the more because it was not in the popular bull's-eye. They discussed it afterwards in the way people do when they discover that funny dark little picture in Aunt Edie's bedroom has turned out to be worth money... "Of course I always rather liked it. I felt there was something about it."

My next adventure in New York was also a flop: Voltaire's *Candide*, adapted by Lillian Hellman into the libretto for a score by Leonard Bernstein. From the start the great risk was that the thing would seem wildly pretentious. And that is just what it did seem. Only Bernstein's mercurial, allusive score emerged with credit.

For my part, I do not at all regret the skirmish. It was an artistic and financial disaster from which I learned almost nothing at all about anything. But it was fun to be closely associated with a group so brilliantly and variously talented.

Bernstein's facility and virtuosity are so dazzling that you are almost blinded, and fail to see the patient workmanship, the grinding application to duty which produces the gloss. This may not be an original or greatly creative genius, but, if ever I have seen it, the stuff of genius is here.

Hellman fought this battle with one hand tied behind her back. We had all agreed that when necessity demanded we would choose singers to do justice to the score, rather than actors who could handle the text but for whom the score must be reduced. Consequently line after line, situation after situation, fell flat on its face because—no blame to them—singers, and splendid singers, were asked to do something for which they had neither gift, understanding nor suitable experience. Miss Hellman stooped fatally to conquer. None of her good qualities, even great qualities, as a writer showed to advantage. This was no medium for hard-hitting argument, shrewd, humorous characterization, the slow revelation of true values and the exposure of false ones.

I wonder whether it was an unconscious reaction to the diamond quality of Bernstein's brilliance? She and I, and an eminent squad of technical collaborators—Oliver Smith for the scenery, Irene Sharaff who designed the clothes made by Karinska—all seemed to lose whatever share of lightness and gaiety and dash we might possibly have been able to contribute. My direction skipped along with the effortless grace of a freight train heavy-laden on a steep gradient. As a result even the score was thrown out of key. Rossini and Cole Porter seemed to have been rearranging *Gotterdämmerung*. I felt sorry for our lady-producer, Ethel Reiner. She and her backers lost a great deal of money; she proved a gallant loser.

Another flop followed: *The First Gentleman* by Norman Ginsbury. This had been a great success in London ten years before. It is a comedy about George IV and his daughter—light, elegant, with a good deal both of wit and pathos. Many producers had considered it for New York, but always the difficulty was to find the right actor for the central part of George IV.

It was a bad day's work when I persuaded the producers, Alexander Cohen and Ralph Alswang, and they, in turn, persuaded Walter Slezak that he was the man. I had seen him and admired his performance in an otherwise boring musical. He had gaiety, elegance, wit and he looked like "Prinny." His very slight accent seemed charming and perfectly plausible for a very Hanoverian King of England. Naïvely I failed to

appreciate that speaking brief perfunctory lines in musical
comedy is one thing, handling the rhetoric and quick-fire lines
in a comedy of style is quite another. Poor Slezak knew so
well what *could* have been done with the lines, what he *could*
have made of them if only English had been his native
tongue. He struggled gamely and with admirable good temper
against a most frustrating situation.

Agonies were undergone during a tryout tour. Wiseacres
would come to New Haven, to Boston, to Philadelphia and
prescribe this remedy and that; the unfortunate author was
persuaded to cut and rewrite and really to harm the style of
a stylish comedy. Everywhere the critics hailed the magnificent performance of Mr. Slezak doing wonders with a stodgy,
verbose English play. It was an ironic situation from which
bad business rather quickly delivered us. One thing delighted
us all: the emergence of Inga Swenson, a beautiful, talented
and clever girl, who in this production had her first leading
part and has since consolidated this early success.

Once again the bitterness of failure was sweetened by the
generosity and gallantry of the management. In Europe we
are rather inclined to purse our lips, to shrug and dismiss
Broadway as an irresponsible pool game. Pool game it may
be; but, as a participant in three successive ringing flops, I
was well placed to observe the good sportsmanship with
which the punters can swallow defeat.

In the fall of 1957, I returned to the Phoenix to direct
two plays—a revival of Schiller's *Maria Stuart* in a new version
by Jean Stock Goldstone and John Reich, and *The Macro-
poulos Secret* by Karel Čapek in a version of my own.

The Čapek play is primarily a vehicle for a star actress.
Eileen Herlie played it splendidly but the revival did not go.
It is true we opened in a week when a bus strike coincided
with a blizzard. But somehow I feel that in similar circumstances *Oklahoma!* or *My Fair Lady* would have survived. We
were one of those marginal cases which favorable circumstances might have saved, but which unfavorable surely destroyed.

I cannot think why Schiller's *Maria Stuart* has been so long neglected in English. Since I do not understand German I suppose I should not presume to judge the original, but whether in a literal translation or in the several "versions," which I have read, it does not seem to be anywhere near the caliber of a masterpiece. On the other hand, it has, quite apart from its enormous and enduring popularity in the German theatre, many of the hallmarks of commercial success: an elaborate but easily apprehended intrigue, rip-roaring parts for two effectively contrasted leading ladies, a great scene of "confrontation," love scenes, scenes of sexual jealousy, an effective farewell for Mary Queen of Scots as she goes to the block, capped by an equally effective dust-and-ashes scene for Queen Elizabeth. It has clearly been designed for production by stock companies—effective roles all around a manageably small cast; with staging which can be as elaborate or simple as resources permit. At the Phoenix on a limited budget we staged it with the utmost simplicity; but, thanks to Donald Oenslager, it looked quite distinguished. Irene Worth came home to her native America from Britain to play Mary, and the role of Elizabeth brought back that splendid actress Eva Le Gallienne after a rather long absence.

We were all nervous about how it would be received, for the version made no concession to prevailing theatrical fashion; it was, like the original, robustly and unashamedly "ham." With any but expert and highly assured performers it would have been deadly. But the company at the Phoenix played it, with total disregard for "Methodist" values, at a spanking pace, attacking the audience head-on with dialogue which, very rightly, did not scorn gambits like "Little does he know!" or "Who could have supposed?" The two ladies writhed and purred and roared their way to a minor triumph, stalwartly supported by a corps of gentlemen mostly recruited from Canada.

The success of this revival was particularly sweet, partly because the Phoenix Theatre, struggling against great odds for survival, needed it badly; and partly because critical and public acclaim for well-propelled "ham" was a needed shot in the arm for a valuable element in theatrical life, which has for many years in America been in a sad decline. So strongly did I feel this that, rightly or wrongly, we imported most of the actors from the Shakespeare Festival Company of Stratford, Ontario. I was convinced that a play like *Mary Stuart*, demanding an operatic breadth of speech and movement, could hardly be cast with American actors. For thirty years they have had no training in the necessary technical equipment. Partly this has been due to radio, movies, and television. Microphone and camera are supposed not to take kindly to big, broad acting; an intimate "natural" style is demanded by almost all directors.

I am convinced that a mere fashion has been glorified into a sacrosanct rule of technique. Some of the finest performances on the screen—by Laughton, for instance, Jannings, Kortner, Pauline Frederick and many of the Russians—have been as operatic as all get-out. Whispering intimacy has been a great cover-up for photogenic men and women with no acting talent, and for giving an air of reality to quite perfunctory material.

Nevertheless, for years it has been a cardinal sin to "act" in front of microphone and camera. Actors for a generation have schooled themselves to work in a manner which at its best can be termed economy of means but is more often just a tiny, constipated manifestation of nothing at all, in which the raw amateur, if he looks and sounds right, can do just as well, probably better, than an experienced and accomplished professional. Moreover, for thirty or forty years the influence of the leading critics in America has been exerted in the same direction. They have disprized and derided anything which seemed even faintly tinged with "ham," and only found that to be true which is naturalistic and life-size.

I imagine that a factor in all this has been the breakaway of the American theatre from its dependency upon European, and especially British, influence, and the welcome emergence of a strong and self-conscious nationalism. Lillian Hellman,

Clifford Odets, Arthur Miller, Tennessee Williams are all best served by "natural," realistic acting; great spouting whales tend in their plays to be irrelevant and out of key. Greek tragedy, French classical tragedy, the Elizabethans, Goethe, for that matter Schiller—the whole classic repertory of the Old World seems at the moment to have little to say to the New World in the first fine careless rapture of artistic nationalism. It is nice, and of course educational, to have an occasional visit from the Old Vic or the Comédie Française. But there is a tendency to regard their performances, not without respect—perhaps, indeed, with too much respect —as imported antiques rather than lively and still relevant comments on the human scene.

An institution like the Old Vic is not so much the Old Curiosity Shop as a supermarket where you may *help yourself* to some of the ingredients, unobtainable elsewhere, but necessary for a balanced and nourishing theatrical diet.

American actors seem to feel that the development of a technique of classical acting, which means, among other things, learning how to manage great rhetorical speeches and how to swish about effectively and without embarrassment in the finery of other epochs, is in no way related to the expression of themselves, the contemporary background and the local scene.

I think that they are very wrong. I have before made the analogy between drama and music. The dramatic classics are to the actor what the Beethoven sonatas and the preludes and fugues of Bach are to the pianist; in my opinion, an absolute necessity as imaginative background and as a means of developing the technique which will free him from a thousand limitations, not merely technical but imaginative. In long term, the content and the manner of artistic expression are indivisible. Little journalistic plays generate a little and limited acting style; such a style, in turn, is inappropriate and inadequate to the performance of great works.

16

Opera

YOU MIGHT THINK that, insofar as a singer devotes himself to opera rather than to lieder or oratorio, he is, therefore, interested in acting, even interested in other forms of theatre.

With rare exceptions, this is not the case. Singers seem to find themselves on the operatic stage not because they particularly want to be there, but because they have been told, often by the oddest people, that that is the sort of voice they have, that is where they will do best.

Looked at another way around: what the operatic stage demands is *vox*. If a person has a great big voice and can sing in tune he can get on better in opera than a more talented and intelligent, and even more musical, person with less of a voice.

Now God in His Almighty Wisdom and Fairness has not always given the greatest voices to the persons with the greatest intellect or the best education, or to the most beautiful of His creatures. Nor is the career of an opera singer calculated to appeal, as a general rule, to such persons; there are, naturally, many and notable exceptions.

Indeed, the dramatic side of opera is not very attractive.

Most operatic artists have to live a vagrant life, and their career, a comparatively short one, is devoted to the presentation of a limited number of roles in circumstances which rarely permit the dramatic side of the performance to be anything but a stereotype surrounded by a shambles.

The musical side of their work tends to be much more interesting, partly because a higher standard is demanded, partly because of the great and fascinating problems which have to be tackled. The vocal accomplishment *demanded* of a singer in a role like Rigoletto or Carmen is very great.

Theoretically a similar theatrical accomplishment should likewise be demanded. But in fact audiences, and promoters too, will settle for vocal accomplishment and let the acting go hang. I will name no names, but go to any great opera house in the world and five nights out of six you will see some internationally celebrated performer singing like an angel and acting like a lump of wood.

If you questioned them, you would find that most opera singers regard acting as a tiresome adjunct to their singing. The performance to them is a purely musical affair, to which for reasons they do not regard as their business, some "actions" have to be tacked on. . . . "On page 11 you have to open the window. At bar 319 you have to pretend to pour wine out of the empty bottle on the table; at bar 426 you have to lie down and pretend that the soprano has stabbed you, and go right on lying there, as still as you can, while she fusses around with candles and stuff."

They are trained, and very rightly, to regard the score of the work as sacrosanct. Musical accuracy is vital and the conductor's word is law. Theatrical accuracy is of no account —"After my aria you'll find me somewhere up by the door, old boy, unless I'm down left—there's a window down there and if I'm not just the thing my dresser hands me in a glass of milk." The stage director is an irrelevant fusspot who concerns himself with all the part of the performance that is most boring and least important.

Hardly any singer will believe you if you suggest that the

singing and acting are simultaneous expressions of the same impulse; that if a singer is standing up like a block of wood, no matter how "beautiful" a tone is pouring out the impression created by the tone will be contradicted by the stance.

It is not, however, true that the wooden stance always produces a wooden tone; it is apt to be so, but not always. Also in this argument a singer can usually win: at some point he is bound to say, "Well, who cares if my stance is wooden? People go to opera not to *look* at acting, but to *listen* to singing." This is incontrovertible. You may say that they should not do so; that if they do, the singers might just as well stand up in evening dress in front of organ pipes, with the chorus ranged behind them as in oratorio. Most singers and a large proportion of the operatic audience would prefer it that way.

Your only answer is that if Mozart, Verdi, Wagner, and Puccini had wished their works to be so performed they could easily have made their wishes clear. But, instead, and maybe it *is* a pity, they preferred the far more expensive and troublesome and cumbersome mechanics of the stage. That being so, then the singers, critics and operagoers who treat operatic art as a solely musical form are wrong.

I question if it should even be regarded as dominantly musical. In practice it always is, because the musical preparation is technically so demanding. Because the professional judgment of opera is almost entirely pronounced by musicians, the fact is glossed over that these musical-technical demands are met at the expense of dramatic and imaginative demands.

My own first experiences of opera were with the Sadler's Wells company during the war. The first big air raids closed all theatres, and, with no financial reserves, we had no option but to disband the company. Within a matter of weeks, however, we re-engaged a small nucleus of principal singers. Four choristers symbolized a chorus and understudied the principals. The musical director, Laurance Collingwood, and a répétiteur accompanied on two pianos. Productions of La Traviata and Figaro were prepared with easily portable screens instead of scenery. This group went out to the smaller industrial towns in Lancashire and Yorkshire. From the first the reception by the audiences was enthusiastic: they were getting, after all, performances from a dozen of the country's leading singers in productions, which were certainly unpretentious and a little austere but very thoroughly rehearsed; though no proper substitute for an orchestra, the piano score had been carefully and expertly arranged and was excellently played.

In the course of two years we were able to turn the audience's good will to account: the company, despite almost overwhelming difficulties of manpower, was steadily increased in size; almost piece by piece, as profits permitted, we built up an orchestra.

Sometime in 1943 Joan Cross, the artistic director of the company, felt that it was time to renew the old productions and add some new ones. She asked Eric Crozier to direct The Bartered Bride, Kurt Joos to make a new production of Figaro, and me to do La Traviata.

It was my first, and last, experience of an operatic production when there was enough time for the dramatic preparation. In this case all the principal singers were not only thoroughly familiar with the work, they also had long experience as a team. Miss Cross, who had sung and acted Violetta with immense acclaim at Sadler's Wells before the war, was not only a top-ranking singer and musician but also a highly intelligent and gifted actress. Her alternate in the role, Janet Hamilton Smith, was also an admirable actress. The rest of the cast were well-suited. We had time for some discussion of the meaning of the work and how we might try to express it with the simplicity and economy which wartime production demanded. We even had time to try things this way and that, adapting the movements and stage business to the various personalities of the artists. Sophie Fedorovitch designed scenery and dresses of masterly simplicity and elegance; the result was an effort upon which I look back with some pride.

After the war, and after I had ceased to be connected with the management, I was asked back to Sadler's Wells to direct productions of *Carmen, The Barber of Seville* and Verdi's *Falstaff*.

Anna Pollak was not afraid to make Carmen the vulgar, violent slut which the story demands, and played with great verve and authority. In this production we made some small, unimportant, but I think sensible, innovations. The first act was set in quite a squalid, sordid sort of environment and the factory girls looked like factory girls, not like operatic choristers whose sole concession to the warm South is to sling embroidered Spanish shawls over themselves, as if they were suburban grand pianos. The last act is set outside the arena where a bullfight is about to take place; in it Carmen bids farewell to the toreador who goes off into the ring. She is then left completely alone. It has always seemed to me that just when the audience's attention should be most firmly riveted, it is disturbed by the implausibility of this deserted scene— no peanut or candy or pop vendors, no check-takers at the arena gates, no latecomers, no chance passers-by. Nor is it a plausible venue for Carmen and José to have their final scene of recrimination and eventual murder. Obviously he could not, and would not, try to murder her just there. Moreover, an enormous empty space, seeming the more enormous and the emptier because a moment before the entire chorus has been present, makes it very hard for two people, with nothing to lean against, nothing to hold on to, no apparent reason to move anywhere on the stage, to take any kind of a shot at acting the scene. The situation seems to demand that José edges Carmen into some position from which she cannot run away, and from which if she screams for help she will not be heard.

Most of the problems, I thought, could be solved if the scene were transferred from outdoors to some interior which did not need to be precisely defined—a room at an inn maybe, or a dressing room behind the arena. We did this: the acting was much more possible and, so far as I am aware, no violence was done to the story and certainly none to the score; the change of scene did not involve changing so much as a semiquaver.

Inevitably, since music critics are the most conservative creatures in the world, these small changes were the subject of unfavorable comment. The merits and demerits of the performance were ignored in favor of shocked squeaks because garbage cans were seen in the first act and because, in the last act, the letter of the stage directions was disobeyed.

The Barber of Seville was a poor effort. From the singers more virtuosity is demanded than the Sadler's Wells company could at that time supply. I do not know quite what is demanded from the stage director; what I supplied contrived to be at once galumphing and stark.

Falstaff was better. This masterpiece is not suited to the enormous dimensions of La Scala, Covent Garden or the Met. It gained a great deal from the comparative intimacy of Sadler's Wells and from the admirable teamwork of its company. Arnold Matters had not either a voice or personality of a scale to dominate a huge house. But the good musicianship of his singing and the deft economy of his acting were just right for the Wells; and I think the direction had more variety and zest than is usual on the operatic stage. The last act in Windsor Forest was a mess; I have never seen it otherwise. Verdi has set his stage directors many a ticklish problem but none less soluble than this: how to make the mature gentlemen and ample ladies of an operatic chorus acceptable when they are dressed up as tiny children masquerading as elves, hopping about *for far too long*, making believe to pinch Sir John Falstaff, with one eye on the beat of an intricate, concerted set piece.

Meantime I had had the opportunity to direct an opera on the grand scale—Britten's *Peter Grimes*. The first production of this work, as I have related, reopened Sadler's Wells after the war. A year or two later the Covent Garden management decided to revive it with Peter Pears and Joan Cross again in the leading roles which they had created at The Wells.

I had admired Eric Crozier's direction of the first production, with rather literal realistic sets and some attempt at intimacy and realism in the acting. But I felt that in the vast dimensions of Covent Garden intimacy was out of all question and that the majestic sweep of the score, the evocation of the sea and its ineluctable influence on the destiny of the characters, could be better interpreted by a simpler, more spacious setting. Tanya Moiseiwitsch designed a superb set using the entire width and depth of the Covent Garden stage. A horizon cloth surrounded a single enormous set piece suggesting a jetty. This worked splendidly for the scenes of storm and stress; but I must admit that it was rather implausible and overwhelming to the moments of intimate and would-be humorous conversation. Britten evidently felt this too, for a year or two later, at his request, this setting and my choreography were scrapped and more naturalistic ideas prevailed.

Immensely as I admire Britten and respect his taste and intelligence, I have never been able to sympathize with his desire for a naturalistic staging of his operas, and for the inclusion in his scores of conversational scenes such as are entirely appropriate in Puccini, who aimed consistently at *verismo*. But Britten, so I feel, is not consistent: snatches of *verismo* are interpolated into the boldly abstract expressions of atmosphere and emotion. These expressions are those of a far-ranging poetic imagination and a superlative orchestral technician. The masterly authority of these utterances makes the little chatty passages seem feebly trivial.

Early in 1952 Rudolph Bing, who had liked *Carmen* at Sadler's Wells, asked me to direct it at the Met, with Risë Stevens and Richard Tucker. Fritz Reiner conducted—a martinet who expected the singers to watch the beat, often a very tiny and inconspicuous beat, every single second of every single scene. We had one or two skirmishes on this topic. I felt that, here and there, dramatic tension was seriously diminished if the singers could not look one another in the eye, and that, if everyone had rigidly to face front, any lively or expressive choreography was impossible to achieve. Reiner was adamant and I gave way. He was the older man, he was on the staff of the theatre, I was only a guest; also when it comes to a showdown the conductor must dominate—he has the responsibility for the performance. Reiner, though autocratic, was a fair and frank opponent; also, he obviously knew his job superbly well, whereas I knew that in opera I was a bit of an amateur. I gave way but I think he was wrong.

Stevens was delightful. A beautiful and intelligent woman at the top of her particular tree, it would have been understandable if she had felt a bit disgruntled about altering a performance which had been greatly admired, if she had felt inclined to fight, point by point, any changes proposed. On the contrary she was delighted to welcome a new approach and would interpret suggestions with the enthusiasm and humility of a neophyte, but also with the accomplishment of a star.

At one point she was to be carried on the shoulders of some of the men. "Do you mind?" I asked. "You'll be singing as they lift you."

"Not at all" was the crisp reply. "I've studied Yoga."

In the second act there is a gypsy number. Carmens usually get up on a table and bash a tambourine while the ballet takes a fling. I suggested that between verses Miss Stevens should take a fling too. "Do you mind?" I asked and got the reply I expected.

"Not at all. I've studied ballet."

Tucker in those days was a newcomer to opera. He had been a silk merchant and a cantor in a synagogue. But already he was a "big name" and immensely in demand. His acting was raw, but he did not lack imagination or talent. The talent was, however, as yet completely undisciplined. The first time we rehearsed the murder scene—it was in the ladies' anteroom of the Diamond Horseshoe, for like all opera houses the Met is short of rehearsal space—he rushed at Miss Stevens with splendidly realistic fervor and flung her across the room. She landed with a sickening thud beneath the piano. "Are you hurt?" I asked.

"Not at all," came the reply from beneath the feet of the pianist. "I've studied acrobatic falls."

Rehearsal time was strictly limited. So long as the Met's patrons demand so many operas in so few weeks, there will not be time for adequate preparation of any of them. The first act of *Carmen* is very complicated choreographically; one elaborate ensemble follows another. So short was the time that one passage had never been rehearsed at all, the positions had not even been "blocked." It was not serious; everyone knew what to do until, let us say, the bottom of page 67, and they knew what to do again from the middle of page 69; they also knew the music. So the conductor went right on beating and, singing away, they all sorted themselves out into the positions which they knew were just coming up on page 69. I must own that this choreographic passage looked no more disorderly, and no less expressive, than the rest.

In 1957 Mr. Bing asked me to return to the Met to direct *La Traviata*. This was to be a bang-up revival with Oliver Smith for the scenery and Rolf Gerard for the dresses. The management hoped that this production would remain in the repertoire for many seasons, and no expense was spared. A star cast was to launch it: Tebaldi was Violetta; Warren, Germont Père; and Campora, Germont Fils. The conductor was Fausto Cleva.

Rehearsal conditions were the very best which, with its unspeakably complicated schedule, the Met could offer. It would have been entirely unreasonable to expect better, but in fact they were not at all good. Reckoning the "breaks," which under trade-union regulations occur for ten minutes out of every hour, we had an average of six hours of rehearsal time for each of the four acts. This meant that there was just time, if every consideration were subordinated to the one idea of speedy and efficient organization, to lay out every scene of the opera so that all hands at least knew where to stand and when to move. There was absolutely no time for discussion with the principal artists so that we might, at least, have a concerted idea of what we were trying to do. They had all sung their roles, and with immense success, hundreds of times and in dozens of productions all over the world.

Tebaldi, divinely gifted with the statuesquely noble appearance which exactly matches the nobility of her voice, has clearly taken great pains to acquire a sort of stage technique which serves reasonably well in all parts. Her Violetta is not noticeably different from her Tosca or any of her other roles. Different dresses are worn but the same graciously Olympian demeanor expresses all the characters in every situation. It is the absolute antithesis of "Method" acting. There are simple rules for the expression of a repertoire of emotions: surprise, fear, horror, joy, eagerness, ennui.

This sort of technique has several advantages: it can be taught, and, unlike many artistic techniques, it can be learned by a process of careful and conscientious imitation. A good practitioner, as Tebaldi certainly is, of such rules need never be at a loss on the stage; and, in the emotional and evocative context of great music, the highly formalized routine can impress and even move the audience. But it can never be more than second best. The rules enable the artist, as it were, to accompany the score, to remain consistent with the composer's intention, but not to interpret it in the uniquely personal way which raises craft to the status of art.

Warren brings to opera far more than a magnificent voice. He is intelligent and cultivated; this shows in all his parts. He has a sense of period and of style. But in the rush and scurry of operatic rehearsal, in the breadth of performance demanded by huge opera houses, he has developed mannerisms and imposed upon his acting a style not nearly so formal as that of Tebaldi but rigid enough to make it easy to mistake dignified economy for stiffness.

Campora, though he does not pack quite the punch of the

other two, has a delightful tenor voice and, rare among tenors, is slim and attractive to look at. He moves easily and has assurance and charm on the stage.

Three artists of this caliber brought to bear on a masterpiece should have added up to a performance of some importance. They did not. For one thing there was no time. Given time we could have had some discussion and exchange of views on the meaning of the work and how to use this particular conjunction of personality and circumstance. But, truly, I am not convinced that such discussions would have been very fruitful. I can well understand that neither Madame Tebaldi nor Mr. Warren would have felt inclined radically to change the styles which have, after all, proved no barrier to world fame and almost unvarying critical acclaim, at the instance of a foreign director with less than a tithe of their own experience in this particular field.

Maybe if one wants radically to change the style of grand opera it would be wiser not to begin at the top. As it was, the three pleasantly went their own separate ways; each emitted glorious sounds but was only part of a highly proficient, highly paid, publicized and applauded but fundamentally empty routine.

The scenery was elaborate and handsome; the dresses were handsome and elaborate. My own efforts were revealed as uninspired but reasonably efficient traffic direction: on the opening performance only two ladies had their crinolines torn and one gentleman's toupee was twitched awry.

At its best, grand opera is the greatest experience the theatre can offer to an audience. It is at its best once in a very blue moon and then, I rather suspect, more by good luck than good management. Opera is such a great, grinding, galumphing behemoth—so much energy goes into battling with the multitude of people concerned, the masses of scenery, the mountainous heaps of coronets, riding boots, fans, goblets, scimitars and rosaries that the purpose of it all gets lost; the great machine churns out a noisy, complicated and almost totally meaningless product.

In my own experience of operatic performances, I can only recall two or three really thrilling nights. Mostly one enjoys moments here and there, but comes out with an over-all feeling of how great it would have been if the performance had been just a little nearer the unattainable bull's-eye. Looking back, I think my two or three great nights were all primarily due to the conductor. He evoked a performance from singers and orchestra better than they customarily gave.

I wonder whether great operatic performance *always* stems from the conductor? I can imagine that from time to time the conductor himself is inspired by the performance of one, or some, of the singers. This, surely, is the strongest argument against the rule-of-thumb sort of operatic acting: it is incapable of the inspiration which alone lifts a performance above the prosaically skillful. On the other side, it must be argued that, if inspiration usually stems from the conductor, if excitement and emotion are primarily generated in the pit, then it is the business of the singers not to be inspired themselves but to be mere channels through which the holy spirit flows, the most prominent instruments in a concerted musical inspiration. If this be granted, then rule-of-thumb acting is justified, because, while enabling the requirements of the stage action to be met, it unquestionably leaves a singer much more freedom to concentrate upon the predominantly musical relation between himself and the conductor.

Each artist has only so much energy. The narrower the channel the more forcible is the flow. It cannot be denied that if a considerable part—I will not say half of an artist's energy—is concerned with theatrical values, with feelings in connection with the story, in connection with the other characters on the stage, such proportion of his energy will therefore be diverted from the psycho-musical relation between himself and the conductor.

Rule-of-thumb acting, by an experienced practitioner, becomes almost a conditioned reflex. If the music is erotic he automatically adopts the formula by which he has learned to denote the man in love; if the music expresses fear, his eyes dilate, he makes gestures symbolic of averting disaster. For any kind of definable noise which the orchestra can make there is a formula, or ritual gesture, which can be made as if in sleep, so that no conscious effort is diverted from the all-important musical task.

There is only one argument on the other side: I have advanced it before. In my opinion, it is a clincher. If operatic composers had intended their interpreters to concentrate their full energy on the music, they would not have planned their work for the stage. That being so, it is the duty of those of us who are concerned with the staging of opera to press our claim with all the fervor we can muster. I hope I have made it clear that I entirely appreciate that the conductor, who takes final responsibility, must have the final say-so; but neither he nor the singers must be permitted indefinitely to hold what still is current operatic dogma: that opera is a musical performance to which is appended, at a late stage of the preparation, like a frill round the bone of a cutlet, a perfunctory and almost meaningless stage routine. We would have a better chance of making our point if opera were ever reviewed by dramatic, rather than solely musical, critics. It was once—in London in the nineties—by a young Irishman with a red beard who called himself **Corno di Bassetto**. He beat the hell out of the whole business.

17

Abroad:
Israel & Finland

ONE OF THE HAPPIEST FEATURES of life in the theatre is that you may get a good many chances to travel and to see the world, not just as a tourist but as a working member of a foreign community. By the end of the war there was hardly a part of the United Kingdom, except Cornwall, with which I was not acquainted. But brief holidays were all I had experienced abroad.

In the winter of 1946 came an invitation from Habimah in Tel Aviv. I had seen the company in London before the war, and had admired immensely its productions of *The Dybbuk* and *The Golem*. I was asked to suggest a play, which would be given in Hebrew; I should have an interpreter.

It seemed sensible to suggest a classic, but not an English classic; something which should be as foreign to me as to Habimah, but which should be of sufficiently universal significance to transcend the geographical and racial differences between us and the temporal difference between all of us and the play. We agreed upon *Oedipus Rex*.

My wife and I left England on Christmas Eve. There was deep snow, a fuel shortage, and rationing was still in full force. A few hours later we were met at Lydda by the Committee of Habimah. My wife was presented with a large

259

bunch of roses, and we all sat down, right then and there at the airport, to roast chicken with all the trimmings, further assisted by an excellent local red wine followed by cognac. We then repaired to Habimah to meet the company at coffee, with more cognac; and finally wound up in a charming hotel looking out over the sunlit Mediterranean. The material circumstances were clearly going to be all that could be wished.

Theatrically, also, it promised to be a rewarding experience. The interpreter, Fanny Lubitsch, was not only a superlative linguist, but also a gifted and intelligent actress in the company. The designer, Shalom Sebba, too, was a remarkable fellow. I had sent out beforehand several long letters outlining how I hoped the production might look, what ideas I hoped the decor would convey, and why: I also sent sketch plans of the set. When I first met Sebba he seemed rather a shy, diffident sort of person, about forty years old, nice-looking, but not at all the conventional notion of an artist. He looked more like a gymnastic instructor. He spoke fluent English. He presented a scale-plan of the set, exactly embodying all my suggestions, then rather shyly said that with regard to the costumes he had ventured to depart somewhat from the scheme I had outlined. He then produced a series of drawings which even I could see at a glance were more thoughtful and infinitely more original than my suggestions, to which they bore not the faintest relation. Of course we adopted them at once.

I did venture to suggest that, though the drawings were wonderful, simply wonderful, it might be nice if one or two of the Chorus of Aged Thebans had a stick or crutch. It was as though I had fired a gun. Suddenly the charming and eager face of the gym instructor became suffused and crimson, the eyes flashed, the mouth twitched and worked. He stamped thrice on the floor, loud thumps like an irate and alarmed male rabbit. Then the words came: "Understand this," he said in a low controlled tone, far more alarming than a scream. "Once and for all, *I Will Not Tolerate Realismus!*"

The paroxysm subsided as suddenly as it began. I was able to assure him that he could not detest Realismus more heartily than I; we had a hilarious luncheon, crowned by cognac, and when eventually the Aged Thebans took the stage there never was seen such a medley of crutches, poles, cudgels, knobkerries and Hellenic alpenstocks—a gnarled and leafless Birnam Wood clumping and thumping up the palace steps.

The actors were accustomed to regarding a director with a respect, even reverence, which at home we are not accorded. The company originated in Moscow, whence it migrated to Israel in the nineteen-twenties. The actors were used to long months of preparation with a wealth of disquisition by the director.

For our first rehearsal a long table was laid with an emerald baize cloth and tiny coffee cups. I was ushered to its head where a stately chair, almost a throne, was set and a coffee cup slightly larger than the rest. At my right hand and my left sat the two senior members of the company, each fully old enough to be my Papa; away beyond them stretched the rest of the group in descending order of seniority; far, far away down that long table were young boys and girls, some no more than forty-six.

I gave a limping, but I hope modest and I know brief, harangue about what I supposed to be the meaning of the play, and how I hoped we might express it. I could feel Fanny Lubitsch striving to make my remarks sound better in Hebrew than they did in English; and I could feel a sense of courteous but grave disappointment that I was not more apocalyptic, more thrilling and emotional, that I had not pounded the emerald baize till the coffee cups shook. There was no coffee, the cups were obviously there to be shaken. From the walls, framed photographs of some of my Russian predecessors looked down. They had beards and deep stiff collars and rimless pince-nez; one of them wore a fur hat. I seemed to feel them frown. *They* would have shaken the cups; *they* would have shouted and whispered hoarsely, but thrillingly; *they* would have wept.

After the first day, we left the green baize table and worked on the stage and in the hands of these wonderful actors the play began to take fascinating shape.

After about a fortnight, we were rehearsing one afternoon when I heard what seemed to be shouting voices in the street outside the theatre. But before you could say Jack Robinson in Hebrew the actors had shut their books and fled; Miss Lubitsch and I were alone on the empty stage. "Curfew," she said. "Those are loudspeakers on the British tanks. Go to the hotel as fast as you can. Any one on the streets ten minutes from now will be shot."

My way led through normally busy streets. Now there was not a creature to be seen or a sound to be heard, save my own echoing footsteps, and, now and again, the repeated warning on the mobile speakers.

Curfew meant that everyone in the city had to stay óff the street until further notice. A few days before our arrival there had been a curfew period which had endured three weeks. People could telephone; a ration of bread and milk was delivered daily at each house by British troops; in case of emergency, such as a death in the house, you could hang out a sign; an ambulance would then come. This time the curfew only lasted forty-eight hours. But from now on the political situation degenerated from day to day; almost every night there would be outrages committed either by British troops or by the members of Irgun Zwai Leumi, or as the British newspapers phrased it, "Terrorists."

It was the beginning of the end of the British Mandate. This is no place to discuss the rights and wrongs of the situation, which very briefly was this: successive British governments had committed themselves to contradictory obligations to both Jews and Arabs. Under pressure of the enormous waves of postwar Jewish immigration, at this time largely from Europe, the British government was desperately trying to fulfill mandatory powers granted by the League of Nations some twenty-five years earlier. In deference to Arab

pressure, further Jewish immigration had been forbidden, and the Jewish population was in a ferment, which was already becoming armed insurrection. Curfew followed curfew until, after about a week, a military order was issued that no British civilians could remain at large. They must either leave the country at once or go into an internment camp pending an improvement in the situation.

This put us in an embarrassing position. Habimah had already spent a good deal of money on our fares and on the preparation for the production which, if I left, would probably be abandoned. To leave would put the theatre into a bad plight. It would also look bad: the production had been widely publicized, and in Israel a theatrical first night is a matter of public interest comparable to a big ball game in the United States or an important cricket match in England. Additional publicity focused upon the engagement of a British director at a time of strong anti-British political sentiment.

I requested and was granted permission to stay at liberty and go on working. My wife refused to desert Mr. Micawber. The same night, as twilight—the spectacularly rapid, rather disquieting Near-Eastern twilight—was falling, two officers brought to the hotel a little paper to be signed. They were nice, pink young officers with stiff upper lips and revolvers in their holsters. In flat Midland accents they trotted out their dialogue: "Nothing to do with us, old boy; your business of course—oh and your good lady's of course—but quite frankly if I were you..." and proffered the little paper. In grand language it stated a simple conditional clause: if anything happened to Dr. and/or Mrs. Guthrie, His Majesty could accept no kind of responsibility. We signed the document with what novelists call a catch at the heart, and twilight turned, almost with a clang, to dark.

Hardly had the officers gone down the passage when a knock came at the door: the hotel proprietor, in his German English, embarrassed but firm: "You must leave. I'm very sorry—very sorry indeed." And he clearly was; a refugee himself, he knew just how we must feel. "I cannot undertake responsibility for your safety. You must leave."

"Of course," we said. "We quite understand. First thing after breakfast tomorrow."

"I'm sorry. No. Tonight. At once."

And now, from the passage, we heard the shuffling of many feet and a low, rather conspiratorial muttering. Could this be It? The Terrorists had certainly wasted no time.

It was the Committee from Habimah. Their oldest member seized me by both hands; his wife was kissing mine. "My darlings, my doves, it is not safe here. With us you will be safe."

The secretary, Ari Warschawer, much younger than his chairman, and his very beautiful young wife took us to their flat. Like most in Tel Aviv it was very small. We had the bed. They prepared to make do on two chairs and a bolster.

Tea was being brewed, when suddenly on the door there was a thunderous knock. Ari flew to the door and opened it. Six enormous young men crowded into the little room with six tommy guns. Clearly this *was* It. They were going to take us out and shoot us right there in the lobby. The leading tommy gunner clicked his heels in a smart salute. "From the Jewish Agency," he said in the perfect English of the London School of Economics and in the manner of Rupert of Hentzau, "we are"—they all saluted—"your bodyguard."

"*How* nice!" said our hostess. "You must all have some tea before you go."

But no; their orders were never, *never*, to let us out of their collective sight. So we all ten settled down for what was left of the night, feeling rather as I imagine some of the less gregarious animals must have felt on the first night in the Ark.

Came the dawn and the bodyguard was relieved by six other young fellows, who took over the tommy guns and us, and let the first lot away to their day's work. They were all volunteers, serving in the unofficial Army of the Jewish Agency, while at the same time following their usual civilian occupation. One was a dental technician, another a medical student, a third a clerk in a bookstore and so on. We gradually got to know and like them very much.

At a quarter to eight we prepared to leave for work at the theatre. But the boys said that to walk through the streets was too risky and that the Agency had arranged transport. And behold, our carriage waited at the door.

It was not quite a pumpkin drawn by white mice, but nearly as fantastic. An English Daimler, vintage 1897, had been converted into a hearse. Where should have reposed the coffin, we piled in like Keystone cops, tommy guns and all. Black-fringed blinds with black tassels were pulled reverently down, and we moved at a solemn foot-pace not to the cemetery but to the fun factory.

This happened every morning. At first the neighbors peeked reverently and sympathetically at this daily funeral. Gradually mourning turned to joy, and at the end of the first week we were one of the sights of the city. People rushed to watch the cortège, children danced beside the hearse. It would have been far, far less conspicuous to have walked through the streets waving a Union Jack and singing "Rule Britannia."

Oedipus Rex opened on its appointed day. The next morning we flew back to England with only one regret: we had spent six weeks in one of the most beautiful and interesting parts of the entire earth and had seen virtually nothing but the darkened interior of a motor hearse.

The following winter I again directed *Oedipus Rex*, this time for the Swedish Theatre in Helsinki. It may seem odd that there is a Swedish theatre in the capital of Finland. Like Ireland, Finland has been throughout her history dominated, often occupied, by her more powerful neighbors. The last occupation was by the Swedes, with the result that, as in Northern Ireland there is a predominantly Scots–Irish element, so in the coastal regions of Finland there is a predominant element of Swedish Finns. They inherit a tradition of superiority to the dispossessed native Finns, poorer than them-

selves but fanatical in defense of their distinctive language
and culture. The two nations have recently lived in reasonable
and increasing amity and the war with Russia drew them
much closer than ever before. The two cultures and languages,
however, remain distinct and Helsingfors, or as it is known
in Finnish, Helsinki, has both a Swedish and a Finnish theatre, each supported by the state, but each with its own company, repertory, and management.

The contrast between Tel Aviv and Helsingfors could
hardly have been more extreme; or the contrast between
Habimah and the blond Scandinavians at Svenska Teatret.

Finland was still reeling from the Winter War, the gallant
defiance of Russia in 1940. One man in five of military age
had been killed or disabled; her economic resources were
being bled by crippling ten-year reparations to Russia of a
tithe of her total production. The Karelian isthmus, one of
the most fertile parts of the country, had been ceded to
Russia—in hostile hands it constituted a strategic threat to
Leningrad.

The Russians had offered to the Karelians the choice of
remaining in their homes as Russian subjects or retiring to
unoccupied Finland. Ninety per cent chose the latter alternative. They were, of course, welcomed with open arms but
tremendous problems of housing and agricultural land tenure
were heaped on an already strained economy.

Karelia was completely cut off behind the iron curtain.
One train a week traveled between Helsinki and Leningrad.
Travelers sat behind metal shutters pulled over the windows,
armed Russian guards paraded the train to make sure that
no one looked out. On its journey this train would pass
through Viborg, ex-capital of Karelia, once a thriving city
with its own university, theatres, symphony orchestra, great
stores and factories, and so on; as near Helsinki as Philadelphia to New York. So absolutely was Karelia sealed off from
Finland that when I met at a party some people who had
lived in Viborg, they did not even know whether the city

were still inhabited. Unconfirmed rumor said that grass was growing in its streets.

Instead of the sunshine, the flowers, the abundant food of Israel in 1947, we had a sub-zero temperature, snow everywhere and darkness from about three in the afternoon till eleven the following morning. Food was expensive and scarce; commodities of every kind were in short supply. Stockman's, the city's great department store, made a gallant Christmas display: the great windows were bright and gay, but everything had been made, with the utmost ingenuity and great taste, out of paper.

The austerity, however, was only material. Nothing could have been more genial and pleasant than the atmosphere of the theatre. It is a beautifully designed small house, elegant but practical, and splendidly managed. A permanent company presents, for an annual season of about thirty-five weeks, a repertory of plays, classical and modern, of very varied character, including one or two musical comedies—the company includes a few singers as well as actors.

All my professional life I had heard theatre people in Britain and America wishing that we had repertory theatres such as exist on the continent of Europe: a permanent company offering not a stock season, but a real repertory. Such a system, I had heard, would relieve actors, directors and technicians of the nightmare anxiety about being out of work, would guarantee them not only security but a wide experience, the chance really to develop both as individual craftsmen and as members of a team.

Our system of casual theatrical employment certainly enables those at the top to make a great deal more money and enjoy more freedom to choose what to do, where and with whom to do it; but comparatively few climb high enough to attain this freedom and affluence; and, of those who do, comparatively few remain at the top for longer than a few years.

For the first time in Israel and now, in Finland, in strikingly different circumstances, I had the chance to observe closely the working of such a system.

It is perfectly true that the relief from insecurity is a great advantage. An immense amount of energy can be diverted from the search for work and from mere worry into more creative channels. It is also true that continuous employment in a constant and wide variety of plays does develop craftsmanship. But the repertory system also has grave drawbacks. The tensions and frictions and factions inside a permanent company are far greater than can ever develop in the comparatively casual and brief professional contacts of our theatre.

But if a permanent company breeds tensions, tyranny and intrigue, it also creates an extraordinary sense of professional solidarity, of mutual dependence and loyalty. Two members of such a company may be deadly enemies, mutual hostility may obsess them as it can only obsess when two uncongenial people are forced into daily proximity and kept there for a long period. It happens in prison, in schools, in families; but it is a byword that outsiders had better not interfere in family feuds. If they do, the combatants are immediately united in an alliance as intense as their hatred. Together they turn and rend the interfering outsider. It is the same in theatre companies. A feeling of solidarity develops, exactly analogous with family feeling. Internecine factions and intrigues are somehow compatible with feelings of intense loyalty to the theatre and to even the least congenial of colleagues.

It is hardly possible to overestimate the importance of this sense of solidarity, not for its purely artistic or theatrical results but as an element in the spiritual life of those who feel it. It is an element which modern life does not encourage.

More and more we are organized into vast groups. It is only theoretically possible to feel any keenly personal sense of loyalty to General Motors, the A. & P. Stores, the bar association. Even loyalty to country or to church is rather abstract and hard to arouse. I doubt if the most devout Roman

Catholics in Ireland or Spain lose much sleep over church events in Adelaide, let us say, Khartoum or Kansas City.

But to the members of a theatre company this loyalty, this sense of belonging to something collectively larger than the sum of its individuals, is one of the central points of their lives. This, more than any of the fine individual talents, more than the collective achievement of two distinguished organizations, was what impressed me about Habimah and the Swedish Theatre at Helsinki.

Without this feeling, our theatre, however glamorous, efficiently organized, or heavily financed, is comparatively poor. It is weakened where it can least afford to be weak: at the heart. It is deprived of an important ingredient of what I consider its most valuable contribution to society: the feeling of intimate companionship between audience and stage.

In our American and British theatre great individual performers can create this feeling—Danny Kaye is a conspicuous instance. But where the host at the party, so to speak, is a single individual there are severe limits to the range of fare which he can provide. The marvelous range and variety of a great masterpiece, *Hamlet*, for instance, *L'Avare* or *The Cherry Orchard*, demand the collective expression of a group. Really superb ensemble playing is never seen at present in America because there are no ensembles to see. Wonderfully efficient performances occur but the players, most of them, had never met before the first rehearsal, many of them may never meet again; they are strangers, they have no bond of even the most commonplace kind except the two-hour traffic of the stage. The ensemble, if it exists at all, can only be technical. There is no collective life of the company which passes like an emanation from the stage to the audience.

The good permanent companies have such a collective life. It is an asset so precious that, in my view, it more than compensates for defects in the system which it would be foolish and dishonest to ignore.

I have alluded to tensions and intrigue: the younger members, like the junior officers in an army, are gnawed by jealousy and frustration because they see their promotion blocked by seniors. The seniors, likewise, live in constant dread of being pushed off the perch and on to the pension list by younger, more vigorous talents. As a result, the old birds tend to be perpetually on the defensive, the young constantly aggressive. The old, more experienced in the use of beak and claws, trading shamelessly on the respect which is rightfully their due, entrenched in the security of a life contract under which they can only be dismissed for gross incompetence or misbehavior, exercise a tyranny which in the occidental world exists in the family, or in academic life, but is unknown in the theatre.

Moreover, security breeds boredom. The actors long for the possibility of freedom, even at the price of insecurity. They envy British and American actors the fat salaries, lavish publicity and glamour which our theatre possesses more than theirs. It is not easy to be glamorous when your audience sees you at least nine or ten times every season, often wildly miscast; when your audience knows where you buy fish and hats and tobacco, and just how much you pay. Glamour depends upon the glamourous ones being completely anonymous except for the brief periods when they are on show; be that on or off the stage. And remember that after a lifetime in a permanent company an actor's every inflection, every movement, every mood is as familiar to his audience as to his wife. In repertory companies it is not only the actors, but also the customers, who get bored with security and permanence.

In my opinion the best arrangement is neither the permanent company, nor the casual catch-as-catch-can of Broadway and the West End. Some, not all, of the advantages of both systems are gained, and some of the disadvantages are lost, in the sort of arrangements which prevail in the British classical companies at Stratford and the Old Vic: a seasonal engagement, covering a series of productions, renewable if both parties so desire for the next season, even season after season if

that were desired, for many years. The drawback, in the two
instances I have quoted, is from the artist's point of view, a
certain monotony of program—classics, classics all the way.
But is there any theoretic, or any insuperable practical objection to applying a similar system to a series of other kinds of
plays?

The Scandinavian *Oedipus* was interestingly northern. It
lacked the great throbs of Jewish emotion which drove the
Habimah production like the engines of a steamship. On the
other hand, the Scandinavian company had an austere dignity
which was noble and moving. Considering how alike in externals they were—similar, but not identical, set, dresses and
choreography—the two performances were quite extraordinarily contrasted. I do not think anyone could say one was
better than the other. The two national approaches made of
the same play two quite different experiences, but each in
its own way was a valid, and, I think, impressive comment
on the play.

It is, of course, foolish to suppose that people are different
just because they live in places which are colored differently
on a map; or to suppose that though there may be racial
and geographical differences, they cannot be transcended.
They can and, if the human race is to survive, eventually
must be transcended. But these two productions nicely high-
lighted some of the potential difficulties.

Since the *Oedipus* productions I have been back both to
Israel and Finland.

Less than two years afterwards we did, in Helsinki, *The
Taming of the Shrew*. It was a very happy time. Frederick
Crooke, a British designer, was also engaged for the production and my wife came with us. Finland was beginning to
recover from the ravages of war. There was more food, more
money, a sensation of life returning. It was golden October
weather. We used to love the market down at the harbor
where boats would come in from the islands—Helsinki is

part of an archipelago—loaded with flowers, dahlias in crimson and scarlet and orange, Michaelmas daisies and pink cosmias; apples, pears and plums; and vegetables, which I suppose were no more luscious, green and fresh than anywhere else, but seemed so by contrast with the gray northern sea.

In the theatre it was gay. The austere actors of *Oedipus* cast dignity to the October winds. Led by a splendid Petruchio and Katharina they produced an uproarious, completely uninhibited explosion of farcical pyrotechnics.

The first night was disconcerting. We three from Britain and our delightful interpreter, Gerde Wrede, now the theatre's directress, hid ourselves in a nook whence we could spy upon the audience. "Everyone" was there, resplendent in full evening dress. I have never seen a comparable display of quiet, dignified elegance. Seldom can an audience have assembled in a spirit of more earnest and solemn enquiry. They had come to observe how a director, imported from the far land of the author's origin, would interpret Shakespeare. Tall iron-gray ladies adjusted fur tippets and lorgnettes; professors opened their marked copies of the play with pencils poised to take notes.

They were dumbfounded.

The actors screamed their jokes, they fell from ladders, sat down in buckets of water, chased one another into cupboards, ran through the antic routine of farce in a silence that could be felt.

Gradually the ice melted. After a particularly outrageous piece of business an actor made an exit on all fours, and a professor, with a face of stone, clapped white-gloved hands. Soon every exit was applauded. Gradually the stone faces softened, very gradually they crinkled into reluctant smiles. It was not until after half-time that anyone dared actually to laugh. But by the end of the evening the frost had completely thawed. The company had a tremendous ovation and for the rest of the season *The Shrew* played to musical-comedy business.

It was twelve years before I returned to Israel. In a decade of independence the country was transformed. It is not my business to discuss the politics, economics, the problems and triumphs of this phenomenal land. I will confine myself to the theatre.

Habimah, like everything else in the country, was greatly changed. It was far less Russian and far younger. As with all great changes, the results were good and bad.

Something, in my opinion, has been lost in the gradual dilution of the company's very Russian individuality. The new productions are more up to date and, in most respects, much more efficient. But they are more like the productions of any other theatre.

Vakhtangov, who set the impress of his style on all Habimah's earlier work, was a genius. He was one of Stanislavsky's young lieutenants at the Moscow Art Theatre and when Stanislavsky decided to take the small group of Hebrew actors under the wing of the Art Theatre he appointed Vakhtangov to direct it. The result was *The Dybbuk*, Habimah's first, and still infinitely its most important, production.

The play, by An-sky, is not a masterpiece, but the production is the most exciting one I have ever seen. It is still, after more than forty years, in its rejection of naturalism, its use of symbolism and ritual, its choreography, its musical approach, more "advanced," more assured and more economical than the work of any director which I have since encountered.

Vakhtangov died untimely. He was dying even while *The Dybbuk* was being prepared. But his influence dominated Habimah and fixed its early style. None of the subsequent directors approached his originality or force, so gradually the style was bound to change. The reforms have been inevitable; but at the present time Habimah has lost its old distinctive style and has not yet found a new one.

On the other hand, there has been a most welcome transfusion of new young blood. Twelve years ago the leading parts were automatically allotted to the senior actors. Ladies and gentlemen of sixty, even seventy, summers would bounce onto the stage in golden wings and a ton of rouge. The roles of their aunts, uncles, aged retainers, or even grandparents, would be enacted by students, their innocent faces streaked with a myriad grease-paint "wrinkles," their youthful forms bent over canes and twitching with simulated palsies and agues.

Today they have reformed all that. There are young actors, and good ones, for the young parts; and young people in the management. Several of the young men, who twelve years ago were students, are now directing productions and are members of the management committee.

This remarkable theatre has rejuvenated itself, a process which must often have been acutely painful and embarrassing. Gradually it will find ways of adapting its style to conditions, which, in the last forty years since Habimah's inception, have changed in Israel probably more drastically and rapidly than anywhere in the world.

18

Abroad:
Australia & Poland

EARLY IN 1947 I went to Australia as the guest of the British Council. The Council had been asked to send someone to take a look at the Australian theatrical scene and then to advise the Premier, Mr. Chifley, who was considering the possibility of an Australian national theatre.

In six weeks I visited the six principal cities, in which dwells more than half the population of the entire continent. I attended endless receptions and cocktail parties, met the federal Premier and the Prime Minister of each state, and saw a great many amateur theatrical performances of widely varying quality. I did not visit a cattle or sheep station— I hardly saw a horse or cow all the time I was there—and I would not dream of claiming that I had seen the real Australia, whatever that may be.

No traveler, however, can help getting impressions. Mine are the rather specialized impressions of someone doing a high-pressure tour in a purposely restricted professional field. I say this because I quickly discovered that Australians, as a whole, have an almost morbidly developed inferiority complex. "How do you like us?" eagerly smiling strangers would ask. "How do you like our country?" The question was strictly rhetorical.

Naturally, after a residence of two weeks, trying manfully to be a gracious guest, I would not be likely to make any unfavorable comment. I would in all sincerity say something to the effect that, immensely as I was enjoying myself, as yet I hardly felt qualified to express an opinion. However pleasantly and warmly I tried to phrase this sentiment, it never failed to displease. Here, the smiling strangers would feel, is one more bloody Pommy, one more sneering, sophisticated, colonial-minded bloody bastard.

It was the same with food. Britain was still rationed. After five years on short commons my appetite, never very large, had become rather small. Hostesses with the kindest intentions would face me at four o'clock of a very hot afternoon with a plate on which in heaped profusion would be half a cow and about a hundredweight of mashed potato. Smiling eagerly, oh so kindly, they would say "How do you like our food?"

After a party till two the night before, after three or four hours in a plane, before making a speech and in a temperature considerably higher than I am used to, I would pick and fumble at the steak, poke tunnels in the mountain of potato and pull heavily at the draughts of hot sweet tea which wash down every item of Australia's rather limited menu. "Go on!" the host would say; "Dig into it. There's no rationing here." But beneath the gleaming smiles, the cordial pressing tones, it was apparent that they thought me one more bloody, sneering, sophisticated Pommy, who turns up his nose at good, plain, hearty, solid Australian food.

The anxiety to be liked by, and to impress, visitors from home—Australians even of the third and fourth Australian-born generation refer to Britain as home—is paradoxically the greatest danger to Anglo–Australian cordiality. Honest visitors cannot accord unqualified admiration and delight to every aspect of Australia. You try to concentrate upon the many things which there are to admire and like; you try to understand the rest. But right off you are put in an impossible position by this almost universal, desperate and transparent desire to impress.

If you gush and rave indiscriminately you will be taken—and quite rightly, too—either for a hypocrite or a fool, probably both. If you express even the faintest implication of criticism, immediately a wire fence springs up between you and your interlocutor, tingling with a dangerous voltage of electricity. One more unguarded word and, amid sheets of blue flame, you will fuse the mother-complex. The visitor has somehow to reconcile an attitude of humility and shyness becoming to a new boy with the benign authority of one who represents home and mother. Neither attitude must be overdone—the humility can so easily seem sissy, the benignity no less easily seem patronizing; and neither attitude must be insincere.

What impressed me particularly in Australia was a rather back-handed reflection on our own society in Britain. I had been very conscious of the same thing the first time I went to Canada and the United States. You suddenly realize how tremendously important, how all-pervading in every aspect of British life is the class structure of society. Of course, class is not a static but a fluid notion; the class structure of even so ancient and elaborately stratified a society as that in England is constantly changing; in the last forty years it has undergone, under pressure of war conditions and postwar economic problems, a revolution quite as drastic as that which occurred in France in 1798.

Nevertheless, even after such a revolution, it is extraordinary to what an extent British life is still dominated by the traditions and opinions of a numerically tiny upper class. You do not realize this until you live for a while in one of the communities that have come into being since the decay of the feudal system.

Thus my dominant impression on this trip was not of Australia at all, but of home, provoked by impressions of a supposedly classless Australia. I do not mean to imply that

British class-consciousness is a good thing or bad. It is both. But not till you get away do you realize how dominant it is. The English village is still, spiritually as well as architecturally, dominated, often resentfully, by the great house and the church. *The London Times* is the house magazine of quite a small, exclusive, but overwhelmingly influential club. To "get anywhere" in England—this applies much less forcibly in Scotland, Wales or Northern Ireland—it is still almost a prerequisite that you subscribe to "establishment" conventions of speech, manners and morals. If you do not, then you must make your way in business, politics or one of the learned professions by enacting, rather cleverly, the character role of an Outsider.

Australian society is no more classless than any other. In the small towns as well as the large, the doctors and dentists and their wives dine with one another, not with the truck-drivers and their wives, for the excellent reason that, by dint of common interests and roughly similar income, the evening is apt to be easier and pleasanter. In new countries like Australia and Canada, it is, of course, very much easier to move from one class to another than in the more ancient and consequently more rigidily stratified communities. And in countries with an expanding economy, again like Australia and Canada, it is far easier to make and to lose money, with consequent change in social position—upwards or down.

In Australia in 1947 domestic service was still considered a degrading occupation, although manual labor—by dint of powerful trades unions—seemed to be rewarded, in proportion to intellectual labor, more highly than I had ever known. But, paradoxically, this made for more, not less, class distinction. Where nearly all homes are run without domestic help, and on a similar scale of expenditure, the cultural standard can still be almost always and immediately assessed; and this, rather than wealth, becomes the distinguishing factor. Indeed, most of the more cultured people seemed to be poor. I suppose it was very snobbish and naïve of me to be surprised, when I gave a lecture at a university, that the gentleman whose duty it was to stoke the boiler arrived in a Cadillac wearing dirty overalls; whereas the Vice-Chancellor, whose duty it was to take the chair, arrived on a bicycle, with clips on his evening-dress trousers.

I did not notice that spiritually the professional classes seemed adversely affected by their low economic status. There must be less time to read Plato if you have to dust the study and wash up lunch. But I guess such tasks are not inimical to contemplation.

Contrariwise, I did not notice that the economically dominant workers were more happy. Nowhere, except in America under Prohibition, have I seen such widespread and brutal drunkenness. But this may not be a symptom of the Australian working man's malaise: for one thing, by no means all the drunks were manual workers. Is it just possible that conspicuous insobriety is, as it was in the United States, one of the consequences of restrictive legislation in connection with the sale of liquor?

One other thing surprised me at the time: I suppose it was the influence of the immigration propaganda—all those high-colored posters of Sunburnt Sicklemen of Autumn Weary—but I had expected to find Australia full of handsome, laconic men; shy but tremendously virile. Perhaps when I was there all these types were temporarily out back. Certainly the cities seemed to be full of excitable, nervous little gentlemen with light voices and rather a lot of jewelry. It was the women who were handsome, laconic and tremendously virile.

I have since wondered if this is perhaps a phase through which all communities pass at a certain stage of development, a certain biological distance from the tremendous effort put out by the pioneers. If your immediate forbears have made a gigantic inroad upon the family's resources of physical energy, will power and courage, it is not surprising that for a generation or two nature should need a rest. Consider how very few of the world's great men have had sons of anything like comparable stature.

It is an ironic fact that the energy of pioneers has all to be expended upon the herculean task of just keeping alive. Consequently, these efforts are inadequately chronicled for posterity and inadequately celebrated. No one had time to record in writing, in paint, music or sculpture achievements of which, in consequence, posterity underestimates the difficulty, the glory—and the cost.

Professionally, my visit was not particularly exciting. There was one moderate semi-amateur production of *The Merry Wives of Windsor*, derivative in style from England, and one rather dreary semi-amateur production of *Rigoletto*, derivative in style from Sadler's Wells rather than Italy. There were sundry one-act plays, an amateur production of Noel Coward's *Bitter Sweet* with some superb singing but feeble acting and production, and the Australian version of *Oklahoma!* received with immense acclaim. I thought it inferior to the London production in about the same measure that the London production had been inferior to the New York original. I can remember nothing which struck me as distinctively Australian. I knew that Covent Garden and Sadler's Wells were full of excellent Australian singers; that many talented young Australians were knocking on the theatrical door in London and New York, to say nothing of slightly older people like Judith Anderson, Coral Browne, Cyril Ritchard and Robert Helpmann, who have gained honorable admittance. Therefore, it was no surprise to find Australia an extraordinary mine of talent. There was at that time no satisfactory organization for its expression, no considerable public appreciation to develop it, and little enlightened criticism to lead the public.

My report to the Prime Minister suggested that the time to *build* a national theatre had not yet arrived. But it suggested several practical ways of developing Australian talent and taste as a preliminary. It was my view that before spending great sums on a building, a much more moderate sum should be spent on equipping the human material of a national theatre. This, incidentally, should apply to the foundation of any national theatre, be it in Britain, Canada, the United States or anywhere else.

My report can hardly have reached Australia before Mr. Chifley's Labour government was replaced by the Conservative government of Mr. Menzies. The Menzies government took a traditionally conservative view of Art, and the report fell upon stony ground.

The suggestion, however, that Australian taste might not be entirely perfect and that Australia might, in certain matters, be a decade or two behind certain other communities, aroused a tremendous head of steam. Persons who would not otherwise have given a snap of their fingers to support a national theatre felt a passionate eagerness for Australia to possess such an institution, and a passionate rage against the sneering, bloody Pommy who dared to suggest that the time was not quite yet. This may have been of some small assistance three or four years later in the promotion of The Elizabethan Theatre Trust.

Under this trust various important interests united to commemorate the first visit to Australia of the Queen, shortly after her accession, by the establishment of a theatre and an opera company. It was a conspicuous recognition of the fact that in the new Elizabethan age Australia recognized the need for such companies as a part of the national life, and recognized, too, that the quality of such things is not estimable in solely quantitative terms; that an opera or a play must not be regarded as a failure if it fails to pay its way.

In the summer of 1947, again through the agency of the British Council, Lionel Hale and I were asked to represent Great Britain at a theatre festival in Poland. Theatres all over the country were presenting plays of Shakespeare. We had no duties other than to see the various productions and, as guests from the land of Shakespeare's origin, be as cordial and agreeable as we could manage.

Hale, at the time one of the leading London dramatic critics, has since made a name as a quizmaster and interviewer. A shrewder, more observant, withal merrier, companion could hardly be imagined.

From the time our plane left Berlin, we were aware of being behind the iron curtain. We had to fly inside a narrowly prescribed route, and two Russian military planes escorted us to see that we did so.

At the airport on the outskirts of Warsaw we were met by a member of the staff of the Ministry of Culture, our host. A car and chauffeur were at our disposal and a charming girl was our interpreter. We drove through acre after acre of complete desolation. Berlin had been bad enough; this was far worse.

Eventually we arrived at the Hotel Bristol, which was rising from the ruins; our rooms seemed to have been plastered not more than ten minutes before we arrived. There was nothing in either room except a bed—very adequate—and a chair and table, but considering the total desolation around us, this seemed quite remarkable. We left our luggage and went out to a lunch party. When we got back later in the afternoon, Lionel, who had been in Intelligence during the war, declared that his luggage had been searched. He was up to all the dodges, had left clothes and papers in a certain way and found that they had been shuffled. I expect mine had been searched too. We neither of us cared; it was just interesting.

That night we were guests at a performance of the National Theatre. Completely pulverized during the war, it and the Parliament House had been the first public buildings to be rebuilt. We thought ruefully of the low degree of priority to which the British theatre had been relegated in the postwar reconstruction.

The play was *Hamlet*. The production and decor seemed to us very old-fashioned. It all looked like what we had both seen in Germany in the early twenties. The performances of the seniors were rather operatic, and the juniors were tentative. When we commented, I hope in a polite and guestlike way, on the disparity of the two styles, the director explained to us that for eight years there had been no theatre; that the casualties among the middle-age group, both men and women, had been enormous; that there literally was no intermediate stage between the veterans, whose performance he too found old-fashioned, and quite inexperienced and untrained youngsters.

The dresses were hideous, but sumptuous to the last degree. Claudius and Gertrude, for instance, never stopped changing from gold lamé to satin brocade to stamped velvet, yards and yards of it, imported, we presumed, from Italy or France at heaven knows what cost. But out of the theatre, clothing was clearly a major problem. Everyone's clothes were threadbare. In a tailor's shop I had seen suit-lengths of material, which rather resembled blotting-paper than cloth, priced at a sum in zlotys which, with the aid of our interpreter, I computed at three months' wages of a skilled workman. In a bank I had noticed quite a large check cashed by a customer dressed in rags, with rags wound round his feet instead of shoes. When we left, I gave to our chauffeur a pair of shoes, bought in Israel a few months earlier. He was almost shocked at the magnitude of the gift and his eyes filled with tears.

We asked the theatre director how he had been able to mount the production so sumptuously. He explained that, just because people were so clothes-hungry, it was the policy of the government to offer them by means of the theatre a vicarious taste of luxury and grandeur.

The next day we left by car for a quick tour. Our party was joined by a gentleman who would have been perfectly cast for the Mysterious Stranger who accosts Peer Gynt just before the shipwreck. He was of indefinite age, spoke almost no English, and as far as we could make out almost no Polish. Indeed, he hardly ever uttered. His suit, his face and hands, his hat, tie and manner all seemed to have the mildew. There were two notes of bright color: his teeth of glistering gold and, on his long thin cheeks, two vermilion smears of the most obvious rouge. We called him Ashes of Roses. Inquiries as to the identity of our new companion were rather vaguely passed off by both the interpreter and the Ministry man: "He is perhaps from one of the other Ministries. You will find him a most cultured person." Lionel and I beguiled some of the more tedious journeys by giving one another, in slow clear tones, information about the battleships on Derwentwater and the underworld of Stoke-on-Trent.

None of the Shakespearean productions seemed to us very inspired. In the provinces they were not so grand as at the National Theatre, but equally old-fashioned—illusionary scenery, involving long hammer-fraught pauses; the grand characters ranted and spouted, the comic characters were red-nosed burlesques from vaudeville. It was none of it in in what we were conditioned to regard as good taste.

Nevertheless, here were ambitious Shakespearean productions in provincial cathedral cities, in remote railroad junctions, in small coal-mining towns. We could not but reflect that if a Polish visitor were sent to Truro or Crewe or Ferry Hill he would certainly not see a performance of Shakespeare, let alone a foreign classic. If he saw anything at all, it would be the twice-nightly performance of a grubby little entertainment entitled *Bottoms Up* or *Stripped for Action*.

The fact that we did not greatly admire their style did not alter the fact that these were serious interpretations of masterworks which were being seen, and evidently enjoyed, by large and essentially "popular" audiences.

At each performance, during one of the many intervals, the manager would come before the curtain and make a speech of welcome to the two visitors from the land of Shakespeare's birth. The speech always evoked a tremendous, an extravagant ovation. We did not get up and bow, and indeed there would have been no point in doing so. Our bows would not have been seen because the house lights were out. Also, we were fully aware that the ovation was not for us personally, two completely unknown and unimportant individuals. It was the fact that visitors from the West were still at large in Poland. It was not till the third or fourth of these occasions that we tumbled to the significance of the darkened auditoria. With the lights extinguished "They" could not see who was, and who was not, joining in the demonstration.

On our return to Warsaw we went to a brilliant performance of *Much Ado About Nothing*. It was given in a small
ramshackle place, a sort of cellar. The decor was simple but
extremely ingenious. The director, quite a young fellow, had
clearly no large subsidy. The single but not inconsiderable
asset was the great talent of the director and his company
of young actors.

Prizes were given by the Ministry of Culture for the productions which were considered best. The National Theatre
was awarded first place; this production of *Much Ado* was at
the bottom of the list. It was never said in so many words, but
we got the impression that this was because the young director and his group were considered politically unreliable.

Hale had to leave at the end of our assignment. But I had
a day or two to put in before a theatre conference in Prague.
I elected to stay on in Warsaw now that there was more
leisure to look around. I was free to wander at will. If Ashes
of Roses were keeping an eye on me, I never noticed.

I wandered about in the utter desolation of what had been
the ghetto and the scene of incredible carnage and horror.
To say that not one stone was left upon another would be
misleading. There were not even stones—just powdered,
totally unidentifiable rubble. The only recognizable article
I saw was a little bit of the hand of a marble statuette. Here
once had been a home, with pictures and books and works
of art; pleasant dinner parties perhaps, with wine and good
talk and afterwards music.

I left the ghetto. A rough, narrow track led through rubble
piled ten or twelve feet high on either side. Eventually I
came to the meeting place of four such tracks. I learned
afterwards that this had once been the heart of the business
quarter—the equivalent of the Wall Street district in New
York.

When I got there it was absolutely deserted and absolutely
silent. The wind stirred some half-charred fragments of paper
and I could hear them rustle. Faintly I heard twelve chime
from the distant ragged belfry of what had once been a

rococo cathedral. Once, this spot must have been humming with cars and buses and taxis and trucks of merchandise and scurrying multitudes pouring out of offices for their midday break. As I looked down one of the four rubble-piled alleys, a little old man scrambled out of a hole and laboriously onto the top of the wreckage. He had a sieve of corn: "Took, took, took!" he called and five or six fowls appeared from the surrounding wilderness; they were perky and plump and their feathers gleamed in the pleasant, soft, June sunshine.

When I left for Prague, the Ministry man and the interpreter saw me off at the railroad— I cannot say station, for there was none. The tracks just ended in a pile of wreckage. It was like, indeed it was, a railhead on a deserted battlefield. It seemed wildly incongruous to climb into an entirely conventional railway coach upholstered in blue velvet.

Just as the train was leaving, a mildewed figure appeared from nowhere. In its dusty hand a dusty handful of faded worts. He thrust them into my hand; the train was now moving, he swarmed onto the platform of the coach.

"See, Mister," he said in ashen tones, "Forget-me-not."

Then two damp and dusty hands clamped themselves to my face. He implanted a sickening kiss upon my cheek.

"Ta-ta, Mister, and forget me not."

I never shall.

19

Ireland

IT IS A MATTER of some regret to me that, so far, I have made no great effort to join in the theatrical life of my own country.

I am just too young to remember the great days of the Abbey Theatre at the turn of the century, when, with the Moscow Art Theatre, it led the world, introducing great new plays and revivifying old ones by the freshness and energy of the acting. In the early nineteen-twenties when I first knew it, the Abbey was past its peak. Synge was dead; Yeats and Lady Gregory were getting old, but O'Casey was at his zenith.

Juno and the Paycock and *The Plough and the Stars* were two powerful fireworks to shoot from a small and lowly endowed organization in a small, remote island. The company which launched them comprised some powerful and brilliant personalities—P. J. McCormick, Arthur Sinclair, Barry Fitzgerald, Sydney Morgan and those two extraordinary sisters Sara Allgood and Maire O'Neill. But gradually the team fell apart, and no new talent of the same quality has yet appeared. Sean O'Casey's two masterpieces have had no successors. The glory has departed.

It is inevitable that theatres, like all other human institu-

tions, should have their ups and downs. Maybe the Abbey
after the incandescent early years is suffering only a long, but
still temporary, decline, and will again shine forth. I hope so.

Let us consider the reason for the incandescence and the
decline.

The theatre was the principal artistic expression of a political and philosophical ferment. Its policy was created, and
its day-to-day decisions taken, by persons in whom were
combined the enthusiastic idealism of political and artistic
amateurs with a great deal of practical good sense and energy;
a background of exceptional cultivation and talent with the
authority of a ruling class.

After 1916, victory in the political battle was assured for
Irish nationalism. As so often happens, the idealism and
enthusiasm which inspire the fighters in a desperate battle
evaporates when the stress of battle is relaxed. The qualities
which win a war are not those best adapted to the entirely
different problems of peace.

Inevitably the victory of Irish nationalism was followed by
the suppression of the old ruling class, the Protestant and
English-educated ascendancy. It is not clear what body has
inherited the ascendancy in political and social power.

Organized labor has never carried great weight in Ireland,
where factory workers are far outnumbered by agricultural
workers, of whom a high proportion own their own farms.

The Catholic hierarchy has always had a powerful hold on
Irish affairs. But simple peasant faith was more easily commanded before motorcars, buses, airplanes, radio and television
began to spread urban sophistication everywhere. Several
times the Church's interdicts or commands have proved
ineffectual. The ever-accelerating rush of young people to the
more lucrative employment available in England or America
seems to indicate that the opportunities for the devout life
which Holy and Catholic Ireland undoubtedly affords can be
outbid by other attractions.

Probably power in Ireland now resides where it does in
most other countries, in the hands of those who control large

business. This is the sort of power which, in the twentieth century, we all seem both consciously and subconsciously to understand, to covet and to fear.

At all events, power has passed completely from the grasp of the old ascendancy. Even were there today a Lady Gregory or a Yeats, they would not, by virtue of their position, command the sort of authority which almost automatically was theirs in the early years of this century. On the contrary, their social and educational background would now be a positive disadvantage, so strong that even talents as outstanding as theirs would find it hard to make headway against the prejudice which such a background now excites.

Thus with the victory of Irish nationalism, the Abbey Theatre both lost the main political and philosophic incentive for its existence, and also passed out of the control of benevolent aristocrats.

In theory, it should have been just as inspiring to express the dawn of a new era, to be the mouthpiece of freedom in the new Irish Free State. In practice, it seemed to have been more inspiring to long for the dawn, rather than to hail the sunrise. In theory, it should have been possible for the new state to throw up new leaders as idealistic, as intelligent, as the old ones, but more representative of the people, the newly liberated nation. In fact, there was no violent overthrow of the theatre's old guard. Lady Gregory, Yeats, and Lennox Robinson all stayed on, respected and loved, till their deaths (Robinson's as late as 1958). But as, one by one, they dropped out, others of like caliber were not there to replace them.

The Free State offered to the Abbey Theatre a subsidy—not very large, but then there was not much to offer. In return, however, for the subsidy the theatre accepted various not very onerous conditions: there would be so many productions each year in the Irish language; the actors must also pass an examination which proved them proficient in the Irish language; the theatre's director must be acceptable to the government.

In the early days of the Free State it was understandable, perhaps right, that there should be an attempt to revive the Gaelic tongue. English, fairly enough, symbolized foreign domination. The native language, as de Valera claimed, was the very fountain of nationhood. In theory it was understandable, perhaps right, that Irish be compulsory in the schools. In practice it simply has not worked. After more than thirty years of compulsory Irish in schools, of concentrated propaganda in favor of the language, it still is no more widely spoken than in the past. Public notices are written in Irish; but whenever it is necessary that the public should be fully aware of their import, an English translation is added. No work of literature has appeared in Irish which has received even local popularity, let alone serious critical acclaim. The Abbey Theatre, by insisting that its company be proficient in the language, have further narrowed the already narrow field from which its actors can be drawn. Instead of making some counterinducement to the higher salaries and great opportunities available in London or New York, they have interposed a barrier between the Abbey and a considerable proportion of would-be actors. And for what practical reason? The Irish-language policy at the Abbey conforms with political doctrine and is a condition of the subsidy. But, in practice, the Abbey plays in English. Occasionally, when the play is short, an after-piece is given in Irish, and once a year, at Christmas, a pantomime is produced in Irish. These Irish pantomimes do not present any serious rivalry to commercial pantomime productions, imported into Dublin from England and indistinguishable from similar productions in Preston, Bradford and other provincial cities. The Abbey pantomime is a good deal more tasteful in decor, but also more amateurish in performance and no more serious in aim. It has no commercial appeal whatever.

For the rest, the Abbey's productions in English tend more and more to be exactly what the founders of the Abbey were trying to avoid: commercialized stereotypes of Irish life, bearing little relation to any realities in Ireland, or indeed to any reality at all. The successful ones exploit old stage situations —Uncle's will is the favorite—are peopled by stagey characters, and differ only from other successful plays in that they are written and acted in a dialect which, though not particularly authentic, is unquestionably a beguiling and effective medium for actors.

For the dearth of distinguished or interesting plays it would be most unfair to blame the directors of the Abbey. They are faced, like all theatre directors outside the great metropolitan centers, with the fact that almost every author will try to sell his work in the most profitable market.

What competing advantages can the Abbey offer to playwrights? Not better casting. There are more Irish actors in London or New York than there are in Dublin, and of just as good quality; indeed most of the best-known Irish "names" are to be found abroad, not at home. A success in London or New York will make a hundred times more money than a success in Dublin; and anyway a Dublin production is bound to follow. Whereas a successful Dublin production by no means ensures subsequent productions elsewhere.

Criticism abroad will tend to be more influential, better informed and far more indulgent than on the home ground. Audiences will be no less intelligent and probably warmer— London and New York are incurably sentimental about what they like to call the Brogue.

The poor old Abbey is left with no trumps in its hand. Authors who are professionals, who have wives, children, rent and income tax to think of, and who wish to eat, cannot afford the luxury of offering their work first to the Abbey just out of sentiment.

So the Abbey, like any other small management, gets very few plays which have not already been rejected by Broadway and the West End of London. Occasionally, of course, the stone which Broadway and the West End reject becomes the head of the corner. But this does not happen often. I for one do not subscribe to the belief that there exists a vast body of unproduced masterpieces just because all the metropolitan managers, agents, producers, actors and directors are too dull to know a good thing when they see it.

As well as the Abbey, Dublin has the Gate Theatre, which has for many years been operated by Lord Longford, sometimes under his own management, sometimes rented to tenants. Distinguished productions were done there by Hilton Edwards and Micheal MacLiammoir. MacLiammoir is easily the most impressive actor on the current Irish stage. He belongs to the old school—broadly, unashamedly romantic. He is a wonderful verse-speaker and has great humor. I admire him because he has stuck to the idea of an Irish theatre in Ireland, although he could certainly have earned more money and recognition in the cosmopolitan market.

Dublin also offers a varied succession of intimate, artistic theatrical ventures—the Pike, for instance, and the Globe. They are what our grandparents called Theatre Royal Back Drawing Room, but the endeavor is often serious and the result sometimes interesting; but not, I think, quite as interesting as enthusiastic admirers of Dublin like to make out. I have seen comparable manifestations, of much the same standard, in Bradford, Manchester, Middlesbrough, Brighton, in American universities and little theatres and even—this will not be believed in Dublin—in Belfast.

Belfast, the only other city in Ireland large enough to support an indigenous theatre, has not the same theatrical tradition as Dublin. Also, although the two cities have populations of approximately the same size, Dublin the capital of Eire has an advantage over Belfast, which, as the capital of Northern Ireland, is the nucleus of a much smaller population.

Nevertheless, in the last twenty years the standard of local theatrical production has in many respects been higher in the north than in the south. In Belfast the Arts Theatre has a respectable record of productions of significant plays in the international field, while the Group Theatre has specialized in the production of plays in Ulster dialect. It is interesting that George Shiels and Joseph Tomelty, the two most successful Irish dramatists of the last twenty or thirty years, are

Catholic Ulstermen writing in the Ulster dialect. Their work has had better productions in the north, where the actors are better able to realize the characterization and atmosphere of the plays, as well as the authentic dialect. But it has been more warmly appreciated in the Catholic south.

The theatre in Belfast is bedeviled with the same basic problem as is Dublin, or indeed any regional center: the irresistible magnetism of London, New York and Hollywood; the centers not only of stage production, but of radio, television and moving pictures. Irresistibly, as promising young people appear and begin to make an impression in the local theatres, whether as writers, actors, designers or directors, they get lured away into the more lucrative and exciting, but also desperately overcrowded, metropolitan field.

It is at the present time a universal disease. It affects the theatre everywhere. The likeliest cure I can foresee is a drastic decentralization of the mass-producing media.

The provinciality of provincial towns is, however, largely of their own making. It is not entirely thrust upon them by the suction of the metropolis. The Glasgow, Belfast, Dublin or Manchester bourgeoisie all hate and despise their own local accent. They ape metropolitan manners and taste, and will only accept artists who are recognized "successes" and "celebrities." Exactly the same principle applies in the United States. It is not the suction of New York, but their own provinciality which draws the cultural life out of other cities.

Success and celebrity are generated only in the metropolitan cities because only thence issue the newspapers, radio and TV programs which command a national circulation. Therefore it is almost impossible for a local writer or actor to gain the celebrity, which commands the respect of his fellow-citizens and a decent wage, until after he has been away and conquered the metropolis. But by then he will tend to have severed his old roots. His home, his friends, his professional contacts will now be metropolitan, the old home town will be home no longer. Both the artist and his provincial audience will be the poorer because their connection is now only a

matter of sentiment, not in any sense an indispensable tie
of mutual interest.

I have felt this lack of local attachment as a considerable
handicap in my own professional life. My principal professional loyalty has been to the Old Vic. It is the nearest thing
I have known to a professional home, an artistic root. But I
was not grafted onto this root until, at thirty-three years old,
the most impressionable and formative years were already behind me. Nor does the Old Vic connect directly with any part
of my family or regional background.

The natural places for me to have worked were Belfast, Edinburgh, Dublin or Glasgow. These are the cities with which
by derivation I am most closely connected, and to whose life
I should most have liked to make some small enrichment.
Belfast and Glasgow gave me my start but, like almost all
other young people in the theatre, I was soon sucked into
the metropolitan vortex. The sunction was hard to resist but
it would not be true to say that it was irresistible. I think I
could probably have made a living in any one of these four
cities. But it would have been uphill work and I do not think
that, quite apart from other metropolitan dividends in the
form of better pay and wider reputation, I could have had the
chance to do half such interesting, serious and varied work
as has been possible through being less firmly rooted and
more mobile.

Shortly after I left Glasgow—somewhere around 1929—
Lennox Robinson took me out to lunch in London and asked
me to go as producer to the Abbey Theatre in Dublin. I
was not free at the time, but I think if I had indicated a real
enthusiasm plans might have been rearranged to enable me
to go there a little later.

In a sentimental way I have often half-regretted that this
connection was never made. But it has only been a half-
regret. I have no belief that I could have arrested the Abbey's
decline; that was beyond the power of any single individual.
And I do not think, feeling as I do about the Irish language
policy, about extreme political nationalism, literary censor-

ship, and the dominance of the Catholic, or indeed of any
other, Church, that mine would have been a felicitous appointment. I would have fought desperately to keep the
Abbey a theatre of ideas, to resist the commercial attraction
of the cosy folksy wee comedies, and to create a company
technically equipped to deal with a classic repertory, albeit
in Irish dialect and with a distinctively Irish slant. But I see
no means by which the bleeding away of the liveliest talent,
the ineluctable flow to the metropolitan centers, could have
been prevented. And that is the final reason why at the
present time, not only the Abbey Theatre in Dublin, but
provincial stages all over the world are in a state of chronic
and pernicious anemia.

Over the years I have worked in Dublin but three times:
a production of *Hamlet* for Ronald Ibbs in 1950 and a radio
production for Radio Eireann of *Peer Gynt* in 1954, and for
Cyril Cusack, a few months later, a production of a new
play of O'Casey called *The Bishop's Bonfire.*

Ronald Ibbs is a very clever English character actor who
married a witty, intelligent Irish girl called Maureen Halli-
gan. For ten years or so they ran their own company, sometimes in Ireland, sometimes in the United States. They managed to "tick-over" financially but a fatal lack of any consistent, or indeed intelligible, policy prevented their efforts
from having artistic significance.

Hamlet was put on as part of a season at the Gate Theatre,
a small art theatre, sandwiched between two ill-assorted English commercial comedies from the company's touring repertory. The actors were a handful of seasoned old touring pros accustomed to quelling the Irish populace from Dundalk to
Kenmare; but, since *Hamlet* demands a larger cast than the
plays they usually presented, the group was augmented at
rather a late stage with some young people of different degrees of talent but alike in inexperience.

We rehearsed for two weeks. Carl Bonn, who designed
and made the set and dresses, achieved good results on a
small budget; Ibbs gave a lightweight, graceful, accomplished

performance; there was a good Horatio from Godfrey Quigley and Coralie Carmichael made of Gertrude a clinging, gauntly feverish neurotic, which was rather hauntingly impressive.

Coralie Carmichael died last year. She was a strikingly beautiful Italian-looking woman with great black eyes and a deep sweet voice. There was something about her of Thackeray's Miss Fotheringay. She was a Jewess, from Manchester I think, and had been, as the saying is, born in a theatrical basket. Her temperament was gentle, serene and kind. Through long experience she was a competent player and often looked and sounded marvelous. But she lacked any spark of artistic originality. On the stage she did what she was told obediently, capably, pleasantly, but added little of her own. And she lacked the push, the restless demonic energy which alone lifts a player into the front rank. Coralie was content to be as she was. She liked the life of a touring, or provincial, player: knitting and companionable chats in drafty, grimy dressing rooms, the brightly lit two hours of painted fantasy, then the long trudge through the rain, under the railway arch, past the gasworks, round by the Sacred Heart Convent to the digs and cocoa in a thermos, with an early rehearsal or a still earlier train call on the morrow.

Radio Eireann occupies two frowsty floors high, high above Dublin's General Post Office. You enter by a sort of tradesman's entrance in a side street. Discouraged elderly attendants tell you that the lift is out of order, so you toil up endless stairs which smell of the lavatories and of mutton fat from the Post Office Canteen. The repertory company consists of fifteen or twenty men and women held captive under long, safe contracts. Most of their tasks are pretty dreary; and it is certainly hard to preserve enthusiasm if you work all day and every day in the airless vaults of a radio studio. I found it hard going to create the slightest sense of occasion, the slightest feeling that *Peer Gynt* was not just one more script to be read aloud, the rehearsals one more tedious chore to be got through. Even the actor who played Peer, a talented fellow, was often late at rehearsals, often inattentive; I could perceive in him little reverence, or excitement, none of what I would consider appropriate sentiments for a young player to whom is entrusted the recreation of one of the greatest characters in all dramatic literature.

The Bishop's Bonfire was a no less unsatisfactory experience. The management, having, apparently small confidence in the commercial aspect of the venture, had hired us all extremely cheap by appealing to our "loyalty"—loyalty to O'Casey, to Ireland, to Art, to the Management—it was never quite clear. After a few days' rehearsal, I learned that the younger members of the company were working almost for nothing and had been told that there was no more money for them because I, the "guest producer," had insisted on such an enormous salary. Since I too was being paid very badly, I made a fuss. I called a meeting of the company, told them the facts about my salary and challenged the manager to deny them. There was an uncomfortable scene, and the lowest salaries were raised; but the morale of the company was lowered and, inevitably, the relations between myself and the management were thenceforth rather chilly.

The play is not of the same caliber as O'Casey's masterpieces. But I think we failed to do justice to both its broad humor, broader satire and rather luridly purple patches. Moreover, the atmosphere of the first night did not help.

The last O'Casey play to open in Dublin had been The Plough and the Stars at the Abbey some thirty years earlier. On that occasion there was a riot in the theatre. Members of the audience, objecting to the rather cruel satire of the play, had stormed the stage; the actors fought them back with fists, nails and teeth; no one was actually killed and a good time was had by all.

Word had got around that The Bishop's Bonfire, like The Plough and the Stars, was not just a bouquet laid at the silver feet of Kathleen ni Houlihaun, nor yet a penitent heretic's apologia to Mother Church. Dublin knew its own

Sean O'Casey; Dublin suspected that there might be some
fun—a body, maybe, swinging from the chandelier of the
Gaiety, an aged widow savaged in the orchestra stalls, a
child or two trampled to pulp.

By lunchtime on the day of the performance you could not
get into the street where the theatre stands. At three in the
afternoon the mounted police were called to clear the crowds.
When the doors opened the police had to be called again,
because about a thousand people were storming into a gallery
which holds less than three hundred. There was another
storm when Catholic students from the National University
started to boo in the street, because they regarded O'Casey
as a renegade Irishman. They were answered by Protestant
students from Trinity College who made a counterdemonstration in O'Casey's favor.

The streets were ringing with boos and cheers when the
little lady who leads the theatre's orchestra—violin, 'cello and
an exceedingly upright Ibach—struck up, for reasons which
she and her God alone can have known, with a spirited rendi-
tion of *The Bells of Aberdovey.* "No!" yelled the gallery.
"Irish music! Make it Irish." Programs were folded into paper
darts and hurled at the orchestra pit. The rest of the theatre
took up the cry "Make it Irish, Irish, Irish!" and likewise
pelted the orchestra pit, where the little lady, in a flutter of
fear, paper darts and sheet music, was replacing Middleton's
Leek with the *Shamrock.*

Meantime, the students, hearing the noise within, re-
doubled their efforts in the street. Soon, however, for reasons
which I do not know, the national faction withdrew, leaving
Trinity in possession of the field. "We want O'Casey," they
chanted. "We want O'Casey." The curtain was now up and
the actors were finding the competition rather severe. The day
was saved by a fatherly old policeman. He stood in a doorway
at the top of a flight of steps:

"Listen," he said to the Trinity boys. "Are youse fellers for
O'Casey?"

"We are. *We want O'Casey!*"

"Well then for Jesus' sake will ye f— off and let them that have paid for it hear what your man wrote."

And straightway they f—ed off, leaving behind them a silence which could be felt, into which the lines of the play fell like thin rain into a bucket.

The actors, all keyed up to do or die, had spent themselves in the play's first forty minutes. At first the audience played up—supposedly anti-Irish or anticlerical lines were received with jeers and hisses or, by the minority, with exaggerated laughter and applause. But gradually it became apparent that the jokes were not of the finest vintage, the satire not very pointed, the plot a little "hammy" and the performance, in spite of manful efforts by Eddie Byrne and Sean Kavanagh, a little amateurish. By the end of the second act the excitement had fizzed away. The audience was like a wedding party after the departure of the bride; after the elation of the nuptials and the unwonted champagne comes the reaction: a melancholy, punctuated by hiccups.

By the end of the last act torpor was turning to positive vexation. Cyril Cusack came forward at the curtain call and made a long, prepared speech in Irish. After thanking the audience for its wonderful reception, he gave a harangue on behalf of tolerance and liberty. Under this final douche of cold water, *The Bishop's Bonfire*, which had never quite blazed, fizzled finally into a heap of damp ashes.

Next day the Catholic and nationalist papers outdid one another in gleeful and ignorant vituperation. The English press, in deference to O'Casey's great reputation, was polite and praised, so far as possible, the occasional flashes of the old fire. It had been an inglorious venture. The play will, I hope, eventually be revived and done well enough to show that it is not entirely unworthy of its illustrious creator.

My theatrical experiences in Belfast have been much happier. In 1950 I was asked to direct a company which the government of Northern Ireland would subsidize and send to London with three productions. We prepared a satirical comedy by George Shiels called *The Passing Day*; a new play,

Danger, Men at Work, by John D. Stewart and an obscure eighteenth-century comedy called *The Sham Prince*, which Jack Loudan adapted so that the action took place in Belfast about 1800.

The Sham Prince was entirely unsuited to the company and only avoided disastrous failure by the skin of its teeth. *Danger, Men at Work* concerns a superior Englishman who is sent to take charge of a big construction job and makes a hash of his relation with the Irish workers. The Ulster actors did splendidly; but the imported Englishman proved unsuitable to his role. His engagement was a misjudgment on my part, which did great harm to the first venture of a highly promising author.

The Passing Day was right in the bull's-eye. In a brilliant composite set by Tanya Moiseiwitsch, the company gave a superb display of teamwork; and in the leading role Joseph Tomelty scored a ringing success.

In 1958 I was engaged by the Ulster Group to present a new play by Gerard MacLarnon. By an odd coincidence this was called *The Bonfire*. Its action takes place against a background of political and religious intolerance, which leads to violence. The crowd scenes, the bigotry and hysteria were wonderfully written and acted and rather overwhelmed the play's centerpiece, the interesting but incompletely realized character of a young woman. The production was to represent Ulster at the Edinburgh Festival; and we played a preliminary week in Belfast to run it in.

The picture of dear old Belfast which we presented was, in my opinion, true to life. But it was not exactly the version that the Tourist Board might care to exhibit to strangers. There was no end of a hullabaloo. Though there was no demonstration in the theatre, letters poured into the newspapers from those regular correspondents, Disgusted, Pro Bono Publico, and Mother of Nine; questions were asked in Parliament; a deputation of enraged councilors waited upon the Lord Mayor, demanding that he have the offending play withdrawn.

Whether it was a good or bad thing I do not know. In the event there was no violence, and I cannot but feel it was good that the goings-on in Belfast on the eleventh and twelfth of July, with which the play was concerned, seemed, at least to some people, shocking and primitive to a high degree. From the limited viewpoint of the company, it was of great advantage. For a brief moment, the theatre in general and ourselves in particular were the topic of the hour—ladies under iron bluebells in the hairdressers discussed *The Bonfire*; gentlemen in clubs, and men in pubs discussed *The Bonfire*; an arty play, which, at the height of summer in a city not renowned for its support of the arts, might have been proud to play to fifty per cent of capacity, played to completely packed houses. Naturally, when we got to Edinburgh nobody felt particularly steamed up about the politics, but the energy and skill of the actors was the object of suitable admiration.

I have had a further contact with the actors in Northern Ireland in connection with programs of reading aloud. These were the idea of Jack Loudan, a bright spark, then acting as the Secretary of CEMA, a body entrusted with the spending of limited public funds upon artistic projects in the provinces.

Loudan believed that a group of good readers with well-chosen material, carefully presented, would be good entertainment; as good as a play, far less expensive to prepare, and more mobile. Loudan was right. Our first program, presented in the hall of the Y.M.C.A., sweet with the odors of sanctity and stale cake, was a distinct success. At subsequent performances we have improved the method of presentation, broadened the repertory and are gradually feeling the way to what I think has great possibilities as a form of entertainment.

It bears to the performance of a play rather the same relation as chamber music to opera. It is not particularly suitable for massive commercial distribution, but for the right audience it can provide, I believe, almost perfect entertainment. It demands, like chamber music, an intimate relation between performers and audience; the audience must be will-

ing to come out to meet the performance. Attention will not
be bludgeoned by great "effects"; this is not the whirlwind,
but the still, small voice.

As a form of entertainment I commend it to concert and
literary societies, and as a substitute for one of the least satisfactory methods of imparting information, feelings or ideas
—the lecture. But mere reading aloud is not enough. The
material should be most carefully fitted to the measure of
each audience; the readers must have skill and charm; and
I hope it is not professional egotism to say that, however
good they are, they cannot just be left to their own devices.
A director is necessary to guide the interpretation, to balance one item against others, and to be responsible for *mise
en scène*.

20

Edinburgh

IN 1947, largely due to the energy of Mr. Rudolf Bing and Audrey Christie, the wife of the founder of the Glyndebourne Opera, the Edinburgh International Festival of Music and Art was inaugurated.

For some years Bing had cherished the idea of Edinburgh as a festival center. Architecturally magnificent, seat of an ancient and distinguished culture—the Athens of the North —it was also exceptionally well provided with tourist accommodation. It was a great triumph for Bing that he was able to "sell" the idea of a festival on the grand scale to a City Council no more renowned than any other for artistic enthusiasm or dashing imagination, to the fathers of the capital city of that nation which exceeds all other nations in caution and clings more strongly than other nations to the appallingly fallacious economic doctrine that "if you take care of the pence the pounds will take care of themselves." Bing could never have succeeded if it had not been for the Lord Provost in office at the time, Sir John Falconer, who put himself heart and soul behind the project and brought to bear his powerful local influence, intelligence, integrity, humor and charm.

The festival was intended to be truly international. Beginning right at the end of the war, it was meant to show that art has no frontiers. The intention has been realized. Each year a visiting opera company plays in the King's, the largest theatre—Glyndebourne, Stüttgart, Stockholm, Hamburg have all been represented. In the smaller Lyceum Theatre "straight" plays are offered, both English and American, with, for one week each year, some celebrated European ensemble—the Piccolo Teatro from Milan, Jean Vilar from Paris, Gründgens from Düsseldorf. In addition, at the Empire, a vast house normally dedicated to vaudeville, there is ballet by all the world-famous troupes.

Then at the Usher Hall there are choral and symphony concerts arranged round one of the great orchestras of the world; and in various smaller halls chamber music, recitals of songs and intimate musical goings-on by internationally known performers. The Scottish National Gallery puts on a great one-man show by a master, whose works are loaned from all over the world—one year Dégas, another Dufy, another Braque; or maybe, as last year, some celebrated collection is loaned entire, like the pictures from Munich's Pinakothek.

On the esplanade of Edinburgh Castle, perched on its precipitous rock in the very center of the city the army puts on a Tattoo, predominantly Scottish in flavor. This occurs near midnight, is a superb spectacle and draws every night a crowd of five thousand, which, if there were space, could easily be doubled.

These are just the centerpieces. There is a mass of other activity. Visitors come from all over the world—the trade in antiques alone must be worth an incredible sum—everyone flies around taking snapshots, drinking whiskey, meeting contraltos from Antigua, admiring the Floral Clock, buying thicker underclothes, gasping at Rizzio's bloodstains, requesting the autograph of a Mrs. Wishart of Motherwell under the impression that she is Katina Paxinou. It is all very gay. Everyone enjoys it, except my Edinburgh cousins who complain of the phenomenal and outrageous rise in the price of carrots.

To get this gigantic program into operation was a truly extraordinary feat, especially as, in the first year, there were still food rationing, clothes rationing and a general and very real exhaustion to be overcome, as well as the traditional caution of the Scots.

Rudolf Bing has told me how, after long and often difficult diplomacy, the great, complicated plan was about to be put into effect. Negotiations were far advanced with orchestras, opera companies, theatres, ballet groups; budgets had been agreed upon; subscriptions had been promised; printing was in proof. Just as the curtain was, so to say, about to go up, Mr. Bing had one of his ideas. Permission was sought, and granted, to put it before the City Fathers.

"How splendid," purred Mr. Bing, turning on the full battery of Viennese charm, "and how entirely appropriate if the Festival could be inaugurated by *High Mass* in Saint Giles' Cathedral."

"*Popery!*" The blood of the elderly bailies first froze, then boiled, in their Presbyterian veins.

"It might," added Bing, aware of the tension, "be the beginning."

"It might also," replied an anonymous bailie, "be the end."

The whole project, Bing says, very nearly collapsed then and there and was only saved by the tact and promptness of Sir John Falconer, who explained how Mr. Bing as a foreigner and an artist, in fact little more than a babe in arms, could not be expected to appreciate the blasphemous enormity which he had uttered. Fingers were wagged, eyebrows raised, shoulders shrugged, and a resolution was passed that *A Service of Dedication* would take place in the Cathedral. The great band wagon rolled on.

The first festival was a resounding success. But here and there voices were heard to protest that the term "international" need not necessarily exclude Scottish art and artists.

It was resolved that one of the offerings of the second festival should be a Scots play in the vernacular.

James Bridie, at the head of a small committee, approached me as a sort of mongrel Scot, who had many associations with and old friends in the Scottish theatre. It was suggested that I produce one of the classics of the Scottish drama. Bridie added that, if you exclude Barrie, and of course he was too modest to think of including his own work, there were really only three Scots plays which could possibly be considered classics. Two were from the eighteenth century: *The Gentle Shepherd*, a pastoral in verse by the portrait painter Alan Ramsay, and *Douglas* by John Home, a historical tragedy in verse greatly admired in its day—indeed, in the hubbub of enthusiasm which followed the first production in London, a Scottish partisan was heard to bawl "Whaur's your Wullie Shakespeare the noo?" The third classic is far older. It was written about 1540 by a prominent official of the Scottish royal court, Sir David Lyndsay, and bears the rather formidable title *Ane Satire of the Thrie Estaites*.

To read it is a considerable chore. It is about three times the length of *Hamlet*—if played entire it would last seven hours, so I have been told; but I think the accuracy of the statement is unlikely to be tested. It is written in a lingo which daunts even enthusiasts for the Doric; "which," for example, appears as "quwhilke"; about thirty per cent of the words sent me scurrying to the glossary.

Gradually, as I toiled through the formidable text, it began to dawn that here was an opportunity to put into practice some of the theories which, through the years, I had been longing to test. Scene after scene seemed absolutely unplayable on a proscenium stage, almost meaningless in terms of "dramatic illusion"; but seemed at the same time to offer fascinating possibilities, if they could be set and acted in a manner which I felt, rather than clearly apprehended; saw—but through a thick glass mighty darkly.

I told Bridie that, of the three scripts, I thought the satire—which had never, so far as record goes, been played since the sixteenth century—was much the most powerful and interesting. We discussed my theory about the staging. We agreed that a version, greatly abbreviated, must be prepared.

"I think I know the right man," said Bridie. "You must meet."

A few weeks later, over drinks, Bridie introduced me to Robert Kemp. I remember him coming in, out of the Edinburgh drizzle, with a thick tweed overcoat, a tweed cap of a kind which went "out" when my father was a lad, with a thick ashplant in his hand, much more like a cattle dealer than an author. We discussed *The Three Estates*, got on fine and have been the best of friends from that instant.

Next day in downpours of rain we set out to find a suitable place to stage the play. Bridie, Kemp, William Graham of the festival office and myself, in a noble old Daimler with a noble old chauffeur, lent by the municipality. We visited big halls and wee halls. Halls ancient and modern, halls secular and halls holy, halls upstairs and halls in cellars, dance halls, skating rinks, lecture halls and beer halls.

The rain continued to pour. We got extremely wet and Bridie, as our physician, advised, as a precaution against the cold, that we sample the demon rum. We looked at several more halls, and several more rums. The quest waxed hilarious. Bridie and the noble old chauffeur began to sing, as our Daimler careered wildly from a swimming bath, which we were assured could be emptied, in the extreme east of the city, to the recreation hall of a steam laundry in the city's extreme west. Darkness was falling; the street lamps were reflected in the puddles. The repertoire of our singers was nearly exhausted: the limousine was out of gas; William Graham was asleep on its flyblown cushions; I was beginning to be acutely conscious that I had led them all a wild-goose chase. Then spake Kemp in the tone of one who hates to admit something unpleasant: "There *is* the Assembly Hall."

The minute I got inside I knew that we were home. It is large and square in the Gothic style of about 1850. It has deep galleries and a raked floor sloping down to where, in the center, the Moderator's throne is set within a railed enclosure. The seats have sage-green cushions; there are endless stone corridors. Halfway up the steep black approach—it stands on one of the precipitous spurs of the Castle Rock—is a minatory statue of John Knox. There are endless portraits of departed pillars of the Kirk, including, as I was afterwards to discover, a very nice one by Harvey of my great-grandfather preaching alfresco in the Highlands.

None of the others thought the Hall particularly suitable; but they were impressed by my enthusiastic certainty and it was agreed that the Kirk authorities be approached as to its use for a play. The Scottish Kirk, with its austere reputation, might have been expected to take a dim view of mountebanks tumbling and painted women strutting before men in its Assembly Hall. On the contrary, no difficulties were raised; no one suggested censoring the bluer portions of the text or issued fussy interdicts about tobacco, alcohol or dressing rooms. There was a single stipulation: no nails must be knocked into the Moderator's throne.

Robert Kemp made a most able version of the play, cutting it down to a length endurable by a modern audience, eliminating a great deal of theological argument which seemed rather to have lost the urgency it may once have possessed—the original play contains a sermon which would last for fully half an hour; removing a great deal of coarseness, though enough was left to make old ladies sit up and blink; clarifying and simplifying the story. We were left with an entertainment in two parts. The protagonist is an allegorical character called King Humanitie. He is surrounded by a group of Young Sparks, under whose influence he admits to his court Dame Sensualitie and her attendant damsels. The Virtues—Veritie, Chastitie and Gude Counsel—are banished; the Vices—Flatterie, Falsehood and Deceit—are made welcome. Humanitie is all set for a grand spree when Divine Correction arrives and calls him to account.

In the second part Divine Correction sits at the King's right hand while various abuses in the realm, political, social and

especially ecclesiastical, are set right. The cause of a down-
trodden Poor Man is powerfully urged by John the Common-
weal, an embodiment of the eloquent and idealistic revolutionary. There is some hard-hitting stuff at the expense of
Ecclesiarchs, and the play ends with the merry spectacle of
a Public Hanging; gallows are brought, the three Vices are
strung up and the cast troops gaily out to Paradise leaving the
bodies dangling.

The cast is huge: thirty speaking parts and cohorts of singers, soldiers and supernumeraries to the tune of nearly a hundred souls. Mollie MacEwan designed the dresses and properties which were all made, and very well made, in Edinburgh,
mostly by volunteer lady helpers ready to stitch to the death
for the artistic glory of Caledonia. Cedric Thorpe-Davie conducted his own excellent score.

The stage was a tryout, on my part; a first sketch for the
sort of Elizabethan stage I had long hoped, somehow and
somewhere, to establish. The Moderator's chair and the table
before it, in the center of the hall, were enclosed under
a platform attainable from each of three sides by steps. Behind, and above the fourth side, a gallery was attainable by
two flights of stairs. The space under this gallery could be
closed or exposed at will by drawing curtains.

I am not sure that some of the liberties we took with
Lyndsay were justified. Robert Kemp was completely faithful
—he merely trimmed and clipped, but added nothing of his
own. I, on the other hand, ventured to present the gay
courtiers and their flighty lady-friends with rather more indulgence than the author may have intended. The Virtues,
on the other hand, were interpreted satirically. Lyndsay indi-
cates that Gude Counsel, Chastitie and Veritie are angels.
But what we showed were a lovable but completely futile
schoolmaster of at least a hundred years old and two formida-
bly vigorous spinster aunts: Chastitie, in a white starched
dress, was like the matron of a very old-fashioned hospital;
Veritie delivered tracts and suggested a Salvation Army lass
or a female Jehovah's Witness. The actors gave broad but ex-

tremely endearing caricatures. The Vices were incredibly
lively and appeared to relish their own malice so heartily that
the audience relished it too.

With no great names in the cast, with the play's daunting
title backed by publicity to the effect that it was a morality
play in archaic Scots, which had never been acted since the
sixteenth century and was now going to be presented in the
Kirk Assembly Hall, an edifice not associated in the public
mind with gaiety and only accessible by climbing eighty-seven
steep stone stairs—thus heralded, we opened with almost no
booking at all.

Appalled by the look of our first-night plan, the festival
authorities scurried around and collected an audience of students, hospital nurses, a handful of fanatical Scottish na-
tionalists, a smaller handful of Scottish litterateurs and the
ladies and gentlemen of the press. Even so, the hall—which
is very large—was far from full.

However, the vigor of the play, matched by splendidly
vigorous performances from the entire cast, carried it home to
a really triumphant success. Suddenly we became the toast
of the festival; everyone wanted to book tickets; everyone
praised the wonderful Scottish actors; everyone declared that
he had known from the start how simply great the play was;
at least six persons claimed that they, and they alone, in the
teeth of fearful opposition, had suggested its production. It is
my belief that the original suggestion came from Harvey
Wood, who soon after left Edinburgh for Paris where for
some years he represented the British Council.

This production had several pleasant results. The piece was
successfully revived for three years running, thereby renew-
ing what was, for all of us concerned, a happy partnership.
Second, it restored *The Three Estates* to the honored place
it deserves in Scottish letters. It is now required reading in
the literature course of at least one Scottish university. This
must, I think, be a first-prize bore for the students concerned;
but at least it shows that the worlds of scholarship and the

theatre are not completely cut off from one another. Third, it put the Assembly Hall firmly onto the theatrical map. In all subsequent festivals it has been used for important productions, especially for those of Shakespeare by the Old Vic.

It is by no manner of means an ideal theatre. But I feel warmly towards it because of this venture. It proved that to produce this play in this particular manner had been more than a wayward intuition. It was a decisive step in a direction, which I had first subconsciously and over many years at the Old Vic meditated, had then consciously wished to take, and had now finally taken.

It is probable that, like everyone else who thinks he has had a good idea, I attribute to this more value and more novelty than it has. But it seemed to me that the performance at the Assembly Hall not only suggested all kinds of interesting and exciting technical possibilities, in staging, grouping, lighting, and setting; but that it threw a new light for me on the whole meaning of theatrical performance.

One of the most pleasing effects of the performance was the physical relation of the audience to the stage. The audience did not look at the actors against a background of pictorial and illusionary scenery. Seated around three sides of the stage, they focused upon the actors in the brightly lit acting area, but the background was of the dimly lit rows of people similarly focused on the actors. All the time, but unemphatically and by inference, each member of the audience was being ceaselessly reminded that he was not lost in an illusion, was not at the Court of King Humanitie in sixteenth-century Scotland, but was, in fact a member of a large audience, taking part, "assisting" as the French very properly express it, in a performance, a participant in a ritual.

I had long abandoned any belief in the idea that the aim of a theatrical performance is to create an illusion. For children it may do so, and for very unsophisticated people. Everyone is familiar with the sailor, who at a performance of a melodrama, rose from the body of the hall and knocked down the actor, who, twirling his moustaches and ogling horribly, had been trying to seduce the sweet village maiden.

But nowadays, with cinemas within reach of the most remote hamlets, with drama squirting out of radio and television sets day and night, so that from breakfast to bedtime, from earliest infancy till our very deathbeds, we are familiar with the idea of dramatic fiction; in an age when the lineaments of popular actors are far, far more familiar than those of emperors, popes, politicians or field marshals, when their witticisms, births, marriages, divorces, remarriages and deaths are the gossip of every factory and farmyard; when their hairdos and handbags are first envied, and then copied, by every shopgirl and typist—nowadays, who is going to believe that the events of a play are "really" taking place?

It is true, of course, that a play can be so absorbing that you are temporarily quite lost to reality. You are, as it were, rapt, spellbound. The same thing can happen when you are reading a novel. You can fail to notice that your left foot has gone to sleep, that it is long past midnight, that the cat is asking to go out, that your wife, who has been asleep for an hour, is snoring, and that the wind has changed. But is this illusion? I think not. It has often been my experience when reading a book, listening to music, looking at pictures, or at a play, to be thus rapt. But it is not my experience, nor I believe is it that of most other people, to mistake figment for reality. Does the rapt beholder of Leonardo's *Virgin of the Rocks* think he is "really" in the presence of the holy beings, that he is "really" in that golden and brown landscape? When you read that famous chapter in *Vanity Fair* which ends: "No more firing was heard at Brussels—the pursuit rolled miles away. Darkness came down on the field and city: and Amelia was praying for George, who was lying on his face, dead, with a bullet through his heart . . ." when you read this, do you really think you are living in 1815? If so, who are you? George Osborne, Amelia, Becky, Rawdon Crawley? Or where are you? In London, Brussels, Brighton? When great music conjures, as the saying goes, the soul out of your body, who, or where, are you then? What is the illusion then? There is no illusion. But unmistakably you are rapt, transported; in that condition you lose almost all sense of identity, of time and place.

I maintain that the aim of the theatre should be to transport its audience, but not by illusion.

21

Stratford, Ontario

IN THE SUMMER OF 1952 I was at home in Ireland. One evening the telephone rang and our postmistress told me that earlier that day a call had come for me which purported to be from Toronto.

Mrs. McCabe's answer had been categorical. "Nonsense," she said, hung up and went to feed her hens.

Now, she said, the same joker was on the line again. Would I speak?

"This is Tom Patterson," said a still, small voice out of the everywhere. "Will you come to Canada and give advice? We want to start a Shakespeare festival in Stratford, Ontario. We will pay your expenses and a small fee."

"When do you want me?"

"At once. Tomorrow, if you can."

Naturally, I said yes. I had some time at my disposal. It would be fun to have another look at Canada after all these years. I did not take the advice part or the Shakespeare festival very seriously.

I got out a map. Stratford was about a hundred miles west-southwest of Toronto, rather near to Lake Huron. It was a railway junction. It did not look at all important.

314

At the airport in Toronto I was met by Tom Patterson, a small mouse-colored person, quite young. Merry eyes glinted behind owlish glasses, a poor crop of hair was receding from an impressive dome. He talked a mile a minute. His enthusiasm was endearing, tempered by a grim, reassuringly Scottish humor and what seemed to me a remarkably detached and philosophic approach.

The festival had been his idea. As a soldier in Europe he had been impressed by the opera in Italy. Later, in London, he had fallen in love with the Old Vic. He had considered the musical and dramatic expressions in Stratford, Ontario, and in comparison with what he had seen, he thought them unimpressive. He thought further that Canadians might very well be as talented, as discriminating and energetic as Europeans, and they were certainly richer. He thought finally that he would do something about it.

Back home at the end of the war he made himself a complete pest, everlastingly nagging people about the inadequacy of Stratford's cultural life. He bombarded the corporation, bewildered the Parent-Teacher Association, bothered the clergy, bored the Rotarians, browbeat the Elks and bullied the Lions, to no avail. God, however, moves in a mysterious way. Something called the Junior Chamber of Commerce voted a small sum of money to explore the possibility of a Shakespeare festival. The inevitable committee was formed. It was to meet this committee and to offer it advice that we were driving to Stratford. The July sun blazed on great golden cornfields, sleek dairy cattle, prosperous little crimson towns, incongruously named after the old-country origins of their first settlers—Baden, New Hamburg and Saint Petersburg.

That night we were to meet the committee. There was an hour or two in which to take a preliminary look at Stratford. There is a shopping center remarkably like a hundred other Canadian or American small towns—the same department stores, the usual raw, red churches, the usual public buildings, ungracious and dull. Around this center the residential areas were dignified and charming: avenues of fine old maples behind which, in lawns and gardens, sat comfortable, unpretentious homes. But the most striking feature of Stratford is its park. A small creek, tributary to the River Avon, has been dammed to form a lake over a mile long; around it are ancient willows, down to it slope wide meadows, almost lawns, airy and quiet and, by Canadian though not Irish standards, green.

In the course of thirty years I have had experience of many sorts of committees and boards who manage theatrical enterprises. I expected that this one would consist mainly of artistic and excitable elderly ladies of both sexes, with a sprinkling of businessmen to restrain the artistic people from spending money. There would also be an anxious nonentity from the Town Hall, briefed to see that no municipal funds were promised, but also to see that, if any success were achieved, the municipality would get plenty of credit. The point about this sort of committee is that the artistic ones have extremely definite views, but so conflicting that it is easy for a tiny minority of businessmen to divide and conquer. Prudent, sensible, businesslike counsel prevails. The result is that nothing whatever gets done. In Britain the average age of members is seventy-three.

My first surprise at Stratford, therefore, was to find that most members of the committee were quite young. I was almost the oldest person present. The second surprise was to find that the males outnumbered the females by about five to one. The women spoke seldom, but when they did their remarks were usually briefer and more practical than those of the men.

The greatest surprise was now to come. The committee was unanimous in wishing to organize a festival; it had given proof of this by raising a fund out of members' own pockets to get me out to give advice; now, instead of excited babble quickly turning to acrimonious dispute, there was a silence. They were waiting, with every appearance of interest, even of respect, for me to give my advice.

I was as disconcerted as a visitor to a sickbed who, instead of listening to the usual invective against the brute of a night nurse, a torrent of statistics about weight, blood pressure, sugar content and temperature, a snip-by-snip description of the removal of the stitches, culminating in an offer to display the scar—instead of all this actually heard the patient asking, with every appearance of interest, for news of the world outside.

I advised against producing Shakespeare in the open air. Even if the weather can be counted upon—and it never can—the open air is full of distractions. Many of these distractions are pleasant, the setting sun, the rising moon, the shimmering of leaves, the scent of flowers. But there are less pleasant ones too, the insect kingdom, the foggy foggy dew, the insistent noises of trains, far-off and not so far-off, of barking dogs, of angry babies. The works of Shakespeare require, if they are to be intelligible, the close and undistracted attention of every member of an audience. Open-air performance is only suitable for the kind of entertainment which can be absorbed with one ear, half an eye and almost no exertion of the intellectual faculties.

We agreed that there was no suitable building in Stratford which could serve as a theatre. To erect a permanent theatre until the festival was an accomplished success, until it had been proved that there was in fact an audience, would be a wild extravagance. We therefore decided to explore the possibilities of a tent theatre.

We agreed—and here my respect for the committee was great; and the more I think of it the greater it grows—that to present Shakespeare even adequately is a very, very expensive proposition; so expensive that there could be no hope of making ends meet in the first year, a comparatively slender hope that ends would ever meet. And still the committee was resolved to raise the needful funds and go forward. I did not minimize the financial risk or technical difficulties.

Since an auditorium of some kind would have to be created, even if only under a tent, we felt that it should not be just in the tradition of a nineteenth-century opera house.

I did not then discuss with the committee all the theoretic considerations. At this point we were discussing the building from a strictly practical point of view, and I was merely suggesting that the best practical results would be gotten from a stage which closely conformed to what is known of the stage for which Shakespeare wrote, and by relating the audience to that stage in a manner which approximated to the Elizabethan manner.

The project must manifestly be of some size, in order to attract sufficient attention; for this purpose one production would not be enough. Moreover, we felt that it was wise to have a second barrel to our gun. If we missed with the first, we would have another chance with the second. More than two productions would be impracticable, partly on grounds of expense, partly because of the time needed for preparation.

Finally, we decided that the project must be demonstrably a Canadian one, carried out not merely by Canadian initiative, and with Canadian finance but by Canadian actors. But this need not prevent the committee from seeking the assistance of a limited number of people from Britain or elsewhere. Not merely the sale of tickets, but the whole status of the project, would be greatly assisted if we could obtain the services of an actor of the highest quality and international fame.

All this was carried through in one evening. Not bad going.

At this time the committee had no legal status. It was no more than a gathering of interested citizens charged to investigate the project, but not empowered to take further action. Shortly after this it was incorporated on a legal basis— The Stratford Shakespearean Festival of Canada Foundation —with a charter setting forth its aims. The ideas upon which we had agreed that night in July were now beginning to take practical shape.

Even before this, however, before the committee was more

than an informal, irresponsible body of enthusiasts, and before Tom Patterson had been appointed general manager, he was sent by the committee to London with power to engage a "star" actor, a director, and a designer.

Our first choice for the leading actor had been Alec Guinness. Rather to our surprise as well as delight, he agreed to accept the Stratford offer in preference to the many other engagements always available to the few at the top of the profession. Certainly other offers were more lucrative and it is probably true to say that the deciding factors were the opportunity to play Shakespeare in the particular conditions which our stage afforded, and also to take part in what he felt to be a pioneering venture of a gallant and unselfish kind, a venture which, if successful, might have lasting and important results.

Other purchases made by Tom Patterson on this eventful shopping trip were Tanya Moiseiwitsch, as designer, myself as director. Cecil Clarke, who for some years had been production manager at the Old Vic, was to join us as my assistant at the conclusion of the Old Vic season.

After this, so far as we on the British side of the ocean were concerned, there was a lull. Guinness and I read all the plays of Shakespeare, met often and discussed, inconclusively, which we should suggest to the committee at Stratford.

Miss Moiseiwitsch and I, who are old collaborators, had long dreamed of such a stage as was now to come into being. We were agreed that, while conforming to the conventions of the Elizabethan theatre in practicalities, it should not present a pseudo-Elizabethan appearance. We were determined to eschew *Ye Olde*. Rough sketches on the backs of envelopes gave place to careful drawings. Like every good designer, Moiseiwitsch knows not only what she wants a thing to look like, but why; and she also knows how it is made. Drawings gave place to detailed construction plans. Finally a model was made—an exact replica of the stage which was eventually built—to the scale of a half-inch representing one foot.

By the end of 1952, Guinness and I had narrowed down the

choice of play. We felt that in one of the two plays he must
play a star part; in the other his part should not dominate,
the emphasis should be on the team. We felt, moreover, that
the two plays should contrast, that it would be a mistake
to suggest two histories, two comedies, or two tragedies.

Richard III was agreed upon fairly soon. Guinness wanted
to play it; I agreed that it was a suitable vehicle. We both
felt that the complicated genealogy, the rather obscure historical background, were probably drawbacks for Canadian
audiences but might be offset by the strong thread of melodrama.

For the second play we suggested *All's Well*, largely because it offers such an even distribution of good parts, and
because of the bold contrast with *Richard III*. Its unfamiliar-
ity, which would be a handicap to popularity in London,
seemed to matter less in Stratford where all the Shakespearean
plays were almost equally unfamiliar. We also felt that it
would make for a better team-feeling between the British
and Canadian actors, if one of the two plays were as new to
us as to them.

Shortly before Christmas 1952, I returned to Canada to see
actors. The project by now had received a great deal of publicity. There was considerable interest among the actors and
I was faced by a formidable list of people who wished to be
considered for engagement.

In five days, first in Montreal, then in Ottawa, and finally
in Toronto I saw three hundred and seventeen people. I narrowed this down to about sixty probables, about whom I had
notes as to size, shape, coloring and my own very personal
reaction to our meeting. In addition, there were about another
sixty who, for one reason or another, were also possibles.

The rejects were those who had no experience or who
failed to convince me that they were seriously prepared to do
a job of work. I turned no one down for being plain or shy
or because of the way he was dressed.

The probables were mostly people who had considerable

experience in some field or other of dramatic art. In Canada it is idle to expect many people to have had professional experience, except in radio or television. But I have never felt the distinction between professional and amateur to have much more than monetary significance.

Letters were sent to the probables saying that we would be grateful if they would tell us before making any other definite commitments between May and August 1953. So great was the actors' interest that only three of those whom we approached turned down our eventual offer.

Meantime, on the administrative side a good deal was happening. A suitable site was found in the park which borders the River Avon. Land was made available by the province of Ontario. Robert Fairfield of Toronto was engaged as architect to design the auditorium and supervise the construction. A firm was found in Chicago willing to make, erect and maintain a tent large enough to cover the stage, auditorium and dressing rooms.

The committee now began to be faced with very large expenditure indeed. It had been foreseen, the budget had been quite sensibly prepared, and the response to the financial campaign had so far been distinctly encouraging. Still, there remained a vast, yawning chasm between funds in the bank and projected expenditure.

It was about now that the Jeremiahs began to have a good time—the headshakers, the fingerwaggers, all the vast majority of mankind who derive almost their keenest pleasure from the words "I told you so." It is at about this period that one must admire and respect the guts of the committee. It was still not too late to withdraw.

From behind lace curtains, discreetly; from neighboring cities, patronizingly; from "well-informed circles," with authority; from the local paper, repeatedly, were heard ancestral voices prophesying flop. "It's never been done before," these voices whispered. "You must have enough money to cover expenses before you begin," they warned. "Canadians just hate Shakespeare." "Where are the visitors going to stay?"

"It's never been done before." "Wait for a year or two." "Where is the money coming from? Where will the audience come from? It's never been done before."

There was still time to withdraw. Contracts had not actually been *signed*. The committee was divided. After a particularly stormy meeting two influential members stamped out and slammed the door. They considered that enough money to cover the entire budgeted expenditure of the project must be in the bank before it was safe, or indeed honest, to go ahead. One of the defecting members was a leading accountant in the city, the other was the proprietor of the local newspaper. Their loss was a serious blow.

The remaining members of the committee were considerably shaken but resolved to carry on. But from now on the project was the target of more and more local snipers. Public confidence had been shaken; and from now on the self-confidence of the committee was only maintained by an ever-increasing effort of will, at ever-increasing nervous cost.

In March Cecil Clarke went out to Canada. He is a short, strong-looking individual. He has worked in the theatre all his life, with the exception of the war years. He joined the army as a private soldier. At the end of the war, and at the age of twenty-seven, he was a colonel.

His first duty in Canada was to see again all the actors whom I had seen, so that there should be two opinions on the casting. Our two opinions, arrived at quite independently, were virtually coincident. We both realized that there were probably many good actors whose services we could not use; but on the whole we were very pleased with those we had, and confident that the scheme would not fail because the acting was inadequate. We also considered it a reassuring sign that such a large proportion of those to whom offers were made were willing to accept. No bushfire spreads faster or can be so damaging as the word-of-mouth reaction of theatrical people to a plan. It was apparent that the professional reaction to the Stratford project was favorable and bespoke some confidence in its success.

The next task for Cecil Clarke was to set up a production mechanism. There were several hundred dresses to be made, armor, jewelry, accessories and properties of diverse kinds. Canada, with virtually no professional theatre, has few resources in these matters. It was agreed that it would probably be less expensive, and certainly a great deal more satisfactory, to employ our own staff to cut and make most of the dresses, rather than to rely on existing workshops. We were able to engage two experienced technicians from Britain, Mr. Ray Diffen, a brilliant theatrical cutter, and Jacqueline Cundall to make accessories and properties.

It is not sufficiently appreciated how much the whole style of a production owes to the work of technicians whose names either do not appear or to whom some form of acknowledgement is made among the advertisements at the end of a program in illegibly small type. If the productions at Stratford had a unified and distinguished visual style, it is not only because the designs of Miss Moiseiwitsch had that style. It is because Diffen, in the cutting of the clothes, and Jacqueline Cundall, in the making of properties and accessories, were able to interpret the designs creatively, not merely to make an unimaginative copy of a blueprint.

This was the great difficulty that faced us in preparing the productions. Canada, like the United States, is organized for mass production. It is possible, once materials and designs are agreed upon, to get enormous numbers of a given article turned out by machinery at a comparatively low price. It is almost impossible to get people to bother to make something for which there is no mass demand, for which no blueprint exists, which requires craftsmanship.

Shoes were the first problem. For *Richard III* we required shoes of a shape, and in materials and colors, which bore no resemblance to the shoes mass produced for the public. Similarly, for military uniforms in *All's Well* we needed boots of a particular style. In neither case could we think of affording the enormous prices commanded by any custom-made article in the New World.

Eventually, an aged European craftsman was located in an outlying district of Toronto, who was prepared to make a sample pair of shoes for *Richard*, after Moiseiwitsch's sketch, out of materials for which he was willing to search. The sample, with some small modifications, was excellent. The old bootmaker was delighted to find that his skill was valued again and would be employed. Too old for the rush and flurry of competitive mass production, he was still a first-rate tradesman. Given time and helped by his son, he turned out over fifty pairs of boots at a most reasonable price; they simply could not have been gotten in any other way. Similarly, a Czech craftsman in another suburb was prepared to make the boots for *All's Well*, when all the big firms had refused to consider the order because it did not conform to any mass production schedule.

It was the same with hats. And in every case the only people who would undertake the jobs involving individual craftsmen were Europeans. I am aware that this is not because Europeans are more skillful and inventive. But in the New World skill and invention have been, and are being ever more and more, diverted from hand craft to mechanical processes, industrial techniques, machines and machine tools, assembly lines.

The emphasis, consequently, shifts from quality to quantity. In less time more people have more commodities, working hours are shorter, machines do more of the drudgery. But there is a danger that, in long term, the joy will be taken out of work, the level of taste will become depressed, and a deadly standardization will be imposed, not just upon commodities but on ideas.

Some formidable indications of this already begin to be apparent in the United States, less so in Canada, less still, as yet, in Europe. But there is no evidence that any part of the world will be able to stand out against the enormous pressure towards an economy based on assembly-line techniques.

From April until my arrival in Canada late in May 1953 I had almost daily letters from Cecil Clarke.

Jacqueline Cundall is established in a workshop at Stratford, he wrote, with a staff mostly recruited from the School of Arts in Toronto and the universities in Toronto and Montreal; the making of armor has begun—felt, stiffened with size; as more than fifty breastplates and fifty helmets will be needed, it is reassuring to know that a start has been made. The little bootmaker has produced another sample, better than the first effort; still not quite the ticket. Ray Diffen has arrived in Toronto and professes himself tolerably satisfied with the workroom.

This was a matter of great relief to Tanya and myself in England. Ray is a star of the first magnitude in his particular firmament; we were nervous that he might have thrown a temperament and walked out.

Next letter: no one will undertake the *All's Well* uniforms. How many crosses will be carried in the scene of Richard's coronation? Please send detailed drawings at once. Meantime actors' contracts have been issued. Work on the site has begun.

The next letter enclosed a photograph of the chairman of the committee cutting the first sod. The Chairman, Doctor Harrison Showalter, is a remarkable character. He graduated with a Ph.D. during the depression and, unable to find suitable scope for his gifts and education, became a manufacturer of soft drinks. He is a staunch and resourceful man in a crisis and a pillar of the Baptist Sunday School. He did not know much, and made no pretensions to know anything, about the art of the theatre or the business of theatrical promotion. Little did he know, when he accepted the chairmanship of this enterprise, what a heavy load of anxiety he was assuming. Little did any of that gallant committee suspect what an unruly, squalling, monstrous brat they were going to bring forth.

Early in May came a letter sounding a faint but unmis-

takable note of warning. The money was not coming in quite
as fast as the committee had hoped.

We had heard that the appeal for funds had made an excellent start in Stratford. Cecil's note was disquieting. By
now there were six of us in England who were committed to
the plan: Guinness, Tanya Moiseiwitsch and myself, and in
addition, Irene Worth, Douglas Campbell and Michael Bates.

Tanya and I were sharing the Clarke correspondence. We
consulted Alec Guinness. Ought we to tell the others that
all was possibly not going to end well? We decided that there
was nothing we could any of us do; that therefore there was
no point in sounding a tocsin to our three friends, and even
less in adding to the embarrassment in Stratford by anxious
cables. We resolved on stiff upper lips and rising above.

The financial crisis went from bad to worse. Work on the
tent in Chicago had been suspended pending the receipt of
an advance payment which the committee at Stratford could
not meet. Only by thumping the table had Cecil been able to
get cash to pay the workers in the wardrobe and property
shops.

In the next letter the financial crisis had got into the
Canadian press. Several of the firms who were supplying goods
were, not unnaturally, insisting on payment in advance.

These must have been bleak days in Stratford. A single
bright spot in the darkness: the contractor who was preparing
the site kept right on working. He had decided that the
honor of the community was at stake, and that, whether he
were paid or no, his part in the whole plan would go forward.

The next event I can remember clearly was a wire from
Dr. Showalter requesting me to be available for a telephone
call from Canada on a Saturday afternoon. By now Guinness
was due to sail on the *Mauretania* the next Monday. Tanya
Moiseiwitsch and I were in the throes of a dress rehearsal for
a large production of *Henry VIII* at the Old Vic. It was
opening on the Wednesday, right after which we too were
due to leave for Canada.

My wife and I rallied Tanya and Alec for lunch at our house. It was a tense feast. Then the telephone rang. I lifted the receiver. The others clustered close. All of us were, to coin a phrase, white to the lips. It was my sister, calling to ask if she had left her spectacles on the mantelpiece. When the bell rang again we all felt better. Harry Showalter gave a brief résumé of the financial situation. It was serious but not yet utterly desperate. The committee was divided as to the best course to pursue. How did I feel about postponing the whole thing for a year?

I should like to be able to report that across the ether my voice rang strong and clear—a rallying call that saved the day, a note of steady confidence, the horn of Roland. In fact I asked a few footling questions, hummed and stuttered, said I must consult my colleagues and would call back in half an hour.

I then reported that we all felt postponement would be utterly fatal. Better to abandon the whole plan than either to postpone or to proceed with faint hearts and a reduced budget.

Of course the committee was in a ghastly position. The tent alone was costing a fortune. They had contracts with forty or fifty actors in Canada, contracts with us, commitments to the architect, to the builder, the butcher, the candlestick maker, to say nothing of the good little boot-maker at that very instant stitching away at the eighty-third boot. To proceed was certainly to court a serious financial risk, but there was just a chance of considerable incomings at the box office and of considerable prestige. To postpone or abandon involved, as I saw it, no very great financial saving —the big commitments had already been made—but removed any possible chance of saving the day. Empty pockets and crimson cheeks were the only possible prospects.

Alec Guinness chivalrously said he was ready, if they wished, to acquit them of any liability in the matter of his contract. But what we all, at our end of the line, agreed we must have, and at once, was a definite decision. We seemed to hear the *Mauretania* hooting weirdly in the trees outside the window. We were sincerely sorry, we said, for the committee; we hated to add to their anxieties, but we must know within twenty-four hours whether the festival were on or off. Also we must have the chairman's personal assurance that, if the decision were to go ahead, it meant going ahead at full steam and not going off at half-cock.

Next day, in the middle of Katherine of Aragon's death scene came a wire: DECIDED PROCEED STOP ASSURE YOU FULL STEAM AHEAD.

Even after this, I understand, there was another major crisis. Again the whole project was almost abandoned. But to none of this was I a witness. I am only reporting what I know at second hand. There was an exceedingly handsome anonymous subscription. There was a telegram of exhortation and encouragement from the Governor-General of Canada, who had read in the press that the venture was in trouble. But the precise factors that turned the scale are unknown to me. By the time we reached Stratford—Tanya, my wife and I—all was relatively calm. The financial situation was still grave but steadily improving.

There was, however, one hangover from the crisis: the tent. It had originally been agreed that it should be ready by the time we began rehearsals, the first week in June. For six weeks we were to rehearse on our stage *in situ*. Work, however, had stopped in Chicago pending the payment of a sum which the committee was only now beginning to be able to meet. No one knew exactly when the tent would arrive. "But don't worry," said the committee, "there's still plenty of time." I regret to say there was also a tendency to add, for the benefit of silly, slow old Europeans: "Things out here move faster than you folks can possibly imagine."

Rehearsals started in a structure out in the fairgrounds. A long wooden shed, roofed with corrugated iron. It was vast. It was dry. It had electric light. It had no plumbing, but the fairgrounds were remote and had been planted with lovely clumps of thick, green shrubs. In the shed a replica of our stage had been built. Here we were to rehearse until the tent arrived.

The whole arrangement was satisfactory except in two respects. The acoustics of the building were such that the lightest whisper became an enormous booming noise. Normal speech was almost too loud to be endured by the naked ear, and totally unintelligible. Giants and giantesses seemed to be shouting through the vaults of a cathedral, jointly designed by Cecil B. DeMille and Orson Welles.

The second drawback was the sparrows. Several dozens of them had built in the rafters of our shed. It was a sparrow slum. By day it was comparatively quiet; but towards evening, when the business sparrows came back home, their love life became most obtrusive. Boy sparrow would meet girl and pursue her all over our stage. They were impervious to fear, or for that matter shame. Scenes of unbridled bird sexuality made the life of *Richard III* seem very anemic and suburban. These dear little feathered friends would not have hesitated to make away with *their* nephews. Why, they had no compunction whatever about the death of their own offspring. As the weeks wore on and their eggs hatched, the nestlings fell to their death on the concrete floor below literally by the dozen.

The weeks wore on. The plays were nearly ready. But still there was no sign of the tent.

Anxiety began again. The financial crisis was over. Subscriptions had now passed the estimated amount and were still coming in. The member of the committee who was also its bank manager was reported to be eating once more and only occasionally walking in his sleep. But now, if one met our chairman, an ectoplasmic tent seemed to form in the air above his hat. A king's ransom was spent on long-distance calls to the tentmaker in Chicago. Fabulous numbers of Women were reported to be stitching day and night.

Days pass. The words of the plays are now known, but owing to the acoustics of the shed, no one has yet heard any

lines but his own. Lips are seen to move, gigantic but unintelligible noises resound in the building, punctuated by the
thumps of baby sparrows hurtling to their doom. These noises
make a Wagnerian accompaniment to the *miming* of two
Shakespearean plays. It is an interesting new art form; avant-
garde but searing to the nerves.

Days pass. No tent. Three members announce that, in the
autopsy which will follow the mass suicide of the committee,
graven on their hearts will be found the name *Chicago*.

Came the dawn; Chicago telegraphed that more Women
than ever before were stitching countless hours of overtime
and that the tent would reach the yards on Tuesday.

Nobody seemed quite to know what, or where were the
yards. I had always thought that the combination of Chicago
and yards added up to innumerable quadrupeds turning, poor
things, in seas of blood, but painlessly, to "Bully." Still, it was
nice to know that on Tuesday a tent was going anywhere
at all.

It was nicer still when Skip Manley appeared. Skip was
the tent man. He travels the world putting up, looking after
and taking down enormous tents. He had come from Iowa,
where he had been in charge of a gospel tent. Nightly, several
hundred people had plunged fully clad into a baptismal tank.
After a season of Shakespeare with us, he was booked to look
after a circus tent in Venezuela.

Mr. Manley was a lean Midwesterner. He brought with
him a ton of hardware and kept making calculations on odd
scraps of paper. He referred to the tent as "she" and the hardware—iron rings, chains, swivels and so on—was all part of
the apparatus which would raise "her" from the ground.

I never saw him except in working dress—he was a hard
and dedicated worker—and for work in all weathers he wore
a white panama hat, with a pink and gold ribbon; a pair of
very old trousers which had once been white; brown shoes of
basketwork with pointed toes and an intricate design, and a
shirt made of pink and silver brocade—the sort of garment
which, in Europe, old ladies wear for evenings *en pension* at

Bath, Lucerne or Wiesbaden. In Bath they call them bridge coatees.

On the bony, workworn fingers of the tent man there flashed and flickered jeweled rings. When at last "she" did arrive from Chicago, half Stratford turned out to see "her" go up. It was a sight worth watching. Four eighty-foot poles of Douglas pine were moored in position by guys of steel wire. Skip directed this operation like Toscanini conducting a symphony. Each pole was drawn up and held in place by four guys. Two of these were operated by hand—two teams of fifteen men; the other two were attached to tractors. Skip would sign first to this group to pull so far, then to that; then, with the sweep of a jeweled hand, he would bring the first tractor into play, holding the remainder of his forces at the ready as though they were trombones waiting to make an entry. The whole tricky, delicate operation took a day and a half. Thereafter the great expanse of canvas was hoisted comparatively quickly and easily. In another day or two we were able to rehearse in the tent.

There remained a great deal of work to be done in the preparation of the building; work which had had to wait until after the tent was put up. The only way for this to be accomplished in time was by arranging a twenty-four-hour schedule of work, night and day, and sticking to it. The chairman called a meeting of all departments: the building contractor, the electrical engineer, the plumber, Skip Manley, Cecil Clarke and myself. We agreed that from 10 A.M. till 10 P.M. the theatre should be available for rehearsal. That meant the suspension of all constructional activities. The various departments agreed that they would work at night. Each day at lunchtime we were all to meet and report progress.

Of course, just by making a schedule we were not getting out of the wood. The electrical department kept lagging behind. A firm of wood polishers, brought in to finish the surface of the stage, imparted so high a gloss to the boards that none of the actors could take a step without slipping. A morning was spent rehearsing *All's Well* on "ice," which could ill be spared from more orthodox production methods. And then a precious night was wasted removing the gloss so laboriously applied.

I cannot pay a sufficiently warm tribute to the people concerned with getting this building finished. First of all they appreciated that it really was necessary to be ready by the appointed date. For people who are not used to that sort of schedule this is quite a hard thing to grasp. If you undertake to build a house by a certain date, you may have to pay some financial compensation if you are late. Some inconvenience may be caused, some angry words exchanged. But the house remains a house. The occupants get in late, disgruntled though they may be by the delay. The builder may lose face and a deposit; the building exists and continues to exist. But if the performance of a play, announced for a certain date, is delayed, its existence is blasted. Occupants of the theatre there are none, nor will be any. Their labor is but lost that build it.

In our case postponement was out of the question. We had to be ready or bust. Our colleagues on the constructional side appreciated that they and we were in the same boat. They were as determined as the actors to be ready on time. Moreover, they appreciated that, when we said it was impossible to rehearse while men banged nails into boards, operated saws, paint-sprays and cement-mixers and, if they felt like it, sang "Sweet Adeline," this was not just the fussiness of pampered and self-important artists. They realized that quiet was essential for efficiency in our department; and that our department was not less essential to the project than their own.

Quiet? I had not realized the acoustic peculiarity of tents. Or was our tent unique in this? Any sound which occurred *inside* the tent seemed of normal size. Any sound from without was enormously magnified. The railway shunting yards were a mile away, yet the engines seemed to clang, the box-cars bang, upon the stage. Ball games on a diamond several hundred yards away seemed to issue from invisible amplifiers in our front row. Most disconcerting of all were our visitors. For the first few days after we moved into the tent, the rehearsals, particularly in the evening, were an object of great local curiosity.

Multitudes would lurk in the spring twilight outside the skirts of the great tent. On the whole their behavior was impeccable. Occasionally, they would lift the skirts and peek; but only surreptitiously, only occasionally. They knew they must not interrupt. But it was the acoustics which made all this so tricky. A juvenile head would appear under the canvas, momentarily, slyly, six inches from the ground. Then an enormously magnified whisper from outside would say, "WELL?" The head would withdraw. Then the huge whisper would reverberate, "YOU'RE SURE IT WAS ALEC GUINNNESS?" The head would reappear. The actors, led by Guinness, would make desperate efforts to get on with the job. Pay no attention. Go ahead. Over the dialogue would float the enormous pervasive whisper: "WELL, WHAT'S HE LIKE?"

Then there were the electric storms. Hardly had we raised our tabernacle before God saw fit to send them—a mighty, rushing wind which made the ropes creak and strain, the canvas flap; the whole great edifice was like a ship at sea, like a film set for *Moby Dick*. Then, bingo! The lightning flashed, the thunder crashed and the rain would beat like a million kettledrums on our roof. She stood it all magnificently; she hardly leaked at all. But great canvas tumors would hang down, where water had collected, diseased-looking, ominous. In the drumming darkness, the actors, rehearsal suspended, would see Skip Manley dash hither and yon, with a knife attached to a long long pole, slashing the tumours. There would be a flash of rubies and diamonds, a ripping sound, and then cascades of warmish, dirty water. Then the sun would burst out and rehearsals would begin again in clouds of steam. It was like preparing a play in a Turkish bath.

The storms passed. But, till half an hour before the public assembled for the opening night, a tiny figure might be seen

clambering about on the enormous sagging expanse of terra-
cotta-colored canvas; rubies and diamonds flashed in the sun-
light, and in the moonlight too, drawing together with exquisite, tiny surgical stitches the wounds he had himself in-
flicted to save her from destruction.

We opened. The plays were ready. The theatre was ready.
But, most important of all, the audience was ready. This was
the reason for the festival's signal success: the audience was
ready. The public wanted it to succeed.

Even before we opened it was apparent that the project
had captured the imagination of the Canadian press and had
behind it a powerful trade wind of public good will.

Canada is now potentially the richest nation in the world.
Canadians know this; and know, further, that riches mean
power and responsibility; that, if Canada is honorably to fulfill its destiny, it is not enough just to be rich and powerful.
Canada must not in the councils of the world use the cracked
brash accents of millionaire adolescence, but must speak with
maturity. To an extraordinary degree this theatrical project
in a small provincial town symbolized Canada's desire for
mature and, if possible, distinguished artistic expression.

But Canada is not only very rich. If you are not passionately
interested in ice hockey, hunting or family bridge in the
Home Beautiful, it is also pretty dull. Stratford was doing
something which dozens of other rich, provincial, unsophisticated but not therefore necessarily unintelligent little towns
knew to be courageous and lively.

Naturally, I do not mean that any more than a tiny minority of Canadians were fully conscious or articulate about all
this. But I deduce that some such feelings existed from the
intense interest in the project, even before the plays had
opened, and the tremendous welcome given to them after.

We were further and powerfully assisted by leading drama
critics from New York, who took the trouble to come to the
opening performances and wrote enthusiastically of what they
saw. This was just what we needed. Canadians, very under-

standably and through the modesty of inexperience, lack self-confidence in artistic judgment. They are apt to wait to be told what to like, and why. They are apt to regard an opinion from New York, London or Paris as carrying more authority than the same opinion, equally well expressed, in Montreal or Toronto. Now, finding the New York critics outsinging even the local newspaper in praise set the seal upon artistic success and ensured the prosperity of the new festival.

In five successive years the audiences have been immense and the prestige undiminished. The tent has been replaced by a handsome and interesting new theatre, incorporating the original stage and original cement arena. The federal government of Canada and the provincial government of Ontario have both subscribed handsomely from the public purse, thereby conferring official recognition of the festival's contribution to Canada. The leading American critics have continued to attend and to praise. Success at this festival has advanced the professional status of Canadian actors in their own country, and has won for several of them prominent engagements in New York and Hollywood.

Credit where credit is due. The most influential factor in the success has been, in my opinion, the timeliness of the project. It symbolized something which, at the moment of its inception, seemed to be important and exciting to Canadians.

The next credit is due to the committee in Stratford. In the early stages none of its members were eminent personages; all were local people. Anyone who has lived in a small community will know the kind of difficulties they faced; not just the inertia of the vast mass of citizens, the total lack of interest, but also the positive hostility which is always aroused by anything new, which is thrice venomous if the innovation is admittedly long-haired, three times thrice when it is also conspicuous, expensive and risky. The committee braved this hostility with absolutely no hope of financial gain if the venture succeeded; and with every certainty not only of financial loss, but moral and social disgrace as well, if it failed.

Third and last credit: the productions were not bad. It is
not for me to assess the quality in that first season, when I
directed both the plays. But I can view most of the later
productions with detachment. The Canadian companies have
been good, but on average, no better than an average company at the Old Vic or Stratford, England. But the productions, in my opinion, have seemed livelier and fresher because of the design of the theatre.

The stage is so planned that no illusionary scenery is possible. Yet with its gallery, its pillars, its various levels and
entrances, the necessary facilities are provided for grouping
the actors and arranging the scenes in a logical and expressive way. The relation of the stage to the auditorium is such
that a large audience—nearly two thousand people—can be
accommodated so near the actors that the farthest spectators
are only thirteen rows from the front. In a prosecenium
theatre of similar capacity those in the back rows would be
more than twice as far from the stage.

Audiences coming into this new kind of relation with the
stage have been intrigued and excited simply by its novelty.
That will wear off. But there remains the important fact that
the actors are closer to their audience. The plays therefore
seem more intimate and the verse does not make the huge
demand upon technical virtuosity as when it has to carry to
the back of an opera house. Also, the stage is planned upon
the theory that illusion is not the aim of performance. The
shape of the auditorium, in which the spectators are constantly and inevitably aware of the presence of other spectators, is a constant reminder that the performance is what
it is: a ritual in which actors and spectators are alike taking
part. This idea appeals, I think, because it happens to be
true; whereas the idea of illusion demands self-deception, demands that you believe that to be "really" happening which
is clearly fictitious.

The Stratford theatre is certainly not perfect. I know well
that, over the years, subsequent directors will make many
alterations and many improvements. But I am convinced,

partly by my own productions there, and far more by those of my successors, that the principle is right.

The principle is that a play can be best presented by getting as near as possible to the manner in which the author envisaged its performance. It is not a question of the open stage being better than a stage with a proscenium arch. It is neither better nor worse. The open stage is no more suitable for the production of *The School for Scandal* than is the proscenium stage for *Hamlet*. It will often be necessary in the future, as it has been in the past, to produce a play on an entirely unsuitable stage; and the many problems thus posed will often be solved with striking success. They remain problems; and the energy expended upon their solution has been, and will be, diverted from more important and rewarding matters.

It is to this point that a long and extremely various theatrical experience has led me. It is not a particularly striking or far-reaching point. It is applicable only to the limited sphere of theatrical production. But it is at least an assertion of principle, something objective in the overwhelmingly subjective world of theatrical art and craft. It is not original. Many of my contemporaries have had the same idea about Shakespearian and classical production, and about theatrical illusion. I just happen, partly as a result of good fortune, partly through a determination sustained over many years, to have initiated, first in Edinburgh and then in Stratford, Ontario, two experiments on a bolder and more elaborate scale than anyone else has yet attempted in this particular field.

It may well be that I both overestimate the importance of these experiments and misinterpret their success. But for me they seem to have given a point and a unity to long stretches of my professional life which would otherwise, except for the pleasure I myself have had in them, have seemed a little purposeless.

22

Conclusion

JUST AS I have gradually abandoned the idea of illusion as the aim of theatrical performance, so I have also abandoned the idea that the theatre has a moral aim: to uplift the public, to instruct it, do it good.

For the greater part of my professional life this aim had loomed quite large. It was an attitude which I had absorbed quite unconsciously from earliest youth. My mother, extremely energetic and practical, had an intense and literal Christian faith. She believed that it was her duty to love her neighbor as herself; she believed with the most noble tenacity and in the face of many serious trials, that a wholly benevolent Father–God was ordering all things for the best; and she never seriously questioned that the best was what she had been taught, chiefly by her own father, to believe in as such. She was not a person of profound intellect, but her great warmth, her energy and the consistency with which she practiced her own principles made her a considerable moral force. Also, like all sons of good mothers, I still, long, long after childhood, felt "naughty" when I caught myself disagreeing with my mother, when I found that many thoughts and deeds which seemed good to her no longer seemed so to me.

338

My mother, with her clear-cut notions of good and evil and of a Christian's duty to society, never doubted for one instant that the purpose of art was to benefit mankind by making him more like her conception of God. It is only fair to say that this by no means ruled out amusement as a subsidiary but entirely permissible purpose.

My father, the son and grandson of ministers, had been grounded in the severe Calvinism of the Scottish Kirk. He had rejected most of its doctrinal conceptions and I do not think that Christianity in him was more than a strong liberalism, a strong conviction that there were two sides to every argument, that our Father's house hath many mansions. At the same time I am sure that he too was convinced that the purpose of art was to do good to mankind. But, more skeptical and analytic than my mother, he was not as she was apt to be dogmatically, if benevolently, aware of just which ideas, actions, objects or persons were good and which were bad.

Neither of my parents was passionately interested in art. We had no writers, painters or musicians in the family; we knew none of any distinction. One of my father's patients was an artist; he wore knickerbockers and a bow tie and, in gratitude for having his appendix removed, he painted a portrait of my father in shades of blue and mauve and a sticky texture. My mother thought, not without reason, that the portrait did not do justice to the sitter. For a few brief weeks it hung in a place of honor over the sideboard. It then mysteriously and forever disappeared. All the same, ours was not a Philistine home. Good books were read and discussed; and in a vague way art and artists were even respected. But I do not think that anyone ever doubted that the purpose of art was to produce beauty, that beauty is truth, truth beauty—that is all we know or need to know; that this composite beauty-truth has been "put into this world" for the uplifting of mankind, is indeed one of the aspects of God made manifest.

When I began in the theatre, I was certainly proud of beginning to be an "artist." I regarded it, and still do, as a useful occupation, defending this view by such maxims as man

cannot live by bread alone. The artist is not useful in the
primary sense, as is the farmer; not even in the secondary
sense, as is the cook or weaver, who turns primary products
into basic necessities of food and raiment. But then who is to
determine the limit of necessity? Everyone dresses, for instance, in a manner more elaborate than is necessary either
for warmth or modesty. Everyone eats more, and more
elaborately, than is necessary for bare subsistence. And is man
satisfied with just being warm, modest, and healthy? The
answer is that obviously he is not; he feels compelled to express himself. He does so not only in the fields of eating,
drinking and clothing, not only in the realm of speculation
about who and where and why he is, but in the further realm
of imitation. Just as God found himself compelled to create
the world and all that therein is, so is man, godlike, compelled to create an imitation of God's world, including imitation—or fictitious—men and women.

Rightly, I think, the good artist in all civilized societies is
more highly regarded than the good baker because it is much
harder to produce a good piece of art than a good loaf of
bread; although it is possible to be so good a baker that your
work can be regarded as art. The bad artist, on the other
hand, is regarded more lowly than the bad baker, because his
product is totally useless; after all, a bad loaf can be offered
to the pigs or the fowls.

I was resolved to be a good artist, and I tried earnestly not
only to equip myself technically to that end but also to decide what I thought constituted the difference between good
and bad art—a decision, incidentally which I have never
reached.

I must not, however, pretend that considerations of this
kind entirely governed my decision to go into the theatre, or
my professional attitude after the plunge had been taken.
As with most youngsters in the theatre, my dominant aim in
the early years was to be successful enough to eat.

In a desperately competitive profession, where there are

always more aspirants than jobs, it is inevitable that an inflated value should be attached to success. In the theatre you cannot succeed unless you have exceptional energy and either exceptional looks, charm or talent. You do not require intelligence, but an element of luck is indispensable. In medicine, for instance, or law, a job is not, as in the theatre, like a succulent morsel dropped into a school of hungry perch. You can live well and usefully as a lawyer or doctor, attain to respected, even eminent eld, with very average abilities. In schoolmastering or the church, the laborer is in a seller's market. You can get a job unless you are patently half-witted or have a record blacker than even the hardest-pressed employer can overlook.

This competitive aspect of the theatre is not in every way a bad thing. It is wonderful for discipline. There exists, I know, a popular idea that the theatre conducts itself in a tumult of what is called "temperament." This is not the case. It would not be true to say that I have never witnessed "scenes" in the theatre. I have witnessed many, and have even created one or two. But nearly forty years of theatrical experience have not been half so rich in exhibitions of temperament as my three terms as a master in an English public school. Never in the theatre have I heard such trumpetings as when the senior maths master was requested by the Head to take prep, such sulks and pouts in the common room, such backbiting and such psychotic jealousy because Westbury and his wife had been allotted more prominent seats at Speech Day than Easterbrook and his sister. This was not a school at which the morale of the staff was low; it was a good school and the masters were not a bad lot. It was simply that in a profession where there are more jobs than applicants, discipline tends to be slack, employees can behave badly and get away with it.

A bad aspect, if not the worst, of the desperately competitive nature of theatrical life is the enormous and symbolic emphasis which attaches itself to success. You see the same thing in business. Success becomes a symbol of manly cour-

A *Life in the Theatre*

age and, at the same time, of prudence, strength and cunning, of all which raises great men of business to eminence, including luck.

Businessmen of any potentiality strive not merely to make money but to make the grade, to justify their existence. Their money is the symbol of such self-justification. It is a club to beat wolves and hostile tribesmen, the scalps of the tribesmen are to dangle from Queenie's belt, the skins of the wolves to wrap the baby bunting in; with the same club he can give to pop those forty whacks he has longed since the womb to administer; to twirl and flourish it is to take the sneer off the superior mugs of aunties and uncles, evokes cheers from women at the doors of other huts, makes feebler males cringe and serve. Like Aaron's rod it can work wonders, can bring forth leaves or a plague of frogs or kill the firstborn of the enemy. But, sweetest of all, in the glow of golden noon, is to take the club and lay it reverently, gently, with no pomp and swagger, like a bone at mama's feet.

Success, on the stage no less than in business, is a matter primarily of prestige, self-justification. It is symbolized by celebrity rather than money. It may seem childish when actors make fusses about their billing, insisting that their name appear in type larger than someone else's, getting angry if it is misspelled and so on. I recall an occasion when a young actor's name was, entirely by mistake, omitted from a poster advertising a performance in which he was appearing. He was a nice lad, reasonable and good-tempered; he was also an international high-jumper. I was therefore a little surprised when, in the middle of a perfectly clear and reasonable complaint, he suddenly burst into a paroxysm of tears like a child of eight. It was because his father was coming to see the performance, traveling by train from Bolton or Sunderland. There would have been posters at the railway station; and the young man was dying for his father to see his name, right there staring him in the face, when he got off the train. There had been a lot of opposition at home to his leaving the little family business for the stage. It was desperately important for

him, by means of this symbol of the playbill, to convince his
dad that he was "doing well."

Of course, in the theatre money too is an important success
symbol. But then I hear that in business they set store by
prestige, they fuss about the billing: International Gearboxes
Incorporated grinds its teeth and takes the squeaks because
Consolidated Midwestern danced the first quadrille with
Milady.

Naturally, the higher the pressure of competition the more
important does the success symbol loom. In the permanent
repertory companies of continental Europe there is remarkably little jostling for better billing or greediness about salary.
Good parts are important, but more for artistic reasons, because they are interesting and technically and spiritually developing, rather than because they are steppingstones to fame
and fortune.

In the most competitive areas success becomes so important
that it virtually overwhelms every other aim. In the New
York theatre just now I do not think that a single management is in business with any other aim. Not all of them are
pursuing a success symbolized solely by money, or even by
popularity; but so inflated are the rewards of success, so severe is the penalty of failure, that it is hardly possible to
think of a production solely in terms of artistic quality.
Equally, actors who all through their early life have had to
fight like beasts for economic survival, can hardly be expected,
when they "arrive," suddenly to abandon the training of a
lifetime, suddenly to lose interest in money, billing, one's
name in Hedda Kilgallen's column, a seat against the east
wall of Sardi's, one's divorce on the front page, one's wife's
funeral on the telly, one's clothes torn and one's arm dislo-
cated by sex-mad fans—all the comforting bonbons of popular
success.

In England the competition is not so tough as in America,
largely because the theatre is still widely dispersed outside
London. And for directors it is not so tough as for actors.
Nonetheless, during my first years in the theatre the dominant

aim really had to be success. I had to take any offer I got; there was no choosing what plays I did, nor where, nor with whom.

Like most other people, I rationalized what I was doing to make it seem more creditable than, in fact, it was. While I was with the B.B.C. I made myself believe that radio drama was a potentially important new means of expression, that statements thus made could have a unique quality simply because the listener was deprived of every faculty except hearing. This I still think is the case; but, now that I am no longer economically or artistically dependent upon radio, it no longer seems quite so important.

While I was in Ireland and Scotland I believed that indigenous drama was a valuable element in both national development and international understanding; that art _must_ spring from the soil; that to be "authentic" was important in speech and action, not just on the stage but always and everywhere. I do not think I ever defined "authentic" very clearly, but it had something to do with not being ashamed of your origins, of trying to assimilate your environment very fully and so on—all quite sound, I still think. But later, in another phase of my life, it has become necessary to rationalize a mode of life which takes me from Tel Aviv to Finland, Canada, Warwickshire, London, New York and County Monaghan, Ireland, in all of which I have contacts, personal and professional, at different levels of depth and intensity, but all of which I value. The "authentic" standards hardly apply; yet I do not find the new mode of existence false or bad because more dispersed; and I do not find the slightest difficulty in inventing a new set of rationalizations to fit it. Yet I do recognize a discrepancy between the new rationalizations and the old, and feel forced to the conclusion that, while neither is wholly false, neither is wholly true. I think the contradiction has made me recognize these rationalizations for what they are: attempts to make my life square with predetermined standards of good conduct.

I worked in radio drama because it was the most congenial

of the limited selection of work then available to me. I became interested in Scottish national drama because, if I did not, I would not have been able to keep a job which, for quite other reasons, I was enjoying. Nevertheless, the interest in Scottish national drama, in regional as opposed to metropolitan art, has greatly influenced both my taste and the course of my life. Again and again, when more choice was available, I have picked the regional, as opposed to the metropolitan, offer.

The point is this: hitherto, apart from the competitive aim of "getting on," climbing the ladder, my professional aims had always, partly in fact, partly as a result of not quite conscious rationalization, been directed to uplift, to doing what I had been conditioned, principally by my mother, to regard as good.

Ideas of this kind certainly permeated, probably dominated, my long connection with the Old Vic. They were encouraged by influences of many kinds: "It's so nice that dear Tony's at the Old Vic," old friends of the family would say. "Miss Baylis is such a fine woman." In the profession, and also in the press, endless lip service was paid to the Old Vic, with its great tradition of social service. Educated persons, who ought to have known better, applauded a theatre devoted to Shakespeare simply because it was therefore supposed to be "educative."

No one seemed to think, or at any rate no one dared to say, that a theatre doing Shakespeare badly was doing Shakespeare a disservice and was not uplifting but downcasting the public. No one seemed to remember that, in the many years since Miss Cons started the Royal Victoria Coffee Tavern, times had changed, that the audience at the Old Vic no longer consisted of the good poor waiting humbly for evangelical peers to lift them out of the gutter. Indeed, nowadays it is the peers who need economic uplift far more desperately than the good poor.

By the time I had reached the Old Vic my professional decisions were beginning to be a matter of choice, not just of necessity. I was now being offered plenty of work. But I chose to stay at the Old Vic at lower pay because I was happy there. And I was happy there because I thought it a good and useful institution, that in helping to keep it going I was doing something "worth while." Therefore, at this period, both during Miss Baylis' lifetime, while I was still the instrument of her policy, and then later when it became my duty to formulate the policy of the theatre, I was forced to consider whether the moral purposes of the Old Vic were justified, whether I really did believe in the elevating moral force of art.

Like almost everyone of my generation whom I knew, I had long abandoned the truth–beauty axis. Beauty appeared utterly indefinable and, through lack of definition the whole conception had become cheap and sentimental. "A Beauty," you said of a chorus girl or a red-cheeked apple or a good stroke at tennis. Beauty parlors supplied aids to make women look less like themselves and more like one another. Beauty, more and more, has come to suggest that an experience plays easily on the tender sentiments—a sunset over the sea is beautiful; soft organ music in an old cathedral at twilight; moonlight, of course, and roses and little children saying their prayers. Well, these things *are* beautiful; no question. But they are obviously and sentimentally so. And, if these things are beautiful, whereas suppurating wounds, screams of engine brakes, Manchester on a wet Sunday, are not; then beauty is just a matter of prettiness and pleasure.

An attempt has been made to define beauty in terms of usefulness, to admire what is hideously termed "functional." But I cannot subscribe to this any more than to beauty equated with truth or moral good or any other abstraction. Any phenomenon and any experience, it seems to me, can be "beautiful" in an appropriate context. The only dictum about beauty with which I can agree is that it lies in the eye of the beholder. The only art criticism which to me has any meaning is enshrined in the much-mocked phrase: "I know what I like." Even then I reserve the right to like something on Monday but not on Tuesday, to like it in sunshine but not in the rain, to like it only when I have influenza, when Menuhin plays it, with trees in the background, diluted with water, in a Dublin accent, at a military funeral.

More and more I drifted away from any idea that art was socially elevating. The Old Vic's value lay, I thought, partly in the fact that it is an institution with honorable, though maybe mistaken, traditions; with some suggestion, if not promise, of stability in the fatally unstable, ephemeral world of the theatre. But I have discussed elsewhere the value of an institution. Partly the Old Vic's value was its policy of producing classical plays; and I have also discussed the merits of a classical program. There is, however, no merit in producing classics unless they are well done. I believed, therefore, that to do my utmost to keep a respected institution in being, and to see that the plays were produced as well as I could manage, was the aim of my professional life.

I say "believed" that this was the aim, because one of the lessons which experience has taught me is that our conscious and our unconscious motives rarely, if ever, correspond. This book is not concerned with my spiritual development, but I suspect that it was some disparity between conscious and unconscious motive which prevented me from building, upon the foundation of Emma Cons and Lilian Baylis, the great theatre of which I dreamed. Had I been surer of myself, my own wishes and beliefs, I should have been able at the end of the war, which the triple institution of ballet, opera and drama companies had survived—ballet triumphant, opera and drama battered but intact—to capitalize the fact that these were repositories of certain indispensable skills and traditions, and to turn them into a real British national theatre.

It was not to be.

Since I left the Old Vic nearly fifteen years ago, I have been in a position to choose what I did, and where, and why. I have not attempted to do the most uplifting plays or to regard the audience in the light of sinners seeking redemption.

I am not always sure why I have chosen to do this or that.

In two instances, *The Three Estates* in Edinburgh and the Stratford festival in Canada, it was primarily in pursuit of the technical aim of getting out of the proscenium arch and back to something near the Elizabethan stage; and, secondarily, to work in a provincial center, with actors who seemed to have no less skill than their metropolitan colleagues, but a rather fresher approach; and to endeavor to please audiences, again no less intelligent than the metropolitan audience, but less sophisticated, and therefore less inclined to judgment based on a preconception of the "correct thing," rather than on the evidence of their five wits.

I have moved further and further from dogmatic judgments about artistic quality. I choose plays partly because I like them and want to direct them. I do not always want to direct what I think I can do well. For one thing, no one is a good judge of his own qualities. I do not fully know what impels me to do this or that. Does anybody?

The aim of all this is not just to have a good time. I have reached an age when for a great deal of the time it is pleasantest to look at trees or at the sea, or to play patience, or to read a book which one has read many times before—an old friend. I go about the world getting up plays partly out of vanity, partly for money, partly out of habit—the compulsion to practice a craft which through the years has become almost as indispensable to life as breathing or eating; and partly—a part which I rationalize to a greater extent than is probably justified—in an attempt to create something which will, if only for a brief moment, transport a few fellow travelers on our strange, amusing, perilous journey—a lift, but not, I hope, an uplift.

I have tried to tell some of the facts about my professional life and tried to indicate a few of the practical conclusions to which I have come. But facts and acts and conclusions must be based upon some kind of belief. Let me end this book with a very brief confession of faith.

I believe that a theatre, where live actors perform to an

audience which is there in the flesh before them, will survive all threats from powerfully organized industries which pump prefabricated drama out of cans and blowers and contraptions of one kind or another. The struggle for survival may often be hard and will batter the old theatre about severely. Indeed, from time to time it will hardly be recognizable; but it will survive. It will survive as long as mankind demands to be amused, terrified, instructed, shocked, corrupted and delighted by tales told in the manner which will always remain mankind's most vivid and powerful manner of telling a story.

I believe that the purpose of the theatre is to show mankind to himself, and thereby to show to man God's image.

I believe that this purpose is ill served by *consciously* using the theatre as a moral, social or political platform. It cannot avoid being all three. Its ministers must not be so arrogant as to suppose that their work is to do good to their fellow men. Their work is to glorify their Creator by expressing themselves. They will choose the material to express themselves which they feel, rather than think, will suit what they believe they have it in them from time to time to express. In this choice they will feel "guided" or "inspired," as all God's prophets have been, from Elijah down to the humblest, dottiest, squalidest persons who have believed themselves to be guided and inspired. If this is not so, then for me the term *artist* is entirely meaningless.

I believe that the theatre makes its effect not by means of illusion, but by ritual.

People do not believe that what they see or hear on the stage is "really" happening. Action on the stage is a stylized re-enactment of real action, which is then imagined by the audience. The re-enactment is not merely an imitation but a symbol of the real thing. If I may quote this instance without irreverence, it expresses the point clearly: the priest in Holy Communion re-enacts, with imitative but symbolic gestures and in a verbal ritual, the breaking of bread and the pouring of wine. He is at this moment an actor impersonating Christ in a very solemn drama. The congregation, or audience, is under no illusion that at that moment he really *is* Christ. It should, however, participate in the ritual with sufficient fervor to be rapt, literally "taken out of itself," to the extent that it shares the emotion which the priest or actor is suggesting. It completes the circle of action and reaction; its function is not passive but active. This, I think, is exactly what happens to an audience at a successful theatrical performance.

Just as the sacred drama of Holy Communion is nonillusionary, so is the sacred drama of *Oedipus Rex*, where the actor, also originally a priest, impersonates a symbol of sacrifice. Equally nonillusionary, though more secular, is *Macbeth*, for instance, where the protagonist performs actions symbolic of regicide, usurpation, remorse, and so on. The same principle can be applied to all drama; and in all drama, even the most frivolous, I think that there is some attempt, rarely conscious, to relate the participants to God, or at least to some aspect of God, albeit such aspects are often those represented in Greece by such figures as Dionysus or Aphrodite, where God is seen not in his capacity of all-wise, all-powerful Father but as the personification of Sex, of Mirth, or as the glorification of youth.

The theatre is the direct descendant of fertility rites, war dances and all the corporate ritual expressions by means of which our primitive ancestors, often wiser than we, sought to relate themselves to God, or the gods, the great abstract forces which cannot be apprehended by reason, but in whose existence reason compels us to have faith.

INDEX

About the Author

For seven years, Tyrone Guthrie was managing director of the Old Vic and Sadler's Wells, and in 1952, he was called to Stratford, Ontario, "to give advice" when the now famous Shakespeare Festival was being organized. In addition to his work in the theatre, Dr. Guthrie has written plays and has contributed to numerous publications in Europe and America. He has lectured at colleges around the world, including Oxford, Cambridge, Yale, Harvard, Melbourne, and Sidney Universities. Harold Clurman, director and critic, has called him "the most gifted director on the English-speaking stage."